Scaling Strategies for Social Entrepreneurs

Urs Jäger · Felipe Symmes ·
Guillermo Cardoza

Scaling Strategies for Social Entrepreneurs

A Market Approach

Urs Jäger
INCAE Business School & VIVA Idea
Alajuela, Costa Rica

Felipe Symmes
Viva Idea
San José, Costa Rica

Guillermo Cardoza
INCAE Business School
Alajuela, Costa Rica

ISBN 978-3-030-31159-9   ISBN 978-3-030-31160-5   (eBook)
https://doi.org/10.1007/978-3-030-31160-5

This Palgrave Macmillan imprint is published by the registered company Springer Nature Switzerland AG
The registered company address is: Gewerbestrasse 11, 6330 Cham, Switzerland

Preface

That scaling is about growth seems obvious. But when Alfred, a friend of ours, learned about this book, he got directly to the point. "What happens if someone doesn't want to scale impact?" he asked. "I'm sure that many social entrepreneurs feel comfortable with the impact they have, and prefer to keep things small-scale and local." Alfred is right. This book does not intend to promote scaling as a universal principle that works for everyone, in every context. In fact, the opposite is true. Intending to grow by scaling impact is not a normative decision, but rather a practical one that depends on each social entrepreneur's multiple internal and external relations with actors that support their scaling efforts.

The last century's global economic crisis has proved the downside of promoting scaling as a universal principle. Today, most sustainability experts criticize large-scale economic growth, calling for "limits to growth," as famously promoted by the Club of Rome in 1972. Since the Brundtland Commission in 1987, which was the first attempt to unite countries in the collective pursuit of sustainable development, discourse on sustainability has questioned the notion of unlimited economic growth, leading to a variety of alternative approaches. One of these alternatives, for example, focuses on economic growth based on a limited consumption of resources and includes principles such as ecosystem rehabilitation and the use of recycled material. These alternative approaches make sense. Unlimited growth in consumption leads to situations such as that of the fashion industry. In response to customers who purchase and discard clothing on a monthly basis, many fashion companies have reduced the period in which they release a new collection from once a year to—in some cases—every month. This increases consumption, creates waste, and has a host of other negative external effects.

As this example shows, critiques of growth make sense. Economic growth is not the end-all solution for all the world's problems. However, many also extend this critique of economic growth to markets, mistakenly throwing the baby out with the bathwater. Markets, for better or worse, are an effective social mechanism. Markets have helped many developed countries reach high standards of living, and have allowed many developing countries to—at least in part—escape from poverty. Even social entrepreneurs, who are the focus of our book, use market mechanisms to accomplish social or environmental goals. They invent business models that function according to market mechanisms, aiming to increase the quality of life for all. They do this by focusing on specific topics—education, for example—in specific regions and by targeting specific groups of beneficiaries, such as their own communities. Most social enterprises progressively grow to the size of micro, small and medium-sized enterprises (MSME).

The new reality, however, is that there are persistent, globalized social and environmental challenges such as climate change, poverty, and inequality. These challenges affect the entire globe and, therefore, call for global solutions. This reality also affects social enterprises, as the rising number of global social and environmental challenges creates new opportunities for them to grow on an international scale.

In the face of these rising opportunities for social enterprises to scale internationally, some business experts argue that social entrepreneurs have the duty to scale their impact. This view, however, is misleading. A universal principle of scaling does not exist. In their day-to-day work, social entrepreneurs operate in relation to many different actors at the same time—they relate to themselves, their employees, their beneficiaries, their investors, their communities, their families, and many others. The decision of whether or not to scale emerges from these multiple relations, each of which can provide the *potential* to scale. For many social enterprises, scaling is the correct decision; for many others, it is not.

We can imagine this potential to scale if we compare it to raising children. As parents, we assume that we are the most important relationship with respect to our children, and we try to educate them toward what we think is best. We guide them to higher education, for example, assuming this to be the baseline for a successful life in our modern world. Taking a view that sees "potential," however, guides us differently. We now see that our children also operate in relation to themselves, to their friends, their neighbors, their environment—to *their* world. In our parenting, we instead help them explore these relationships, particularly how they relate to themselves, guiding them to discover their strengths and desires. The life they live is what emerges from their multiple relationships—not just what their parents, grandparents, uncles, and aunts assume to be the best path for them to take. Social entrepreneurs are in a similar position, with many international experts adopting a typical "parenting" role that assumes they need to convince social entrepreneurs to scale their impact. But social entrepreneurs will likely fail if they decide to scale simply because their investors or a given expert has advised them to do so. Whether or not a social enterprise needs to scale depends on the specific challenges it faces and the multiple relations that emerge in its day-to-day work.

From this perspective, planning to scale means understanding the present social context in which the social entrepreneur works to explore growth potentials and express them in customized scaling plans. This is much easier said than done. To do this, they must visit their customers and beneficiaries personally and establish a close relationship with them. Statistics are helpful, but not enough to gain a deep understanding of their reality and define where the enterprise can create value based on "potentials to scale." For example, during extensive field visits, the Guatemalan social enterprise, Kingo, recognized rural consumers who live in extreme poverty and recharge their smartphones at their local neighborhood shops. Kingo's leadership saw this as a potential to scale, and started to sell its services on a prepaid system that is very similar to the telecommunications industry. Leveraging this potential to scale allowed Kingo to increase its impact by extraordinary measures. To explore the multiple relations of a given social enterprise, such as what Kingo did in the rural areas of Guatemala, social entrepreneurs need frameworks that allow them to analyze the present situation of their enterprise in a holistic way—to understand its environment, its available resources, its operations processes, and its leadership structures. Then, based on this deep understanding, they can identify potentials to scale and express them in customized plans.

This brings us back to Alfred and his thought-provoking question—why write a book that helps social entrepreneurs grow by scaling their impact? What we told him, was this: True, aiming for growth by scaling impact is by no means a universal principle. The decision of whether to scale impact depends on the multiple relations around which a given social enterprise works, and out of which potentials to scale can emerge. If social entrepreneurs understand that their enterprise has potentials to scale and, therefore, the potential to make a greater impact on the social and environmental challenges of our time, then they should scale. If they do not perceive potentials to scale, however, then they should remain in their status quo. However, it's also important to consider that, should the potential to scale emerge, then they likely need to leverage it. Not doing so risks going against their social enterprise as it *is*. This perspective becomes clear if we view scaling like life. Repressing the potential to grow, represses life—just like when parents repress their children's explorations of a career in music, or art, mistakenly guiding them toward what, according the parents' understanding, is a safer life journey.

The idea of exploring and leveraging growth potential leads back to our meetings with numerous entrepreneurs over the last seven years. We visited them in their offices, homes, and markets, and had the opportunity to learn from them about the potential to scale and the creation of scaling plans as presented above and outlined in the book. Many of these entrepreneurs have become famous in their communities, cities, and countries, and are well-recognized for the social and environmental impact they have created. Others are silent stars, so to speak, with monumental impacts and relentlessly creative entrepreneurial minds. These entrepreneurs have led impressive lives, careers, social enterprises, impact missions, and visions for the world they live in.

Executing research in environments where basic needs are visible and acute makes research for books such as these a difficult task to pursue. We could have used the money we've invested in it for other projects with an immediate impact on poverty alleviation or other issues that affect our lives in Latin America. We decided to work on this book in hopes of inspiring social entrepreneurs around the world to scale the impact of their enterprises and, therefore, to scale our own impact through the innovative work of others. This vision is also the vision of VIVA Idea, a Latin American think-action tank founded by Stephan Schmidheiny, a Swiss businessman and a pioneer and leader in the global sustainability movement. VIVA Idea believed in this project and invested the necessary resources. Supplementary to this book, VIVA Idea also encourages all interested readers to share their own experiences of scaling impact and, thus, to jointly support social entrepreneurs in solving the major challenges of our century.

Alajuela, Costa Rica	Urs Jäger
San José, Costa Rica	Felipe Symmes
Alajuela, Costa Rica	Guillermo Cardoza

Acknowledgements

We are grateful to Adriana Aguerrebere, Tasso Azevedo, Carolina Benavides, Diego Cárdenas, Carolina Cruz, Liliana García, Andrea González, Cristian Gutiérrez, Jorge Jiménez, Alexandra Kissling, Paula Mosera, Lina Nunez, María Pacheco, Octavio Perera, Claudia Ritzel, Vania Alejandra Rueda, Lina Tangarife, Joaquin Tome, Renata Truzzi, Diego Usatinsky, Chrishian Verdugo, Daniel Villafranca, Renata Villers, Claudia Werneck, Laura Zommer, Lucha Bio, Eric Dijkhuis, Andrea Escobar, Fabián Ferraro, Francisco Garcia, Jorge Gronda, Francisco Gutiérrez, Inge Hernández, Marcos Heyd, María Guadalupe Ibarra, Ignacio Soto, Pamela Landini, Juan Lapetini, Adán Levy, Felipe Lobert, Pedro Mérida, Francesco Piazzesi, José Luis Robles, Albina Ruiz, Luis Fernando Sanabria, Luis Szarán, Daniel Uribe, Luis Wohlers, Ximena Arrieta, Carlos Ballesteros, Daniel Buchbinder, Andres Cavalcanti, Mauricio Gaitán, Thiago Pinto, Jefferson Ramírez, Mario Roset, Andrés Rozo, Jessica Altenburger, Mariana González, Camilo Herrea, Enrique Lomnitz, Oscar Méndez, Rodrigo Pino, Diana Quintero, Nicolás Schiffman, Juan Fermín Rodríguez, Manuel Laredo, Antonio Laredo, Elfid Torres, María San Martín, Pablo Villoch, Ezequiel Escobar, and Juan Nicolás Suarez. All these social entrepreneurs helped us understand how to scale impact and, therefore, to grow our capacity to develop frameworks to solve the great challenges of our times.

We are particularly thankful to Ligia Chinchilla, Rosario Quispe, Helvio Quispe, Juan Collado, Gaston Aróstegui and Sebastian Mealla for their intensive discussions on the challenges of scaling impact. So many others supported us that we cannot mention them all.

None of the authors are native English speakers. Thus, we are very thankful for Stephanie Ament's and Joselyne Hoffmann's intense and efficient work on this text. They were not just proofreaders but partners in our thoughts and mission; this made them capable of deeply understanding our ideas and expressing them with comprehensible arguments.

Finally, we express our gratitude to the Palgrave team for accepting our book and, in particular, we thank Jacqueline Young for guiding and pushing us to finishing the text in a reasonable time frame.

About This Book

Social entrepreneurs often experience difficulties when attempting to scale. The reason for this is that scaling isn't just about an entrepreneur's willingness to grow, but also—and, perhaps, even more importantly—his or her capacity to develop a scaling strategy that reflects an understanding of the various components that must be adjusted to accomplish scaling goals. Once entrepreneurs decided to scale the impact of their enterprise, they must develop new capabilities in order to access new resources and skills.

This book will help social entrepreneurs create effective scaling strategies by providing a detailed, three-phased market approach to scaling. Cases based on social entrepreneurs who have successfully worked in low-income markets in Latin America then illustrate three main strategies for scaling impact: cocreating in low-income contexts, collective impact, and replicating business models. The market approach to scaling described in this book is based on the theory of negotiating impact for resources, as introduced in this book, and a corresponding study of more than 100 entrepreneurs in the Latin American region.

By offering a conceptual three-phased approach as a guide for reflecting on practical case studies, this book appeals to business teachers, leaders of incubators and others working with social entrepreneurs, social entrepreneurs seeking to improve their management practices in order to scale their impact, and those considering creating a social enterprise.

Contents

About the Authors

Urs Jäger is an associate professor at INCAE Business School and Research Director of VIVA Idea. He focuses his research on inclusion of formal and informal actors, low-income markets and social entrepreneurship. He has more than 7 years of experience in teaching experience-based courses in low-income markets. He is the co-author, most recently, of the article "Cocreating with the Base of the Pyramid" published with Ted London in Stanford Social Innovation Review.

Felipe Symmes is a senior researcher at VIVA Idea and Ph.D. Candidate in Organizational Studies and Theory of Culture at University of St. Gallen. He has a master's degree in Studies of development at Université Paris I Panthéon Sorbonne and a business economics degree from Pontificia Universidad Católica de Chile. His work focuses on social entrepreneurship, sustainability, informal markets, indigenous communities, and innovation. He has led consulting processes in the private, public, and civil society sectors in different Latin American countries. He is also a literature writer, publishing in 2016 his first book called *Writings of a Lost Man*.

Guillermo Cardoza is a tenured professor and researcher at INCAE Business School. He is an expert in innovation, change management, and internationalization of SMEs from emerging economies. He has more than 30 years of experience in the world of teaching, research, consulting and management of academic institutions. Guillermo has advised several governments in Latin America and has worked as a consultant for various international organizations. He has taught executive training programs on issues of innovation, change management and international competitiveness for multinationals such as Pfizer, P&G, Roche-Pharma, Nestlé, Cargill, Walmart, Santander Group, 3M, and Telefonica. He studied at Sorbonne Nouvelle University in Paris, where he obtained a Ph.D. in Business Economics as well as master's degrees in Latin American Studies, International Relations and Business Administration. He has been a Visiting Scholar at Harvard University and the MIT-Sloan School of Management.

List of Figures and Photos

List of Tables

1

Introduction: Scaling a Social Enterprise by Exchanging Impact for Resources

This book introduces a market approach that social enterprises can use to scale their impact. We *show examples of how social entrepreneurs have successfully scaled the impact of their organizations by exchanging impact for resources* [1].[i] In this approach, social entrepreneurs connect buyers (such as impact investors) and sellers (such as social enterprises) in order to negotiate positive social and environmental impacts in exchange for resources. While the social enterprise model is often considered up-and-coming, in many countries it is well-established and has been promoted by business scholars since the 1980s [2].[ii] What *is* new, however, is that emerging challenges such as global poverty, inequality, and climate change are driving a large number of social enterprises to scale their impact [3]. A growing number of actors are poised to support these efforts, such as government programs that foster entrepreneurial solutions to social problems, or organizations that provide standards related to impact measurement, investment, and production. Although many resources are available to social entrepreneurs in national and international arenas, this book focuses on impact investors as one of the most important drivers for scaling impact.

We introduce *exchanging impact for resources* as a practice that social entrepreneurs are already using to create new markets and scale their impact. This practice is an extension of the multiple books and articles that propose an "*and*" *approach* to social enterprises, meaning that social entrepreneurs and the organizations they lead set both economic and social objectives [4]. What social entrepreneurs now need, however, is guidance on how these objectives relate to one another—in other words, what the "*and*" means.

© The Author(s) 2020
U. Jäger et al., *Scaling Strategies for Social Entrepreneurs*,
https://doi.org/10.1007/978-3-030-31160-5_1

We argue that the tension between economic and social objectives particularly increases once social entrepreneurs attempt to scale the impact of their enterprises, as this increases their need for resources. Thus, social entrepreneurs intending to scale their impact first and foremost need guidance on how to connect their economic goals with their social ones. Based on our observations of social enterprises that have successfully scaled their impact, we propose a market approach to scaling in which social entrepreneurs obtain the resources they need to scale by negotiating impact for resources.

Based on this approach, we propose three phases through which social enterprises can sustainably scale their impact:

- Phase I: Negotiating impact for resources
- Phase II: Designing operations
- Phase III: Integrating financing and impact logics.

The knowledge presented in this book is based on seven years of research, including more than one hundred cases of social enterprises in the Latin American region that have successfully scaled their impact through a market approach. To show how each of the three phases above play out in the real world, we present examples in the form of illustrative, real-world cases that can be used for training and teaching purposes. Each includes a teaching note to help participants create solutions to the problems presented in the case. A summary of these teaching notes is included in this book, and the extended version of each illustrative case is available via an online platform in which instructors can access additional information, other cases, and discussion boards where they can converse with colleagues on classroom experiences.

This book is for entrepreneurs seeking to scale their impact, nonprofit organizations and for-profit companies that wish to shift toward a social enterprise model, and educators and students in classroom settings who teach or learn about social entrepreneurship in general and scaling impact in particular. We expect that many of our readers are already familiar with terms such as *social entrepreneur* and *social enterprise*, but perhaps need guidance on scaling impact in the face of new global challenges.

The origins of the market approach to scaling impact dates back to the 1980s, when a global economic crisis resulted in nonprofits receiving fewer government grants and private donations. This was a tricky situation for nonprofit organizations, as most had excluded a market approach from their organizational model. For many, their *raison d'être* was to address the social and environmental issues that government and companies were unable to address [5]. However, the nonprofit model failed to offer a solution to the scarcity of resources from grants and donations, and the need arose for new organizational forms and financing mechanisms that would create economically sustainable impacts on existing social and environmental issues.

The social enterprise model emerged, at first mainly in developed countries of North America and Europe, as a solution to this new challenge. These enterprises went beyond the nonprofit model, using a market approach to create impact. Their initial success fostered their growth, not only in developed regions, but also in developing regions such as Latin America. Since the late 1990s, a rising number of social enterprises have begun to explore how they can scale their impact both regionally and globally and, therefore, how they can access more resources. A Thomson Reuters Foundation survey shows that while Canada, Singapore, and the United States are considered the most likely places for social entrepreneurs to access impact investments, more than 60% of all respondents of all 43 countries surveyed report that social enterprises are gaining momentum.[iii]

Social enterprises with intentions to scale are part of a rising number of actors that support a market approach to scaling impact. At least four groups of such actors have emerged:

First, is the *general public*. Many populations are experiencing a rise in awareness of major global challenges such as climate change and poverty, which, in turn, creates a demand for economically sustainable solutions. Social networks are the driving force behind this public awareness. For many people around the globe, access to platforms such as Facebook, Twitter, YouTube, and Instagram has exponentially increased, fostering the visibility of social and environmental issues, as well as their potential solutions, on a regional and global scale. Social network communities discuss major challenges across national boundaries, with significant influence. As of 2019, 4.2 billion of the world's 7.7 billion inhabitants were internet users,[iv] and 3.3 billion were active social media users.[v] Margaret Chang, former Director-General of the World Health Organization, argues that social networks have become an important new voice in the political arena, although many of the arguments within are not based on hard data or evidence.[vi] Whether evidence-based or not, however, the information on social media can construct public meaning. Thus, these platforms have begun to disrupt established hierarchies of communication and erode the power of traditional gatekeepers such as large media companies, political parties, and scientific organizations and journals. This also means that it has begun to elevate the potential of individuals to reach large numbers of people as never before. Twitter, for example, became a crosscutting networking mechanism in an ecological protest that included various gatekeepers and eventually culminated in the 15th United Nations Conference of the Parties on Climate Change (COP15) in December of 2009 [6].

Second, is the increasing numbers of organizations that define and structure the standards of *impact trading* (norms that structure the exchange of impact for resources). The Global Impact Investing Rating System (GIIRS), for example, aims to shift investor behavior toward a standardized way of measuring impact, and the B Corporation has established a set of standards through which companies can integrate social and environmental criteria into all areas of their enterprise.[vii] Such organizations promote the standardization of impact indicators and social impact practices and influence public policy to promote related laws and government services [7]. In countries around the world, these organizations are working to strengthen the institutionalization of social enterprises. In Chile for instance, the B Corps national headquarters works at the public policy level to promote *B Corp Certification* as a mechanism that permits social enterprises to access public funds. Likewise, a rising number of impact investors, governments, social movements, advocacy organizations, and even the social enterprises themselves have begun to contribute to an emerging standardization of a market approach to scaling impact.

Third, is the rising number of impact investors interested in initiatives that address *regional and global challenges* (e.g., those focusing on the United Nations Sustainable Development Goals) yet expect an economic as well as a social or environmental return on their investment [8]. Generally speaking, impact investors focus on both a geographical and economic scope. Those located in developed regions such as Europe, the United States, and Canada are often interested in investing in developing regions such as Latin America, Africa, and Southeast Asia, in such diverse issues as water, economic development, climate change, and poverty.[viii] These investments expect both an economic and an impact return. They are often willing to accept a lower financial return than they would from a for-profit enterprise—but only if the trade-off is a measurable and relatively high social or environmental impact. Compared to financial markets, impact investment funds are still relatively small; however, they are expanding rapidly. A Global Investing Network (GIIN) survey of 229 impacts investors reports that there were USD 35.5 billion in investments in 2017, compared with USD 38.5 billion in 2018—an increase of 8%.[ix] Further, the United Nations supported impact investment on a global scale by strengthening the Global Steering Group for Impact Investment (GSG), which intends to catalyze impact investments in social enterprises through various regional and global working groups that connect and align investors, states, social enterprises, incubators, and other relevant actors. The GSG also provides a platform through which actors can discuss the relevance of social and environmental issues such as poverty, water, health, nutrition, education, and climate change, and search for collaborative solutions on a regional and global level.

The fourth group supporting a market approach to scaling impact includes *social entrepreneurs aiming to impact low-income regions* [9]. Until the late 1990s, development organizations such as the Inter-American Development Bank and multinational companies that source resources in low-income regions (e.g., the coffee industry and its grassroots producers) conceived these populations as solely comprising basic needs—not necessarily as viable markets. Thus, their efforts focused mainly on philanthropic projects that aimed to help people escape from poverty. These projects focused, among other things, on the empowerment and inclusion of poor and informal actors into established global value chains. However, they ultimately failed to create new, viable markets in the region [10]. The rising discussion surrounding the *base of the pyramid* changed this discourse entirely [11]. Social entrepreneurs now increasingly perceive low-income contexts as potential markets in which they can base a profitable business while still making a positive impact. In this sense, contexts featuring poverty and informality also include paying customers. While they may only be able to afford to pay minimal prices, they can help cover the costs of the products and services a business provides and even produce profits. For instance, Dr. Jorge Gronda is an Argentine gynecologist who devised innovative ways of providing poor indigenous communities with affordable healthcare services [12]. One day, an indigenous woman told him she intended to visit a private hospital. Dr. Gronda warned her about the high costs, but the woman responded that she could gather the funds from her community. The response surprised him, and he realized that even poor people can be viable, paying customers. He just needed to create a suitable system that reflected their financial possibilities. In many cases, these customers can only afford minimal prices, and depend on the support of their families or communities—but they can pay *something*, and, more importantly, are *willing to pay* something. Based on this insight, Dr. Gronda built Humana, a private healthcare system for the poor. This group of paying customers is immense, as low-income regions account for roughly 60% of the world population, with a spending power of more than USD 5 trillion a year.[x] This is also the group that most significantly feels the negative effects of climate change, hunger, access to water, and other major challenges. In these regions, institutions such as public education, healthcare systems, and the rule of law do not work as efficiently and effectively as they do in more developed areas [13]. Furthermore, most of the profit-oriented markets rarely function here, as extreme poverty and weak market institutions make access to financing systems difficult—particularly with respect to opening new markets with customers that lack the capacity to pay higher prices.

Rather than become paralyzed by the immense number of unmet basic needs and other social and environmental problems that exist at the base of the pyramid, effective social entrepreneurs have a unique capacity to identify opportunities to negotiate impact for the resources they need to scale their business. Whether in high-income or low-income regions, social entrepreneurs and the organizations they lead can exchange impact in return for resources.

Social entrepreneurs can explore these opportunities to scale their impact by first identifying actors that are willing and capable of exchanging impact for resources. The key is to identify how the impact their social enterprises creates, or can create, is of interest to other actors on a regional and global scale. Using a market approach to scaling impact is profoundly different from how non-profit organizations and for-profit companies work (Figs. 1.1, 1.2, and 1.3).

Nonprofits aim to *serve and help*, based on a philanthropic approach [14]. Social enterprises intending to scale, on the contrary, follow a market approach. They explore negotiation opportunities related to the social problem they address, and focus on social or environmental problems that are of interest to market actors that have resources (e.g., impact investors). These investors can expect a return on their investment, as many social enterprises provide services or products to customers who can at least pay low prices, or have customers, as companies do, but also serve beneficiaries—target groups

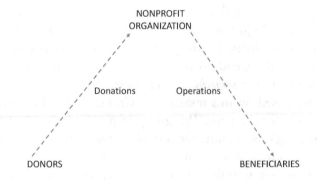

Fig. 1.1 Nonprofit approach to impact

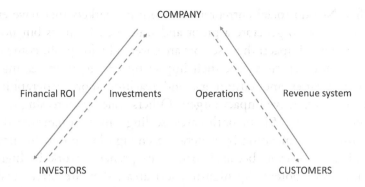

Fig. 1.2 For profit approach to markets

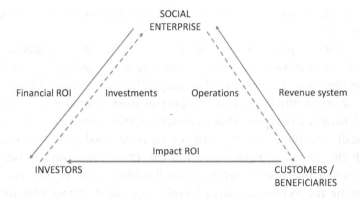

Fig. 1.3 Market approach to scaling used by social enterprises

that are unable to pay for services or products at all. In each model, social enterprises exchange the impact they create with actors who are willing to inject the financial and non-financial resources needed to scale. In return, they report to the investor on the impact they have created, and return the invested money after a certain period of time. In many cases, the social enterprise pays a surplus margin on the money they return to investors.

Social enterprises also differ from for-profit companies in that their core business focuses on both impact and financial sustainability, rather than on paying customers alone. In situations of trade-offs between impact and income, they may prioritize impact over profit, or the other way around, but some degree of tension between the two is always present. Consequently, social enterprises typically do not work in markets where there are social or environmental challenges to tackle, but no investors interested in financing their solution nor potential paying customers that could contribute to the development of a self-sustainable business. These markets are covered by nonprofits. Nor do social entrepreneurs work in markets that have enough paying customers to generate a profit and scale their business but no social or environmental impact; these sectors are covered by for-profit companies.

Some social enterprises scale their impact by serving an increasing number of beneficiaries and customers, and reaching more geographic areas through their respective impact targets. Others scale by increasing the quality of their impact [15]. In both cases, scaling can be attempted through internal financing, meaning by generating enough income to finance their scaling plans. However, because social entrepreneurs work in high-need (and, thus, most potentially high-impact) areas, they are often unable to create enough income to finance their scaling plans internally. Therefore, most social enterprises require external financing to scale. Exchanging impact for the resources needed to scale is an effective way to secure external financing.

For instance, Juan Fermín Rodríguez, a social entrepreneur from Guatemala, discovered that most of his country's rural, poor, indigenous communities lacked access to electricity. Through a crowdfunding campaign that eventually gained the support of international organizations, he founded Kingo, a company that developed a solar technology device that is now installed in homes throughout several poor, rural zones of Guatemala. Through this device, Kingo's customers can choose how much energy they use and when they use it, giving them flexibility at rates they can afford. After testing the technology, Juan Fermín negotiated impact with interested investors. These resources then permitted his enterprise to develop a financially sustainable business model that succeeded in creating a market for solar energy poor, rural regions and was even able to scale its impact to other parts of the world.

Thus, social enterprises that successfully scale:

- Use a market approach to scaling impact.
- View impact as the core of their business model.
- Address social and environmental problems that are of interest to impact investors.
- Pay a financial return to the investor, or at least repay the original capital invested.
- Often sell to paying customers; however, in most cases this income is not enough to cover the cost of scaling.
- Measure their social and environmental impact and report it to current and potential investors.

These criteria show how social enterprises intending to scale their impact differ from other closely related forms such as social innovation initiatives, enterprising nonprofits, and companies with corporate social responsibility (CSR) programs (Table 1.1).

Social innovation initiatives link ideas and find creative solutions to certain social problems. Impact is the core of the resulting business model. For example, young people and organizations often come together in entrepreneurship hubs or other collaborative spaces and find new ideas to addressing social or environmental problems. Nevertheless, innovation is an investment for organizations and does not necessarily generate solutions that *scale impact*. What scales impact from innovation is the organization's ability and willingness to standardize, routinize, and constantly improve the products, processes or interventions that generate impact [15]. We extend this discussion, arguing that social enterprises exchange impact for resources and develop efficient operations and systems of revenues in order to scale and address social or environmental change.

In the case of *enterprising nonprofits*, market activities are not directly related to impact [14]. To understand this, it is important to know the difference between a business model and an operational model. A business model is formed in simple terms of a financing model (where resources come from) and an operational model (how products and services that reach the target group are created). Nonprofits are mainly financed by donations (financing model), and their operations focus on social impact (operational model). Market activities are fairly limited and are used to increase funding, and not directly linked to the core social mission. This is why nonprofits commonly focus their products and services solely on their beneficiaries' needs. To secure additional resources through market activities, enterprising nonprofits create an organizational unit through which to sell additional products or services, aiming to generate income outside of their operational model, which focuses on impact. Furthermore, based on their nondistribution constraint, they do not offer financial return to their donors, nor do they repay the capital they received. Many nonprofits serve as an example of this organizational type. UNICEF, for instance, sells Christmas cards to raise funds. However, Christmas cards are not how UNICEF creates impact. Rather, it uses this market activity to fund core impact activities that are focused on children. Social enterprises intending to scale are different from enterprising nonprofit organizations such as UNICEF, in that exchanging impact for resources is at the core of their business model. They focus on social problems that are of interest to impact investors and, by exchanging impact for resources in impact markets, create self-sustaining business models.

Table 1.1 Differences between organizations with impact goals

Organizational form	Relationship between impact and economic return	Impact in the core business model	Impact reporting	Impact investor	Financial distribution	Paying customers
Social enterprises intending to scale	Exchanges impact for resources (economically sustainable impact)	Impact is at the core of the business model	Reporting needed	Address social and environmental problems that are of interest to impact investors	Pay a financial return on investment, or at least repay the capital provided	Sell to paying customers, but this income is not enough to cover scaling costs
Social innovation initiatives	Undefined	Impact is at the core of the business model	Undefined	Undefined	Undefined	Not defined
Enterprising nonprofits	Impact first	Impact is at the core of the operational model	Reporting needed	Non-existent	Nondistribution constraint	Focus on beneficiaries who do not pay for the value received, or if they are the income generated is marginal compared to fundraising efforts
Companies with CSR	Economic return first	Impact is not part of the core business model	Reporting needed	Non-existent	No direct financial return on investment CSR activities	Beneficiaries of CSR activities are not paying customers

Scaling social enterprises also differ from *profit-oriented companies* that follow CSR guidelines and practices as a way of helping to solve social and environmental problems faced by the society in which they operate [16]. The multinational Swiss bank UBS, for example, has a CSR budget, which it spends on various social initiatives. Companies such as UBS separate their business and social focuses, addressing social issues through their CSR departments, which are often divorced from the core business strategy and are not part of the core profit goals. Social enterprises intending to scale are different from companies with CSR programs because financial sustainability and impact are integral components of their core business model.

This book seeks to help social entrepreneurs take a market approach to scaling impact, incorporating three phases that depict the elements around which they reflect to construct their scaling strategy. We understand scaling strategies to be guidelines for scaling, rather than rigid structures.[xi] Unlike structures, strategies establish goals for the scaling process and help define how to accomplish them. They serve as a compass throughout the scaling process. Thus, an enterprise's scaling strategy is its guide to negotiating impact for the resources needed to scale. The reason we support a three-phased, market approach to scaling is a practical one: scaling isn't just about an entrepreneur's willingness to grow, but also—and, likely, more importantly—about using the right method to develop strategies.

Phase I: Negotiating Impact for Resources

A market approach to scaling takes an "outside-in" perspective. Social entrepreneurs begin compiling their strategy by first exploring actors with whom they can potentially negotiate impact in exchange for the resources needed to scale. This includes actors that are in the area where social enterprises work as well as national and international actors that are interested in the issues they address. A market approach assumes that the value of a social enterprises' impact depends on how others evaluate impact. For example, a particular impact investor's means of evaluating impact opens space to negotiate the amount of resources that he or she is willing to put toward the issue the social enterprise is trying to tackle, and at what percentage interest. A contextual study can help social entrepreneurs map accessible sources of resources (i.e., public organizations, international nongovernmental organizations (INGOs), private companies, individual impact investors, institutional impact investors, customers, etc.). These actors have economic and/or non-economic resources and are interested in negotiating the provision of these resources in exchange for measurable impact. In the case of impact investors, the contextual study also helps social entrepreneurs understand the current standards, or norms that structure the practice of negotiating impact for resources, for both financial and impact return (e.g., rates of interest, social impact indicators, etc.). In the case that such standards don't exist, social entrepreneurs can advocate their creation in order to support their negotiation and scaling strategy. Thus, Phase I includes an analysis of: *impact*, *resources*, *standards*, and *negotiation*.

Phase II: Designing Operations

Once social entrepreneurs define how they intend to negotiate impact for the resources needed to scale, they design the organization's operations that allows them to generate revenue and create impact. On one hand, social enterprises link their operations and revenue processes by creating products and services and distributing them to their target customers. On the other hand, they link these processes via revenue systems to current and potential customers who can pay for these services. These were explored in Phase I, when listing actors who can help negotiate impact for resources. Social entrepreneurs must design efficient and effective operations that can help deliver the impacts that are most of interest to potential customers or beneficiaries, as well as impact investors. The goal is to reduce operating costs in order to design self-sustaining business models. One way to do this is to create standardized products or services that focus on a specific need of their target customers. In this way, enterprises can increase their impact in quantitative terms, often reducing operating costs all along the value chain. Apart from streamlining operations, social enterprises must also design a revenue process. Some choose to provide products or services to customers who can at least pay a minimal price and are positively impacted by the product or service they purchase. Others have traditional (non-impact) customers and, rather, serve beneficiaries by including them as employees or providers in their business's value chain. In either case, social entrepreneurs must carefully design pricing and payment processes for their target customers. The elements analyzed in this phase are: *supply and assets*, *products and services*, and *distribution and revenue*.

Phase III: Integrating Financing and Impact Logics

A "logic" is a way of seeing the world. Employees of social enterprises use different logics when arguing for or against a scaling strategy—some may adhere to an impact logic, while others adhere to a financing logic. It becomes challenging for social entrepreneurs when those arguments between employees who adhere to different logics become intense, with belief standing against belief. The more social entrepreneurs intend to scale, the stronger the risk of conflicts between different logics. The reason is that the importance of the financial logic rises and, thus, so does the need to integrate this logic with the impact logic of their mission. Social entrepreneurs work on this integration based on three elements that need to be analyzed in this phase: *mission*, *leadership*, and *communications*.

A market approach to scaling uses the information mapped in Phases I, II, and III to design a strategy that explores and leverage scaling opportunities per the various elements included in each phase. This provides the necessary components of the social enterprise's scaling strategy. Designing a scaling strategy is often a creative process based on open, unstructured communication within the social enterprise team.

To illustrate these three phases, we present several illustrative cases from social enterprises in Latin America. These examples show how the practice of exchanging impact for resources allows social enterprises to scale their impact. To introduce the three phases and their respective cases, we build our argument as follows. In Chapter 2, we introduce the market approach to scaling impact, and highlight how our definition of scaling a social enterprise as exchanging impact for the resources needed to scale expands the current literature on social enterprises, impact investment, and scaling. In Chapter 3, we introduce Phase I: Negotiating impact for resources and a case to illustrate it. In Chapter 4, we present conceptual guidelines and a case illustrating Phase II: Designing operations. Chapter 5 focuses on Phase III: Integrating financing and impact logics, and its respective case. In Chapter 6, we introduce three examples of scaling strategies that are widely discussed by practitioners that can be deduced from the three-phased approach to scaling. Finally, in Chapter 7, we discuss the challenges of teaching social enterprises to scale (or learning how to scale, if the reader is an entrepreneur aiming to scale impact).

Notes

i. The concept of exchanging impact for resources was theoretically developed by Urs Jäger and Andreas Schröer and published in the article *Integrated Organizational Identity. A Definition of Hybrid Organizations and a Research Agenda, Voluntas,* Vol. 25, pp. 1281–1306 in 2014. In 2014, this article won the "Best Paper Award" from Voluntas. Jäger and Schröer call this exchange approach "functioning solidarity." In this understanding, social enterprises (hybrid organizations) are "characterized by an organizational identity that systematically integrates civil society and markets, exchanges (negotiates) communal solidarity for financial and non-financial resources, calculates the market value of communal solidarity, and trades this solidarity for financial and non-financial resources. In other words, they 'create functional solidarity' (2014, p. 1281)."

ii. Dennis Young (1983) authored one of the first books on social enterprises.

iii. See https://poll2016.trust.org.

iv. See internetworldstats.com.

v. See slideshare.net/DataReportal/digital-2018-q4-global-digital-statshot-october-2018-v2.

vi. Seehttps://www.who.int/dg/speeches/2017/address-university-washington/en/.

vii. See https://bcorporation.net.

viii. A good example of the different views of impact held by organizations that focus on standards versus those that focus on processes is found in the paper: Reinecke, J., & Ansari, S. (2015). When times collide: Temporal brokerage at the intersection of markets and developments. *Academy of Management Journal, 58*(2), 618–648.

ix. See Global Impact Investing Network (2018): Annual Impact Investor Survey, 2018.

x. See The World Bank's Global Consumption Database: http://datatopics. worldbank.org/consumption/ and the United Nations efforts to achieve the Sustainable Development Goals: https://sustainabledevelopment.un.org.

xi. For explanations of strategy as a combination of planning and process through practice, see: Chia, R., & Holt, R. (2009). *Strategy without design: The silent efficacy of indirect action.* Cambridge: Cambridge University Press.

References

1. Jäger, U., & Schröer, A. (2014). Integrated organizational identity: A definition of hybrid organizations and a research agenda. *Voluntas, 25,* 1281–1306.
2. Young, D. (1983). *If not for profit, for what? A behavioral theory of the nonprofit sector based on entrepreneurship.* Fallbrook, CA: Aero Publishers Inc.

3. Dees, G., Anderson, B., & Wei-skillern, J. (2004). Scaling social impact: Strategies for spreading social innovation. *Stanford Social Innovation Review*.

4. Dacin, M. T., Dacin, P. A., & Tracey, P. (2011). Social entrepreneurship: A critique and future directions. *Organization Science, 22*(5), 1203–1213.

5. Evers, A. (1995). Part of the welfare mix: The third sector as an intermediate area*. *Voluntas, 6*(2), 159–182.

6. Segerberg, A., & Bennett, L. W. (2011). Social media and the organization of collective action: Using Twitter to explore the ecologies of two climate change protests. *The Communication Review, 14*, 197–215.

7. Ebrahim, A., & Rangan, K. (2014). What impact? A framework for measuring the scale and scope of social performance. *California Management Review, 56*(3), 118–141.

8. Höchstädter, A. K., & Scheck, B. (2019). What's in a name: An analysis of impact investing understandings by academics and practitioners. *Journal of Business Ethics, 132*, 449–475.

9. Webb, J. W., Kistruck, G. M., Ireland, R. D., & Ketchen, D. J. (2011). The entrepreneurship process in base of the pyramid markets: The case of multinational enterprise/nongovernment organization alliances. *Entrepreneurship Theory and Practice, 34*(3), 555–581.

10. Jäger, U., & Sathe, V. (2015). The importance of vision and purpose of BoP business development. In S. Hart et al. (Eds.), *Base of the pyramid 3.0: Sustainable development through innovation and entrepreneurship* (pp. 12–30). Sheffield: Greenleaf.

11. Prahalad, C. K. (2007). *The BOP debate: Aneel Karnani responds*. http://nbis. org/nbisresources/sustainable_development_equity/bottom_of_pyramid_debate_with_prahalad.pdf.NextBillion.net.

12. Bucher, S., Jäger, U., & Prado, A. M. (2015). Sistema Ser: Scaling private health care for the base of the pyramid. *Journal of Business Research, 69*(2), 736–750.

13. Godfrey, P. (Ed.). *Management research in informal markets*. London: Routledge.

14. Anheier, H. (2014). *Nonprofit organizations: Theory, management, policy* (2nd ed.). London and New York: Routledge.

15. Seelos, C., & Mair, J. (2019). *Innovation and scaling for impact: How effective social enterprises do it* (256 pp). Stanford, CA: Stanford University Press.

16. Porter, M. E., & Kramer, M. R. (2002). The competitive advantage of corporate philantrophy. *Harvard Business Review, 80*(12), 5–16.

2

A Market Approach to Scaling Impact

A market approach to scaling argues that *social entrepreneurs scale the impact of their enterprise by exchanging impact for resources.* In this chapter, we explain how this approach expands the current understanding of contextual approaches to scaling social enterprises [1, 2]. We further explain how it contributes to the current literature on impact investment, particularly focusing on the relation between impact investors and social enterprises. Finally, we explain the three-phased approach to market-based scaling, how this differs from the popular concept of a business canvas, and how our three phased-approach can help teachers and practitioners create successful scaling strategies. Chapters 3–6, below, dig more deeply into each of the three phases and provide cases as an illustration and as a baseline for teaching, with corresponding teaching notes.

How a Market Approach Supports Efforts to Scale Impact

Scholars generally define markets as social places where exchanges occur between buyers and sellers under certain standards that structure their interaction [3, 4].[i] In private marketplaces, for-profit companies sell products and services to clients who pay a price to the company. In other words, actors exchange products or services for money. Social enterprises, however, are different. They trade positive social or environmental impacts—not simply products or services, as for-profit companies do. They are "sellers" of

© The Author(s) 2020
U. Jäger et al., *Scaling Strategies for Social Entrepreneurs*,
https://doi.org/10.1007/978-3-030-31160-5_2

impact. We thus use the expression "market approach to scaling impact" to define the practice through which social enterprises and other actors, such as impact investors, *negotiate impact in exchange for financial and non-financial resources*, under a certain set of standards. Using this definition, we expand the current understanding of social enterprises in three ways. First, we outline a contextual approach to the impact logic model that prioritizes the processes of negotiating impact for the resources needed to scale. Second, we define how social enterprises relate to different actors in order to scale under a market approach rather than a non-market approach such as stakeholder relations. Third, we introduce an "outside-in" approach to scaling impact, composed of three phases that can help entrepreneurs integrate financial sustainability and social/environmental impact.

A Contextual Approach to the Impact Logic Model

Much of the discussion surrounding the impact created by social enterprises has so far focused on the impact logic model, which illustrates the various steps that social enterprises follow in order to achieve impact: *inputs, activities, outputs, outcomes,* and *impacts* [5]. *Inputs* are the resources required for impact; *activities* are the injection of inputs toward specific actions that create impact; *outputs* are the immediate results of these activities; *outcomes* are the medium-to-long term effects of outputs; and *impact* reflects the long-lasting, systemic societal change that occurs over the years. These five steps help social enterprises structure their social and environmental impact [6].

The established impact logic model was originally created in the 1970s by Larry Posner and a colleague, and became known as the Logical Framework, or LogFrame, model [7].[ii] Posner and his colleague developed the LogFrame model to help traditional NGOs and governmental development initiatives to increase the efficiency and impact of their projects. Since then, the concept has changed slightly in terms of the number of steps, but its original structure remains the same. The LogFrame model, however, is not designed to include market-based mechanisms in an impact-driven business model, thus does not explain the relationship between impact and markets that is at the core of social entrepreneurship and social enterprises. Rather, it follows a nonprofit approach that focuses solely on impact. Observing this shortcoming, scholars began to call for the development of models that integrate both the organizational and contextual aspects of social enterprises [5].

The three-phased approach to scaling introduced here—negotiating impact for resources, designing operations, and integrating financing and impact logics—responds to this call by proposing a model that integrates a market approach with an impact logic model and explains how entrepreneurs can exchange their impact for the resources needed to scale.

Extending the Ecosystem of Social Enterprises by Establishing a Market-Based View

The term "ecosystem" has been widely used in management studies as a metaphor to depict the relational nature of human activities that function as a system, similar to a biological ecosystem [8–10]. Business scholars often apply the term "ecosystem" to describe the complex relationships and diversity of actors with whom a social enterprise must relate in order to successfully achieve its goals [11, 12].[iii] For example, governments, advocacy organizations, financing organizations, partner organizations, social enterprises, customers, and other groups form part of a social enterprises' ecosystem.

In line with the concept of a *social enterprise ecosystem*, our market approach to scaling impact highlights how important it is for social enterprises to collaborate with different actors and consider institutional frameworks such as laws and market regulations that can support their activities [13, 14].[iv] However, we go beyond the concept of ecosystems, as the latter does not illustrate how social enterprises can exchange impact for the resources needed to scale their impact. We propose extending the concept of ecosystems to encompass a *market view* that explores and leverages opportunities to trade impact for resources. We define all actors involved with social enterprises as "traders" who exchange impact for resources within negotiation processes. This definition specifies the relationships between the actors involved in scaling processes as part of a market that has its own set of standards which are norms that structure trading impact in exchange for resources. Within this market, actors such as impact investors have economic and non-economic resources, in exchange for which they demand a social or environmental impact. Other actors, such as social enterprises, provide this impact. Therefore, the markets in which social enterprises reside operate according to a demand and supply function of impact. For example, impact investors (the demand side of impact) purchase impact from social enterprises (the supply side of impact) for a price (the investment).

The Roles of Actors Who Interact with Social Enterprises Throughout the Scaling Process

A market approach to scaling impact highlights the role of social enterprises and impact investors as traders of impact. This does not mean that other actors are not important. The book focuses on impact investors as key actors for social enterprises that intend to get access to resources to scale. In addition to impact investors, social enterprises can negotiate impact for resources with diverse actors. These include international organizations, advocacy organizations, governments, partners of social enterprises, and other actors that are relevant to the development of social enterprises. These actors play various roles in negotiating impact for the resources needed to scale. Below, we will briefly review some of their roles.

As outlined in Chapter 1, standard-setting organizations define the standards that structure impact trading [15].[v] Examples such as the Global Impact Investing Rating System (GIIRS) and B Corp Certification illustrate how these organizations provide tools and standards through which to assess the impact of a given social enterprise and set investor expectations, as well as normative guidance for companies wishing to integrate social and environmental criteria into all of their areas. These organizations are key to establishing a common understanding between social enterprises and impact investors that considers both impact and financial returns. Social enterprises benefit from these organizations by obtaining standards by which to assess the success of their endeavors, whilst impact investors receive guidance on where to spend their money in order to achieve their financial and social or environmental impact goals. These standards thus act as a normative framework that sets the stage for relations between social enterprises and impact investors and, in turn, facilitates the process of trading impact for resources.

Governments are also key actors [16].[vi] They play two roles. First, governments establish legal frameworks in the countries in which social enterprises carry out their work. These legal frameworks can either inhibit or facilitate the impact of a social enterprise, such as by enacting public policies or incentives that promote the enterprises' activities. The United Kingdom, for example, developed specific legal forms of social enterprises in order to facilitate their foundation and development. Other governments, as in the case of Chile, create round tables in which advocacy organizations, standard-setting organizations, impact-focused organizations, academia, social enterprises, and impact investors can discuss issues and provide recommendations for how to create an institutional setting that favors the founding and growth of social enterprises. Second, governments establish the legal framework for the contracts that bind investors to the social enterprises they invest in. For example, in order to be able to receive an investment of over US 500 thousand dollars from a European institutional investor, the Peruvian social enterprise Ciudad Saludable Group, which cleans up cities by partnering with impoverished grassroots recyclers, had to route the investment through one of its for-profit branches. Although the impact investor was extremely interested in Ciudad Saludable Group's impact mission, Peruvian law did not permit such investment in nonprofit organizations. Similarly, creating legalized entities with both a for-profit and nonprofit focus can open new external investment possibilities that will help social enterprises to scale their impact.

Another critical actor for social enterprises intending to scale are collaborating partners [17].[vii] Collaborating partners are individuals and organizations that have economic and/or non-economic resources, and establish a collaborative relationship with social enterprises in order to help them achieve their goals. A for-profit company, for example, might help a social enterprise establish efficient operations and achieve its final impact goals. Social enterprises also partner with NGOs that are more embedded in their contexts in order to establish better distribution channels [18]. As we will see in Chapter 6, many social enterprises develop collective impact strategies that include working with other actors that have similar goals.

Standard-setting organizations, governments, and collaborative partners are all part of the markets within which social enterprises operate. However, the key actors with whom social enterprises negotiate impact for resources are impact investors.

The Relationship Between Impact Investors and Social Enterprises

Impact investors are key to a market approach to scaling impact, as they comprise one of social enterprises' most important sources for financing scaling endeavors [19].[viii] Impact investors possess valuable economic and non-economic resources that can be used to help scale social enterprises [20]. In addition to financial backing, impact investors bring valuable business advice to key areas related to scaling, such as financial and talent management. Impact investors can also provide support in legal matters, networking opportunities to build new partnerships, and mentorship for strategic decisions about growing the social enterprise.

In this book, we examine impact investment from the social enterprise perspective [21–25].[ix] This means that, while investors are key actors for social enterprises, in most cases they do not control the social enterprise's scaling processes. There are some exceptions, such as in cases where impact investors provide a high percentage of the social enterprise's equity capital [26]. Generally speaking, however, impact investors act as collaborators in terms of financing, social capital, business advice, and other financial and non-financial resources that can help the enterprise scale its impact. A market approach uses three elements to define the relationship between impact investors and social enterprises wishing to scale: (a) negotiating impact for resources, (b) defining standards that structure the relations, and (c) avoiding mission drift.

Negotiating Impact for Resources

Impact investors are rooted in the world of global finance and capital markets and, as such, think in terms of return on investment (ROI). At minimum, they ask that their invested capital be returned. More importantly, however, they have certain expectations regarding the *social* return on their investment [27].[x] Thus, they demand that their investees have clear impact goals and strategies for how to accomplish them. Furthermore, they typically request the expected impact be assessed through measurable indicators.

For most impact investors, scaling strategies are a precondition for investing in a given social enterprise. As impact investors conceive impact in terms of future ROI, they want to be familiar with the enterprise's strategy—mainly in terms of the expected (and measurable) social or environmental impact, the estimated financial return, the resources needed, the existing business and operational models, and the organization's human resources and internal culture. If a social enterprise is unable to provide this information, impact investors will likely decline the offer to collaborate, as they lack the information they need to mitigate the risk of not receiving the expected ROI.

Social enterprises create impact, but—paradoxically—are often not accustomed to discussing impact in terms of returns. Therefore, many social enterprises find themselves unprepared to work with impact investors. Albina Ruiz, for example, founder of Ciudad Saludable, initially struggled with the due diligence process in terms of understanding impact investors' language and goals. She viewed them as cold-shouldered and not clearly aligned with the mission and social spirit of her enterprise, which worked with impoverished grassroots recyclers. As discussed above, the tools that social enterprises use to construct their business and operational models often fall short of fully integrating the impact element with the market element. This often results in barriers to taking advantage of opportunities to scale.

The three-phased market approach to scaling social enterprises proposed in this book begins with mapping actors with whom the enterprise can engage in negotiation. The goal of this analysis is to explore opportunities to exchange impact for resources. As explained in Chapter 1, revenues for social enterprises intending to scale are not easy to obtain [28, 29].[xi] Many social enterprises struggle to create a business model that allows them to obtain the economic and non-economic resources necessary to scale their impact based on the sale of products and services alone. Negotiations with interested parties who can provide the necessary resources to reach scaling goals is the way out of this dead-end situation. A market approach searches for organizations, groups, and individuals that are both willing and capable of exchanging resources for impact within a given set of standards (Fig. 2.1) [30].[xii]

Impact investors (on the resource side) focus on specific impacts, and often define the geographical scope they intend to reach when investing in a social enterprise [23]. Their impact and geographical focus may or may not coincide with one of the social enterprises looking for resources. Thus, both parties must negotiate and explore their common interests in order to reach an agreement. In this negotiation process, social enterprises may be more or less flexible with respect to their impact, depending on the importance of the resources they have available and those they need for their scaling processes. If all of the actors had the same interests and coincided in how they evaluate the methods and importance of a given impact, then negotiations would be unnecessary. However, this is often not the case. This is neither good nor bad. It simply means that exchanging resources for impact is a process of negotiation. The case of Mamut, a social enterprise in Bolivia that transforms used tires into floor tiles to restore public parks and social places,

Fig. 2.1 Market approach to scaling

among other services, provides an example. When seeking impact investments, they realized that the environmental impact of recycling alone was not enough to exchange impact for resources from investors. "Many companies around the world are already doing this," thought its founder, Manuel Laredo. He then established a more ambitious impact for his enterprise to be attractive for investment—the construction of sustainable cities. This implied creating a sustainable value chain that would generate a positive impact on grassroots recyclers. Framed as such, Laredo was able to negotiate with investors and obtain the resources he needed to successfully scale Mamut's impact.

Defining the Standards that Structure Relations

A market approach to scaling impact includes the institutionalization of both financial and impact return standards that structure the nature of negotiations between social enterprises and impact investors. This is why it is key for social entrepreneurs to execute an analysis of the norms or standards currently in place (for example, those set by organizations such as GIIRS or B Corporation, or legal forms of social enterprises that determine which modes of financing are eligible) and what norms or standards are needed to make negotiations more effective and efficient. The case of Ciudad Saludable, introduced briefly above, can help illustrate what we mean. Ciudad Saludable's leadership reached an agreement with the impact investor regarding mutual goals—not only in terms of the indicators that would be used to measure impact, but also regarding the incorporation of international standards of professionalization, such as ISO norms. They also agreed to advocate on the public policy level, lobbying for a national law that could empower and accelerate the social enterprise's impact.

Standards that structure the negotiation of impact for resources can spur changes in the social enterprise's operational model. In the case of Ciudad Saludable, for example, the impact investor asked the social enterprise to standardize the services it provided to grassroots recyclers (such as training workshops) by adhering to internationally recognized operational norms. In addition to its operational model, a social enterprise's revenue process can be affected by adherence to new and existing standards. Social enterprises that sell products or services to benefit customers who can pay a minimal price and are positively impacted by the service need to find suitable pricing solutions for their clients. These solutions respond to the reality of customers who are extremely low-income and do often not have access to banking services. Social enterprises that sell to traditional paying (non-impact) customers and serve beneficiaries by including them as employees or providers in their value chains establish revenue models that permits the generation of income via a traditional customer based that essentially funds the services the enterprise provides to beneficiaries. Structuring revenue processes is a challenging task; however, analyzing international pricing standards and learning from the experience of impact investors can help.

Significant tension between social enterprises and impact investors can arise during the process of defining the standards that will structure their relations. Many impact investors have already created standards for tasks such as impact assessment, which rely on global standard setting organizations like the Global Impact Investment Rating System. Social enterprises intending to scale will likely need to analyze and negotiate how these standards will be employed in a way that complies with impact investors' expectations, yet is feasible for the social enterprise. This isn't always easy, as impact investors often base their decisions on quantitative data, while social entrepreneurs base their decisions on contextual knowledge [31]. This difference is a structural one. Impact investors, on the one hand, are typically at a geographic distance from the impact generated by social enterprises and, therefore, use a combination of standards and quantitative data to monitor the impact of their investments. Social enterprises, on the other hand, work within a specific and often local socio-economic context and, thus, accumulate empirical knowledge of their impact. Integrating the systematic and quantitative driven approach used by investors with the experiential and contextual approach used by social enterprises often becomes the main challenge in negotiations.

Avoiding Mission Drift

Social enterprises always face a tension between two goals: social impact and financial sustainability [32]. However, this is particularly strong when an enterprise wishing to scale enters into negotiations with an impact investor. If the impact investor expects the economic return to be higher than the impact return (financial-first impact investors), significant tensions can arise in terms of maintaining the enterprise's social mission [33]. The ability to successfully balance the impact and finance logics becomes a vital factor for social enterprises wishing to scale, particularly if they are to avoid mission drift. Mission drift occurs when an enterprise adheres so strongly to an investors' economic or social expectations that it shifts away from its original mission, which comprises both social impact and financial sustainability, to a purely nonprofit or purely profit-oriented one [34].

An enterprise's mission is a relatively short statement describing its primary purpose. The mission statement is essential, as it serves as the "north star" that guides the enterprise's work over time. For businesses, the guiding star is financial return. For nonprofit organizations, it is their social or environmental mission. Social enterprises are different from both of these. Their guiding star isn't just impact, as with nonprofits, but *functional* impact [35].[xiii] An impact is functional if it is attractive to investors, and therefore allows the social enterprise to secure the resources it needs to achieve its planned impact continually over time. This leads us to a simple yet key point. Some social or environmental missions are inherently more attractive to impact investors than others. A social enterprise working to protect a certain species of insect, for example, might inherently attract fewer investors than helping children in the slums of Brazil gain access to better education. Social enterprises looking to scale must frame their impact in a way that attracts potential investors. The enterprise whose mission is to save an insect species, for example, might need to frame its impact in terms of the broader concepts of biodiversity and fighting the consequences of climate change.

Dialogue in the Dark, a social enterprise that is structured as a social franchise organization and operates globally is a good example. Its mission is to "facilitate [the] social inclusion of blind and disabled people on a global basis," with the goal of "changing [the] mindset of the general public on disability and diversity and to increase tolerance for 'otherness,' and [provide] employment for blind and visually impaired people around the world."[xiv] This mission statement defines a specific target population (the blind and visually impaired), and adopts a long-term vision of extending this impact around the world. Furthermore, it highlights the changes it wants to see in relation to the target population and defines demonstrable achievements (a change in mindset and employment opportunities) that can be analyzed and monitored. The mission is clearly formulated, and is inspiring for stakeholders and investors.

When social enterprises intend to scale, challenges can arise with respect to their mission. The process typically goes something like this [36]: The enterprise tries to reach more beneficiaries and begins to take a more market approach, as proposed in this book. To do this effectively, the enterprise's leadership hires market experts such as business school graduates.

These market experts begin to create communications materials, strategies, budgets, marketing plans, performance analysis tools, and other modern management structures. These structures are attractive to investors, and the social enterprise secures more investments. However, the investors expect the social enterprise to be increasingly aligned with modern management techniques, which begins to shift the balance away from its mission statement. This emphasis on market orientation often clashes with staff that is working toward the enterprise's social or environmental mission on a day-to-day basis. These employees begin to question the investors' expectations and argue that the social enterprise's identity—that is, its social or environmental mission—is at risk. Questions such as, "How many management tools do we need?" or "At what point do we become *too* much like a for-profit enterprise?" can start to circulate. These examples illustrate the tension that can arise within a social enterprise that is in the process of scaling. Often, some employees are more impact-oriented, while others are more market-oriented. Even more severe tensions can arise when discussing the parameters by which to measure the social enterprises' performance. Market-oriented employees might argue that creating financial value for investors takes priority, while the mission-oriented employees might feel that value creation for the beneficiaries takes priority [37]. Explicit or implicit conflicts will inevitably rise. Many leaders of social enterprises believe they can navigate this tension by judging performance based on financial return only. However, this puts the social enterprise at a heightened risk of mission drift, particularly at this juncture. Focusing on financial return alone fails to account for whether the enterprise is executing its stated mission efficiently and effectively. Investments, therefore, cannot be any social enterprise's sole "north star." They are just one indicator of effective, efficient management, and financial sustainability.

The Three Phases of a Market Approach to Scaling

While studying more than 100 social enterprises in action, we learned that social entrepreneurs who successfully identify scaling opportunities: (1) negotiate impact for resources, (2) design operations, and (3) integrate financing and impact logics. By completing these phases, social entrepreneurs can develop a successful scaling strategy for their enterprise (Fig. 2.2) [38, 39].[xv]

Fig. 2.2 Three-phased market approach for developing a scaling strategy

The three-phased market approach to scaling provides a practical guide for how to create a successful scaling strategy that will increase a social enterprise's impact. The model effectively guides complex discussions on how to create scaling strategies. It creates a common language among actors who are willing and capable of negotiating impact for resources—such as impact investors, private companies, incubators, consultants, business school teachers, and others who are interested in fostering the capacity of social entrepreneurs to scale their impact.

At first glance, creating a new framework for scaling might seem redundant, as in recent years an existing tool, the Business Model Canvas, has gained widespread use in business modeling. An increasing number of business schools, incubators, and investors are using the Model Canvas to help social entrepreneurs craft their scaling strategies and mitigate the challenges they encounter while implementing it. However, while the Model Canvas helps startups create their initial business model, on closer examination practitioners are recognizing that it provides minimal guidance for social entrepreneurs with intentions to scale. We have come to this realization as well. Like many business schools and incubators, we began our exploration of a market approach to scaling by first using Osterwalder's Business Model Canvas in our workshops.[xvi] When discussing the tool with practicing social entrepreneurs, however, we realized its limitations in addressing the specific challenges they face with respect to designing a scaling strategy. Thus, we have spent the last several years developing this three-phased approach to market-based scaling, which addresses the Model Canvas's gaps regarding certain areas of interest to social entrepreneurs (Table 2.1).[xvii]

Table 2.1 Difference between the three-phased market approach to scaling and the Business Model Canvas

Elements of scaling	How the Business Model Canvas incorporates the elements of scaling	Scaling challenges faced by social entrepreneurs	How the three-phased market approach to scaling responds to the scaling challenges of social entrepreneurs
Phase I: Negotiating Impact for Resources			
Impact	Focuses on customer segments	Focusing on positively impacting the life quality of entire populations and specific target groups	Social entrepreneurs map and frame their impact to be attractive for getting resources to scale
Resources	The canvas implicitly assumes that paying customers and traditional investors are the sole income and financing sources	Including resources other than paying customers, including contributors of both economic and noneconomic resources	Social entrepreneurs map accessible resources and define what they need to scale
Standards	Not part of the model. The canvas implicitly assumes to adapt to established standards that define business relationships	Developing standards that structure relations in terms of both financial and impact returns	Social entrepreneurs map current standards and define those that support their impact and financial return
Negotiation	Value proposition of product/service for specific customer segments	Providing products/services with an impact that is valued differently by different actors	Social entrepreneurs map how they exchange their impact for resources and design arguments and practices to ensure successful negotiations
Phase II: Designing Operations			
Supply and assets	Competition through business models	Creating scalable solutions through solid operational and revenue processes	Based on mapping their supply and assets, products/services, and distribution and revenue, social entrepreneurs design their operations to reduce costs and increase efficiency. In terms of revenue, they design solutions to either: (a) sell products or services to clients who pay low prices and receive impact, or (b) sell products or services to traditional paying customers and provide services that impact beneficiaries
Products and services			
Distribution and revenue			
Phase III: Integrating Financing and Impact Logics			
Mission	Profit-driven	Structuring in a way that includes both financing and impact logics	Social entrepreneurs map how they previously balanced different logics within their mission, leadership, and communications. They also design solutions to increase their capacity to balance these differing logics
Leadership			
Communication			

Phase I: Negotiating Impact for Resources

The first phase in our market approach to scaling includes the elements of *impact*, *resources*, *standards*, and *negotiation*. These elements differ from the Business Model Canvas in the following ways:

Impact: While the Business Model Canvas focuses on value creation for customer segments, social enterprises focus on creating social or environmental impacts on entire populations or specific target groups. In our three-phased market approach to scaling, "impact" is broadly defined as changing the present condition of the many actors with which a social enterprise is involved.

Resources: The Business Model Canvas assumes that traditional paying customers are the business's main source of income and traditional for-profit investments their way of financing stages of growth. Likewise, social enterprises receive financial resources from paying customers—either from beneficiary customers who pay minimal prices for products or services that positively impact their present condition, or from traditional paying customers who finance services to non-paying beneficiaries. However, social enterprises also include actors who provide financial and non-financial resources to help the social enterprise scale its impact—typically impact investors.

Standards: The Business Model Canvas assumes that the business model is embedded within an established market structure that operates per specific behaviors and relationships. In contrast, social enterprises must analyze the standards that structure their relationships with actors that have resources of interest. They must identify existing standards that can support their scaling efforts, as well as those they must adjust or create.

Negotiation: The Business Model Canvas focuses on creating value propositions in the form of products or services for specific customers. Social enterprises, however, face the unique challenge of simultaneously maintaining relationships with various different market actors, each of which may evaluate the enterprise's impact differently. Thus, our three-phased market approach to scaling differentiates impact (changing the present condition of the many actors with which the enterprise is involved) and assessment (the subjective evaluation of the impact created by the enterprise). Based on this information, social enterprises identify opportunities to negotiate impact in exchange for resources.

In Phase I, social entrepreneurs are guided by the following questions:

1. What kind of *impact* makes a measurable difference for our target group? What kind of impact do we intend to achieve in the future?
2. Which actors are interested in our impact, and what *resources* are available within these markets? What additional resources will we need in the future in order to scale our impact?
3. What are the current *standards* guiding our relations with impact investors, and what standards do we need to create to facilitate our scaling efforts?
4. What practices can we use to *negotiate* our social or environmental impact in exchange for resources? What practices can we use to increase our access to resources?

Once the current situation has been identified and future plans have been defined, social entrepreneurs can then move on to Phase II.

Phase II: Designing Operations

The second phase of our market approach to scaling aligns with the Business Model Canvas. It includes *supply and assets*, *products and services*, and *distribution and revenue*. In the Business Model Canvas, however, the *distribution and revenue* element assumes that other companies compete with the overall business model. In contrast, social enterprises that intend to scale their impact are focused in the scaling potential of their business models—not just differentiating themselves from competitors. Therefore, social enterprises design operations and revenue solutions to increase their capacity to build solid internal processes to create products/services and efficiently deliver them to customers and beneficiaries.

In Phase II, social entrepreneurs are guided by the following questions:

1. What *assets* do we have? What assets do we need to scale impact? How do we organize the supply of raw material and other inputs into our production in a manner that is both cost-effective and impact-generating?
2. What *products and services* should we specialize in to increase the value we create for our customers or beneficiaries? What practices do we need to have in place in order to standardize our products and services to successfully scale impact?

3. What processes do we use and should we use to **distribute** our products and services in a manner that is both cost-effective and impact-generating? What **revenue processes** can we use to support our customer's capacity to pay? What processes will increase our revenues while also keeping our products and services financially accessible for our customers?

Phase III: Integrating Financing and Impact Logics

In Phase III, social entrepreneurs reflect on the tension that scaling creates between the two logics, impact logic on the one hand, and financing logic on the other. This phase differs from the Business Model Canvas, which assumes that every business model is profit-driven, while the structure of social enterprises encompasses both economic sustainability and social or environmental impact. Thus, the third phase of our market approach to scaling includes **mission**, **leadership**, and **communication**, which are used to map how the enterprise currently balances the two logics and design solutions that increase its capacity to do so.

In Phase III, social entrepreneurs are guided by the following questions:

1. Where in our **mission** do the financing and impact logics unite? What elements can we add to our mission to increase the overlap between these two logics?
2. How is our **leadership** structured, and what types of interactions does it promote inside and outside the organization? What kind of leadership structure and interactions would support the overlap between the financing and impact logics?
3. What are our **communication** practices? What practices do we use to foster internal and external communication in a way that unites the financing and impact logics?

While many social entrepreneurs are interested in scaling, few achieve it. Through our empirical studies we have learned that effective social entrepreneurs typically use an "outside-in" approach to scaling, first negotiating impact in exchange for resources from various actors, then focusing on organizational aspects such as (re)defining the products and services it offers to target groups and integrating the financing and impact logics within their mission, leadership, and communications efforts.

Having outlined the theoretical background, the basic structure and the process of working through the three phases to scaling in practice, we will further detail each of these phases and introduce specific cases to illustrate the challenges an enterprise might face during each phase.

Notes

i. For more on the definition of markets, see (1) Fligstein, N., & Dauter, L. (2007). The sociology of markets. *Annual Review of Sociology, 33*, 105–128; (2) North, D. (1990). *Institutions, institutional change and economic performance.* Cambridge University Press.

ii. One of the original documents was created for trainers to teach the Logical Framework. Posner, L., & Rosenberg, L. J. (1970). *Guidelines for teaching Logical Framework concepts.* Washington, DC.

iii. For more on the social enterprise ecosystem, see (1) Mc Mullen, J. (2018). Organizational hybrids as biological hybrids: Insights for research on the relationship between social enterprise and the entrepreneurial ecosystem. *Journal of Business Venturing, 33*(5), 575–590; (2) Roy, M. J., McHugh, N., Huckfield, L., Kay, A., & Donaldson, C. (2015). "The most supportive environment in the world"? Tracing the development of an institutional 'ecosystem' for social enterprise. *Voluntas, 26,* 777–800.

iv. The discussion on "ecosystem" is in line with Kerlin's [13 and 14] research on contextual influences on social enterprises.

v. An example of advanced international standards is the industry of Social Impact Assessment. Vanclay, F. (2001). International principles for social impact assessment. *Impact Assessment and Project Appraisal, 21*(1), 5–11.

vi. FAB Move, an International Research Project on social enterprises organized by Annette Zimmer, highlighted the importance of governments to foster social enterprise ecosystems on a national level. A recently published article explains how the government and nonprofits facilitate "Impact Investing Marketplaces". The authors introduce four ways in which these actors facilitate impact investing marketplaces: (1) enabling optimal infrastructure for marketplaces, (2) improving fixed marketplaces through information exchanges or reducing entry barriers, (3) moving markets on their margin by providing efficient approaches (such as the one we introduce in this book "negotiating impact for resources"), and (4) launching assets to markets [16].

vii. An empirical study showed that the creativity of collaborating partners is a success factor for partnerships. The study specifically showed how positive externalities of entrepreneurship hubs help other hubs to contribute to the success of entrepreneurs when these neighbors hold creativity-focused roles, yet the negative externalities of hubs hinder their neighbors' contributions when they hold efficiency-focused roles [17].

viii. The GSG supports a global movement on impact investment based on the assumption that the status quo of Impact Investors in 2019 on the level where

Venture Capitalists were in the 1980. This movement assumes Impact Investors to have the same impact on social enterprises as Venture Capitalists have on innovations in for profit enterprises. See: https://gsgii.org and Letts et al. [19], who proposed the idea of impact investment more than 20 years ago.

ix. Although practitioners have been recognizing the importance of impact investing [20, 22], the research on this phenomenon is rather at its beginning, see [23, 24] and for a recent literature review Hockerts and Agrawal [25].

x. Höchstädter and Scheck define impact investing as "generally defined around two core elements: financial return and some sort of non-financial impact. The return of the invested principal appears to be a minimum requirement. Generally, however, there are no limitations with regard to the expected level of financial return, that is, whether it must be below, at, or above market rates. With regard to the non-financial impact, impact investing is typically defined around a social and/or environmental impact. In addition, a number of definitions further require that the non-financial return be intentional and measurable or measured, respectively" (p. 454).

xi. For more on earned income strategies used by social enterprises, see (1) Moizer, J., & Tracey, P. (2010). Strategy making in social enterprise: The role of resource allocation and its effects on organizational sustainability. *Systems Research and Behavioral Science, 27*(3), 252–266; (2) Santos, F., Pache, A.-C., & Birkholz, C., (2015). Making hybrids work. *California Management Review, 57*, 36–58.

xii. For more on the tendency of social enterprises to work with actors that share their impact goals, see [30].

xiii. The concept of "exchanging impact for resources" was theoretically developed by Urs Jäger (the first author of this book) and Andreas Schröer and published in the article *Integrated Organizational Identity. A Definition of Hybrid Organizations and a Research Agenda, Voluntas*, Vol. 25, pp. 1281–1306 in 2014. Jäger and Schröer call this exchange approach "functioning solidarity." In this understanding, social enterprises (hybrid organizations) are "characterized by an organizational identity that systematically integrates civil society and markets, exchanges (negotiates) communal solidarity for financial and non-financial resources, calculates the market value of communal solidarity, and trades this solidarity for financial and non-financial resources. In other words, they 'create functional solidarity'" (2014, p. 1281).

xiv. Downloaded in 2014, http://www.dialogue-in-the-dark.com.

xv. Other researchers [38] explored organizational capabilities a social enterprise needs to scale its impact. Those are staffing, communicating, alliance building, lobbying, earnings generation, replicating and stimulating market forces. All of these elements are included in our three phase model. Our three phases can even guide entrepreneurs and their team to explore latent issues, that are described as a main challenge of current management environments [39].

xvi. https://www.strategyzer.com/team.

xvii. Other models, such as the Social Business Model and the "B" Canvas have tried to adapt the Business Model Canvas to the work of social enterprises. These models included the impact variable under the terms "value proposition for users" and "purposes." However, they have the same weaknesses as the Business Model Canvas, as they focus neither on scaling itself nor the resources needed to scale through a market approach. Furthermore, they illustrate issues similar to those outlined at the start of this chapter regarding the use of frameworks such as the impact logic model that don't account for the negotiation processes that entrepreneurs must enter into in order to scale impact.

References

1. Dacin, P. A., Dacin, M. T., & Matear, M. (2010). Social entrepreneurship: Why we don't need a new theory and how we move forward from here. *Academy of Management Perspectives, 24*(3), 37–57.
2. Dacin, M. T., Dacin, P. A., & Tracey, P. (2011). Social entrepreneurship: A critique and future directions. *Organization Science, 22*(5), 1203–1213.
3. Fligstein, N., & Dauter, L. (2007). The sociology of markets. *Annual Review of Sociology, 33,* 105–128.
4. North, D. (1990). *Institutions, institutional change and economic performance.* Cambridge: Cambridge University Press.
5. Wry, T., & Haugh, T. (2018). Brace for impact: Uniting our diverse voices through a social impact frame. *Journal of Business Venturing, 33,* 566–574.
6. Ebrahim, A., & Rangan, V. K. (2014). What impact? A framework for measuring the scale and scope of social performance. *California Management Review, 56*(3), 118–141.
7. Posner, L., & Rosenberg, L. J. (1970). *Guidelines for teaching Logical Framework concepts.* Washington, DC.
8. Luhmann, N. (1995). *Social systems.* Stanford: Stanford University Press.
9. Shrivastava, P. (1995). Ecocentric management for a risk society. *Academy of Management Review, 20*(1), 118–137.
10. Whiteman, G., Walker, B., & Perego, P. (2013). Planetary boundaries: Ecological foundations for corporate sustainability. *Journal of Management Studies, 50*(2), 307–336.
11. Mc Mullen, J. (2018). Organizational hybrids as biological hybrids: Insights for research on the relationship between social enterprise and the entrepreneurial ecosystem. *Journal of Business Venturing, 33*(5), 575–590.
12. Roy, M. J., McHugh, N., Huckfield, L., Kay, A., & Donaldson, C. (2015). "The most supportive environment in the world"? Tracing the development of an institutional 'ecosystem' for social enterprise. *VOLUNTAS: International Journal of Voluntary and Nonprofit Organizations, 26,* 777–800.

13. Kerlin, J. A. (2010). A comparative analysis of the global emergence of social enterprise. *VOLUNTAS: International Journal of Voluntary and Nonprofit Organizations, 21*(2), 162–179.
14. Kerlin, J. A. (2013). Defining social enterprise across different contexts: A conceptual framework based on institutional factors. *Nonprofit and Voluntary Sector Quarterly, 42*(1), 84–108.
15. Vanclay, F. (2001). International principles for social impact assssment. *Impact Assessment and Project Appraisal, 21*(1), 5–11.
16. Tekula, R., & Andersen, K. (2017). The role of government, nonprofit, and private facilitation of the Impact Investing Marketplace. *Public Performance & Management Review, 42*(1). Published online 5 December 2018.
17. Clement, J., Shipilov, A., & Galunic, C. (2018). Brokerage as a public good: The externalities of network hubs for different formal roles in creative organizations. *Administrative Science Quarterly, 63*(2), 251–286.
18. Gutiérrez, R., Márquez, P., & Reficco, E. (2016). Configuration and development of alliance portfolios: A comparison of same-sector and cross-sector partnerships. *Journal of Business Ethics, 135*(1), 55–69.
19. Letts, C., Ryan, W., & Grossman, A. (1997). Virtuous capital: What foundations can learn from venture capitalists. *Harvard Business Review, 75*(2), 36–44.
20. O'Donohoe, N., Leijonhufvud, C., Saltuk, Y., Bugg-Levine, A., & Brandenburg, M. (2010). *Impact investments: An emerging asset class*. J.P. Morgan.
21. McWade, W. (2012). The role for social enterprises and social investors in the development struggle. *Journal of Social Entrepreneurship, 3*(1), 96–112.
22. Leme, A., Fernando M., & Hornberger, K. (2014). *The state of impact investing in Latin America*. Bain & Company.
23. Achleitner, A.-K., Heinecke, A., Noble, A., Schöning, M., & Spiess-Knafl, W. (2011). Unlocking the mystery: An introduction to social investment. *Innovations, 6*(3), 145–154.
24. Emerson, J. (2003). The blended value proposition: Integrating social and financial returns. *California Management Review, 45*(4), 35–51.
25. Hockerts, K., & Agrawal, A. (2018). Impact investing: Review and research agenda. *Journal of Small Business & Entrepreneurship*. Published online 31 January 2019.
26. Brown, J. (2006). Equity finance for social enterprises. *Social Enterprise Journal, 2*(1), 73–81.
27. Höchstädter, A. K., & Scheck, B. (2019). What's in a name: An analysis of impact investing understandings by academics and practitioners. *Journal of Business Ethics, 132*, 449–475.
28. Moizer, J., & Tracey, P. (2010). Strategy making in social enterprise: The role of resource allocation and its effects on organizational sustainability. *Systems Research and Behavioral Science, 27*(3), 252–266.
29. Santos, F., Pache, A.-C., & Birkholz, C. (2015). Making hybrids work. *California Management Review, 57*, 36–58.

30. Powell, E. E., Hamann, R., Bitzer, V., & Baker, T. (2018). Bringing the elephant into the room? Enacting conflict in collective prosocial organizing. *Journal of Business Venturing, 33*(5), 623–642.

31. Aschari-Lincoln, J. (2017). *Determining characteristics of social organizations for their financing* (Doctoral thesis). University of St. Gallen, St. Gallen.

32. Austin, J. E., Gutierrez, R., Ogliastri, E., Reficco, E., & Fischer, R. M. (2006). *Effective management of social enterprises: Lessons from business and civil society organizations in Ibero-America.* Cambridge, MA: Harvard University Press.

33. Smith, B. R., Kistruck, G. M., & Cannatelli, B. (2016). The impact of moral intensity and desire for control on scaling decisions in social entrepreneurship. *Journal of Business Ethics, 133*(4), 677–689.

34. André, K., & Pache, A. C. (2014). From caring entrepreneur to caring enterprise: Addressing the ethical challenges of scaling up social enterprises. *Journal of Business Ethics, 133*(4), 659–675.

35. Jäger, U. (2010). *Managing social business: Mission, governance, strategy, accountability.* Houndmills and New York: Palgrave Macmillan.

36. Jäger, U., & Schröer, A. (2014). Integrated organizational identity: A definition of hybrid organizations and a research agenda. *VOLUNTAS: International Journal of Voluntary and Nonprofit Organizations, 25.* Published online 3 July 2013.

37. Kreutzer, K., & Jäger, U. (2011). Volunteering versus managerialism: Conflict over organizational identity in voluntary associations. *Nonprofit and Voluntary Sector Quarterly, 40*(4), 634–661.

38. Bloom, P. N., & Chatterji, A. (2009). Scaling social entrepreneurial impact. *California Management Review, 51*(3), 114–133.

39. Bansal, K., Kim, A., & Wood, M. O. (2018). Hidden in plain sight: The importance of scale in organizations' attention to issues. *Academy of Management Review, 43*(2), 217–241.

3

Phase I: Negotiating Impact for Resources

This phase is the first step to creating a scaling strategy. In this phase, social entrepreneurs explore how they can negotiate impact for the resources they need to successfully scale. In this analysis, social entrepreneurs take an "outside-in" approach to scaling as they explore actors with whom they can potentially negotiate impact in exchange for the resources needed to scale. This includes actors in the same geographical area where the social enterprise works, as well as national and international actors interested in the issues it addresses. A contextual study can help social entrepreneurs map accessible sources of resources (i.e., public organizations, international nongovernmental organizations (INGOs), private companies, individual impact investors, institutional impact investors, customers, etc.). These actors have economic and/or non-economic resources and might be interested in negotiating the social enterprise's impact in exchange for these resources. The contextual study also helps social entrepreneurs understand the current standards for both financial and impact return (e.g., rates of interest, social impact indicators, etc.), which can support or hinder their negotiation efforts.

Exploring Actors That Can Support a Market Approach to Scaling

Four elements (*impact*, *resources*, *standards*, and *negotiation*) illustrate the process of negotiating impact for resources. We will use the social enterprise uSound to illustrate each of these elements, and support related conceptual arguments for this phase of our market approach to scaling (Fig. 3.1).

© The Author(s) 2020
U. Jäger et al., *Scaling Strategies for Social Entrepreneurs*,
https://doi.org/10.1007/978-3-030-31160-5_3

Fig. 3.1 Phase I: negotiating impact for resources

Impact

Defining **impact** establishes a starting point for the social enterprise's scaling strategy. As we have previously explained, however, this impact must align with the expectations and interests of market actors if the enterprise hopes to negotiate the additional resources needed to scale its impact. More specifically, impact investors have a special interest in measuring and reporting on the impact of their investments [1]. Therefore, one of the main challenges of the impact element is to define impact in the language of "impact return." Social and environmental impacts can be very difficult to measure, however, so negotiating impact for resources presents added challenges. Successful social entrepreneurs find ways to measure their impact. This, in turn, allows them to be confident that (a) their actions are indeed having the intended impact; (b) they can communicate this impact effectively; and (c) they can convince potential investors to provide economic and/or non-economic resources in exchange for this impact. In this sense, successful social entrepreneurs leverage their previous and potential impact as a means of obtaining resources.

Consider "uSound," a social enterprise founded in 2015 by Ezequiel Escobar and three of his MBA colleagues from Jujuy, an impoverished region in northern Argentina. The team's initial motivation was to support a fellow student who suffered from hearing loss. They created an app that allowed him to use his phone as a hearing aid. It worked. Ezequiel and his partners then learned that 5% of the world's population suffers from hearing loss, many of whom cannot afford to purchase expensive hearing aids. Observing that both rich and poor citizens have access to modern mobile phones, they developed a high-quality product that could be used as an app/headset package and would cost 20% less than other hearing aids. Further, Ezequiel and his partners could measure the number of times their app had been downloaded. To further measure their impact, they executed empirical studies of select customers to monitor how the hearing device had changed their lives. The number of apps downloaded, coupled with empirical studies, allowed the partners to measurably demonstrate how uSound's app increased the quality of life of their customers. This, in turn, helped them negotiate financial support from the government and other public authorities. In the end, the local government agreed to purchase a certain number of apps for a defined population. By 2017, the app had been downloaded more than 350,000 times in 150 countries.

Guiding questions:
What kind of ***impact*** makes a measurable difference for our target group?
What kind of impact do we intend to achieve in the future?

Resources

This element refers to the financial and non-financial ***resources*** needed to scale impact, as well as the actors who can provide them. It is extremely common for social enterprises to lack the resources they need to scale their impact, so a key challenge is to identify potential resources in their surrounding environment. Social enterprises, whether they operate in high- or low-income contexts, explore and exploit resources to scale their impact. Resources can come from investors, customers, and partners specifically interested in negotiating impact in exchange for resources. To illustrate the point, we will return to the case of uSound. Once uSound's leaders had explored and analyzed the context in which the enterprise operated, they identified and targeted different impact investors, finally agreeing to launch a negotiation process with the regional government. The regional government was not only a potential source of financial resources, but would also provide access to other investors and other contact networks, such as media outlets that could help market the organization's impact.

Guiding questions:
Which actors are interested in our impact, and what ***resources*** are available within these markets? What additional resources will we need in the future in order to scale our impact?

Standards

Standards are norms that structure negotiations between social enterprises and impact investors. Those norms guide the expectations that the sources identified in the previous element have regarding financial and impact return, and those held by the social enterprise. Impact investors, for example, are interested in receiving a financial and social return on their investment and often expect clear results reporting from the social enterprise, according to international standards such as GIIRS. To meet these expectations, successful social enterprises take the time to review internationally established reporting standards. In addition, both social enterprises and impact investors analyze the creation of new standards that facilitate impact in order to define how they can overcome any barriers that might impede their impact goals. When standards, such as laws and market regulations, are well-established and support the investor's impact targets, they can be leveraged by the social enterprise to scale impact. However, if the institutional settings are weak or nonexistent, as is common in many low-income market regions due to a high degree of informality and poverty [2, 3], the enterprise must create or transform the standards in a way that supports its efforts to scale. Social enterprises can also face a much more nuanced setting, in which some standards support their mission while others represent obstacles. Social enterprises intending to scale must identify and leverage the standards that will help them scale their impact [4]. This is a complex process, and can take several years, but building and/or changing standards can be an extremely effective strategy for scaling impact—particularly in developing countries.

In the low-income markets of Jujuy, for example, where uSound was founded, many laws and public institutions do not function efficiently because of high levels of corruption. This affects the healthcare market, which at the time was dominated by public hospitals and doctors that operated within a bureaucratic system that resulted in high costs and poor health outcomes for patients. When it came to positively impacting people with hearing loss, uSound's leaders realized they could not be successful within the current system of standards. So, Ezequiel and his partners took their online hearing aid app directly to the regional government, which had shown interest in providing hearing devices to poor customers. The parties agreed that it was vital to change the standards of the healthcare market by providing certain services via the internet, without the intervention of a doctor. So, they constructed a business model that could sidestep the bureaucratic system via technological tools.

Guiding questions:
What are the current **standards** guiding our relations with impact investors, and what standards do we need to create to facilitate our scaling efforts?

Negotiation

Once potential sources have been identified and alignment has been achieved by analyzing (and potentially creating or adjusting) the standards that structure the relationship, social enterprises then **negotiate** with investors to exchange their impact for the resources needed to scale [5, 6]. Negotiation is a practice in which social entrepreneurs explore their own interests and expectations as well as those of the negotiation partner, search for common interests and expectations between the two parties, and seek mutually-beneficial solutions. At this stage, it is particularly critical that social entrepreneurs analyze the values and interests of potential investors and only select those that most align with both the commercial and impact value of their enterprise. For example, uSound received an offer from an investor to open an office in the United States. As the young company understood that it was not yet prepared for this, its leaders declined the offer. It's important to remember that not all investors fit the needs of a given social enterprise.

Guiding questions:
What practices can we use to **negotiate** our social or environmental impact in exchange for resources? What practices can we use to increase our access to resources?

Table 3.1 presents further examples of the elements of **impact**, **resources**, standards, and **negotiation**.

The Diseclar Case

The first step to create a scaling strategy is to negotiate impact for resources that are relevant to the social enterprise's scaling efforts. With respect to impact investors, most social entrepreneurs have a hard time establishing opportunities to raise investment funds, for one of two reasons. On the one hand, social enterprises that were initially founded as nonprofit organizations rarely perceive their impact as negotiable. These organizations tend to look for resources in the form of donations, which they use to develop products and services that impact their target groups. On the other hand, other social enterprises that began as for-profit companies often fail to recognize the need to make their impact more visible and measurable in order to attract investors who expect financial and social returns.

Table 3.1 Examples of Phase I elements

Elements	Examples
Impact	*Impact on systems*: Tasso Azevedo, a Brazilian entrepreneur who works to protect the Amazon has created various organizations, including law firms, nonprofit organizations, and for-profit companies in order to strengthen inter-sectoral collaborations *Impact on communities*: Luis Szarán, a Paraguayan music director, founded Sonidos de la Tierra to strengthen community development through the establishment of community orchestras *Impact on organizations*: Puntaje Nacional in Chile helps primary schools increase the quantity and quality of teaching and learning materials, therefore strengthening the quality of schools
Resources	*Non-financial resources 1*: EUVestment (pseudonym, see Chapter 6) advised Albina Ruiz, founder of Ciudad Saludable, on products and services for grassroots recyclers *Non-financial resources 2*: USound, an Argentine company that created an app that works as a hearing aid, found that establishing business in the low-income context of Jujuy had the benefit of offering a high-quality skilled technical labor at a lower cost compared with high-income contexts *Financial resources*: FUNDES, a social enterprise that supports SMEs in Latin America, identified large companies as a key customer group interested in its services to help them increase the efficiency of their value chains
Standards	*Impact return through changing existing laws*: Albina Ruiz, a Peruvian environmental engineer, collaborated with the Ministry of the Environment to create a law that professionalizes informal recyclers *Financial return*: Juan Fermín Rodríguez, a Guatemalan entrepreneur and founder of Kingo, an organization that provides solar energy to isolated and poor communities, developed a revenue system based on modern analytics that track profitable and unprofitable consumers
Negotiation	*Sustainability*: Nicolás Suárez, the founder of Diseclar, a company that produces furniture from recycled plastic material, included sustainability in its business model in order to access impact investors *Subsidies*: Five young university graduates who founded Ilumexico negotiated with the Oaxacan government to subsidize 40% of their enterprise's project costs

The following case illustrates the challenges faced by social entrepreneur Juan Nicolás Suárez in negotiating impact for resources when his enterprise, Diseclar, was at its early stages of development. Juan Nicolás's decision was to either (a) negotiate with investors that were only seeking a financial return on their investment, or (b) frame Diseclar's impact in a way that would attract impact investors to enter into negotiation with

Diseclar. This dilemma of framing a business model as primarily impact-oriented or primarily financial-return-oriented is quite common for social enterprises working in Latin American markets, as most venture capitalists in these markets manage their risk by investing in ventures that already show strong market proof—thus, are already in advanced stages of development—and expect a high financial return on investment, with which most social enterprises in the region, especially in their early stages of development, can scarcely comply [7]. The rising number of impact investors in Latin America, however, evaluate financial risk differently from these profit-oriented investors [8]. Impact investors are typically willing to accept a higher financial risk if they can invest in a social enterprise that shows a high probability of having a significant and measurable social or environmental return.

Juan Nicolás recognized the difficulties associated with accessing profit-oriented financing and explored the possibility of negotiating impact for resources from two different perspectives: negotiating primarily based on Diseclar's expectations of financial return, and negotiating primarily based on impact return.

The Case: Securing Venture Capital for a Social Enterprise in Latin America[1]

Just under three years after launching his journey as an entrepreneur, Juan Nicolás Suárez (Photo 3.1) was at a crossroads regarding the destiny of Diseclar, a recycled furniture manufacturing company that he had founded in Cali, Colombia.

Diseclar originated from Juan Nicolás's idea to produce a raw material from recycled waste products that could compete with wood in terms of durability, cost, and aesthetics. With some assistance, he created and perfected the material, and explored various applications such as tables, pergolas, floors, chairs, and benches.

Juan Nicolás's connections and past experiences with the beverage industry and its distribution channels had revealed the local market's need for low-cost tables and chairs. Thus far, he had only sold his products to individual consumers through direct references and had tried—without much success—to sell his outdoor pergolas and floors wholesale to large

[1]Authors: Randall Trejos, Researcher INCAE Business School and Urs Jäger, Associate Professor INCAE Business School and Academic Director VIVA Idea.

Photo 3.1   Juan Nicolás Suárez, founder of Diseclar, sitting in one of his products

distribution companies. Though aware of the stark differences between these two types of customers, he decided to target both because he needed all the income he could gather if he wished to scale his business.

For over two years, Juan Nicolás had produced his initial prototypes by outsourcing manufacturing, and had sold his products to anyone who was interested. During this time, he received funding from entities that supported social entrepreneurship, and earned awards from business plan competitions. Thanks to USD85,000 raised in this way, along with some of his personal savings, Juan Nicolás was on his way to obtaining one of the seven machines he would need to move the manufacturing process in-house. He saw the acquisition of machinery as the next step in Diseclar's development, as this would reduce his reliance on third parties and allow him to cut costs. The cost of all seven machines was USD500,000.

It was another hot day in Cali, and Juan Nicolás had just arrived at his workshop after meeting with a prospective customer. As he sat at his desk, he returned to a question he had been entertaining for several months, "How can I raise half a million dollars?" He turned to look at the one thing that comforted him during difficult times. Spread across his desk were various certificates from prizes that his business had won, along with multiple newspaper articles praising Juan Nicolás as an example of a successful Colombian entrepreneur. He knew that this display of support had to mean that he was onto something big. Juan Nicolás continued to reflect. "I've not always been 100% sure for what kind of investor I should look for. Some want financial results, while others are attracted to sustainability or the social aspect of my business." For the nearly three years he'd been in business, he had met various for-profit investors who offered support, most of them foreigners who were only willing to invest in Diseclar if it could expand into other countries. "What if I focused entirely on our sustainability and social impact?" he thought. "I am coming across an increasing number of organizations that care about these things." He knew this was not going to be an easy decision. "You never want to close a door to a potential investor…but it's becoming harder and harder to please everyone at once," he had told a friend during lunch the day before. "On one hand, I feel like if I focus too much on sustainability and social impact, instead of profits and ROI, then I might lose access to more traditional angel investors and VC funds. On the other hand, I don't want my business to only be about profit and growth, because that risks losing the soul of what Diseclar stands for. To be honest, I don't know how to pitch this business anymore."

Recycling in Colombia

Diseclar was competing with several companies that manufactured furniture from real wood, as well as others that used plastic or faux wood (priced slightly lower). A real wood table and four chairs were priced at USD210, while plastic ones costed about 40% less. These competitors sold through major retailers such as Homecenter, Jumbo, Tugo, and PriceSmart, and their value proposition was based on low prices. However, none of these companies shared Diseclar's approach of using recycled materials.

Colombia's, National Study of Recycling [9], conducted from 2010 to 2011, showed that 25,999 tons of solid waste was being produced daily, 6025 of which was recovered from recycling over 312 days of operation (16.54%). Experts believed that with adequate public policy and a greater public awareness regarding recycling, Colombia could aspire to achieve recovery rates of 20–25%. However, the country was still far from these levels. Medellin, the city with the most positive figures, was recovering 17% of its solid waste, with Bogota at just 3.9%. Of this, nearly 60% was organic, 8.4% was cardboard and paper, roughly 13% was plastic, 2.4% was glass, and 16.7% was an aggregate of metals, electronics, wood, batteries, and other materials.

The recycling industry generated significant economic value. In 2011, experts estimated that more than 50,000 of the country's citizens practiced recycling as their primary occupation, and at least 200,000 people were indirectly related to the industry. Despite its size, however, economic value was not distributed evenly throughout the value chain, and the recycling market presented considerable challenges for each of its stakeholders.

For collection—the first step in the value chain—the average monthly income of male and female workers ranged from USD21 to USD218, with most receiving 80% below the legal minimum salary of roughly USD192.[i] The vast majority of collectors worked under precarious conditions, did not have healthcare coverage, and had a guild associativity of less than 30% with little opportunity to organize and improve their conditions.

The collection, transportation, and processing of materials—representing the second step in the value chain—was largely concentrated, with a few companies controlling pricing. This issue was exacerbated by minimal state intervention to restrict monopolistic practices. Representatives of the sector thrived on this lack of public policy and used it to protect their particular interests.

Companies that transformed recycled material—representing the third step in the value chain—required high volumes of material to sustain operations because of the scale requirements that came with large manufacturing equipment. Because of the way that the value chain was set up in the previous two steps (with individual collectors gathering very small volumes and pricing being controlled by the monopolistic practices of the collection companies), manufacturers were often exposed to fluctuations in the availability and price of raw materials, forcing them to import.

Actors from the recycling sector felt that public institutions did not make enough of an effort to promote recycling as a source of income and did not advocate the separation of private, household garbage as a citizen responsibility. A systematic and sustained effort to raise awareness about the importance of recycling, as well as the implementation of regulations that would require the public to separate its waste, were still missing.

In addition, the payment model structure for sanitary landfills, along with the existence of waste disposal concessionary companies, generated incentives that were contrary to recycling efforts. Local governments paid per ton of waste, so it was in the companies' interest to move the greatest amount of waste possible to the landfill.

Development Stages of Diseclar

Stage 1: The Idea

One of Juan Nicolás's earliest positions was an eight-month project at SAB Miller, in which he was charged with overseeing campaigns and brand activation events for the beverage company Bavaria. During that time, he witnessed the excessive plastic waste generated by the drink factories, as well as by many distributors (e.g., small bars and restaurants). He also noticed that only a small portion of this plastic waste was being reused or recycled.

As a result of his contact with restaurants, bars, and small shops, he also came to understand that these businesses had a need for low-cost furniture. This furniture (sometimes purchased, and other times on loan from the beverage companies) consisted of affordable yet short-lived plastic or wooden tables and chairs.

If he could find a way to utilize the waste produced by the beverage industry to manufacture the plastic chairs and tables that its establishments required, he could solve both problems. Companies such as Bavaria could reuse their waste responsibly, with the incentive of getting back the low-cost chairs and tables they had lent to their distributors. The distributors would have better quality, more durable furniture at a lower cost. In the end, all parties would be helping the environment.

Stage 2: Incubation at Campus Nova

In 2011, shortly after the SAB Miller project, and while he was working for Corbeta, Juan Nicolás received an award from the Pontifical Xavierian University, which resulted in USD2500 in seed capital and the opportunity to join Campus Nova,[ii] the university's incubator and entrepreneurship center, with the pilot project that would later be named Diseclar.

Campus Nova was created in 2010, after the university decided to make entrepreneurialism a cross-cutting subject for all majors (rather than just an elective). Now, under the Academic Vice-Chancellorship, the initiative would provide students with the option to go from being an employee to generating employment. Campus Nova seemed to be the most concrete way to support entrepreneurs both inside and outside the university.

Like many other incubator programs, Campus Nova supported ideas that were in their early stages of conception with market testing and, in cases where a project was determined viable, the formalization of the company. By 2014, the initiative had incubated 2000 entrepreneurs and created 210 companies. Each month, 50 new people entered the program, 40% of which had no affiliation with the university. The majority of the incubated projects (70%) were considered traditional companies, 20% were of a cultural or artistic nature, and just 10% were social or environmental businesses.

Under the mentorship of Oscar Mauricio Vásquez, the Campus Nova director, Juan Nicolás began to refine his idea, taking the first steps toward turning it into a company. One of these steps was to decide what raw materials he would use and how he would process them. However, neither Diseclar nor Campus Nova had adequate technical knowledge, nor the facilities needed to perform the necessary tests. They decided to contact the Servicio Nacional de Aprendizaje[iii] (SENA) for support.

Stage 3: SENA and the Emprender Fund

Thanks to his relationship with Campus Nova, in 2012, Juan Nicolás met with Andrés Fernando Tellez, an adviser for SENA's Entrepreneurship Unit. Tellez became key to the project's development, because he gave Juan Nicolás access to chemical and material engineers who were experts in polymers, as well as professionals who were researching the use of organic waste to replace the petrochemicals used in plastics.

With the help of SENA, Juan Nicolás decided to compete for support from the Emprender Fund, a government initiative to support projects demonstrating either a strong component of either innovation or social/environmental impact. The fund was offering a USD50,000 award and the opportunity to participate in SENA's mentorship program for one year. This consisted of two to three monthly sessions that would help entrepreneurs accelerate their projects. In November of 2012, Diseclar became one of the award winners, leading Juan Nicolás to resign from his job and devote his time entirely to his company.

In February of 2013, the company became incorporated—though Juan Nicolás was still waiting to receive the USD50,000 in funding. Eager to move forward, he and his adviser, Andrés, began to test the materials. One of the first challenges they faced was that the material, made entirely from plastic waste, was aesthetically unattractive. It was lightweight and low cost but would not be well-received by consumers. The pair began to experiment with a combination of materials, particularly those of organic origin. Bagasse coffee, once dried, mixed well with the plastic to provide greater flexibility, which was a desirable characteristic when using it for furniture. It also had a more attractive color and texture than the previous versions but was still a product geared toward a market motivated by low cost and durability, rather than design and aesthetics.

Once they had solved the problem of what material to use—at least partially—Juan Nicolás and his colleague took on the task of defining their target audience, identifying its needs, and whether or not their company could successfully compete with other products on the market. At the time, they focused solely on tables and chairs. They started by polling restaurants that served traditional foods, since these customers typically needed low-cost furniture and would not be discouraged by a simple, rustic look. Although Diseclar's value proposition was largely based on the environmental impact of making products from recycled materials, they realized that the restaurateurs' main priority was that the furniture be as cheap as plastic and as attractive as wood. For this audience, environmental impact was secondary.

The results of the market study and the possibilities that arose from a new material based on recycled plastic and bagasse coffee provided Diseclar with an approach that went beyond the provision of alternatives to plastic chairs and tables—it would also be able to market an alternative to wood. According to Juan Nicolás and his partners' calculations, if produced internally, they could offer a product that was as cheap as plastic but aesthetically capable of competing with wood.

Stage 4: Financial Awards as a Source of Funding

The concept of using waste materials while creating low-cost furniture capable of replacing wood was certainly an attractive idea. In an effort to publicize the project and seek funding alternatives, in 2013 Juan Nicolás entered several business and innovation competitions (Photo 3.2).

The Stephan Schmidheiny awards[iv] recognized Diseclar in its Environmental Innovation category, granting it a USD20,000 award. The Chivas Venture contest[v] also awarded the initiative with USD10,000, and a competition organized by the United Nations awarded it with USD5000.

These distinctions, in addition to providing a financial boost at a time when he was still waiting for the financing promised by the Emprender Fund, were key to motivating the entrepreneur to press on. "Receiving so many awards convinced me that this was a good idea; that it was worth continuing to fight for, even at a point when I hadn't yet seen any profit," said Juan Nicolás.

Stage 5: Formalization and Development of a Minimum Viable Product

In September 2013, still awaiting the receipt of the money from the awards he had already won, Juan Nicolás began to plan the first steps he would

Photo 3.2   Juan Nicolás Suárez, founder of Diseclar, in a pitch for raising funds

take once the funds arrived. Initially, he thought the first step would be to acquire an extruder machine to process the material and manufacture the basic parts with which to assemble his products. However, this would cost USD100,000—nearly all the funds he had raised to date.

Still under the mentorship of Andrés Fernando Tellez, Juan Nicolás opted for a more cautious approach: to outsource manufacturing and generate some prototypes to test the market reaction. Meanwhile, he decided to spend some time learning about the manufacturing process before investing in machinery. This would allow him to invest in marketing and building up an inventory of raw materials without incurring significant sunk costs. Outsourced manufacturing, however, entailed certain risks. Much of his value proposition laid precisely with the material that he had perfected over the past year. Furthermore, processing it at an outside plant would involve sharing the formula with a third party. He decided to take the risk and, by the end of the year, had the parts ready for assembly.

In April 2014, with the first pieces assembled, he launched a marketing campaign focused on the segment targeted during the market study: small restaurants serving simple menus. The response was not encouraging, as many indicated that they had already met their need through other channels, such as plastic and wood furniture suppliers.

In June, drawing from his network of acquaintances, Juan Nicolás began to visit potential customers who had shown an interest in the material but were inquiring about other potential uses apart from furniture. Some saw it as a durable replacement for wood and asked if it would be possible to use it to manufacture pergolas and outdoor flooring. Though unexpected, Juan Nicolás found this application was attractive, and he decided to produce both products: furniture on the one hand, and pergolas and flooring on the other.

With the feedback provided by these first customers, he decided to rethink Diseclar's brand, logo, and positioning strategy. He distanced the logo from the notion of chairs and tables for restaurants and incorporated other products such as pergolas and outdoor flooring, in addition to other applications of his material.

By mid-2014, Juan Nicolás finally received the money from the Emprender Fund and, after several months of market testing and accumulating lessons learned, he was finally in a position to acquire the extruder machine that would help cut his dependence on third parties for the manufacture of parts. This independence was only partial, however, as the initial processing of the material from plant fibers and recycled plastic continued to be outsourced.

Diseclar as of 2015

Mission and Vision

Diseclar's mission was to contribute to the culture of recycling and environmental conservation, and to the improvement of Colombian citizens' quality of life. Its four-year vision was to meet the needs of the national and international furniture market, using eco-friendly raw materials while generating a viable social impact.

Target Market

Although Diseclar initially intended to exclusively serve corporate customers such as restaurants as a B2B company, by 2015 its sales were primarily to end users who purchased furniture, outdoor flooring, and pergolas for their homes.

Aware that negotiations with large companies tended to move slowly, Juan Nicolás chose to serve the general public as a way of publicizing his products and generating income. As he saw it, at this stage, they couldn't afford to say no to any potential customer.

Later, Juan Nicolás tried to get a foot in the door of the construction and real estate industries, seeking larger sales with housing developments.

On the institutional end, the company was contacted by the city government to bid on a USD500,000 project to build low-cost stands for street vendors. Due to the volume required and its dependence on outsourced manufacturing, however, Diseclar was unable to participate in the bid.

Products

By July 2015, Diseclar's sales were evenly divided between furniture (50%) and outdoor flooring and pergolas (50%). The material was durable and resembled wood, but was considerably heavy. The fact that the products were made from recycled materials generated a positive image, but it was rarely a decisive factor in the Colombian market.

Costs and Competitiveness

Before purchasing the extruder machine, Diseclar had depended on outsourcers for two key operations processes: the processing of raw materials from waste (recycled plastics and plant fibers) and the assembly of the resulting parts into furniture. Its outdoor flooring, for example, was cheaper than fine wood flooring (such as teak) but couldn't compete with low-cost products imported from China. In terms of tables and chairs, however, outsourcing these processes allowed Diseclar to offer prices that were 15% lower than wood alternatives and 25% lower than what was known as "plastic wood."

Juan Nicolás purchased the extruder machine in order to manufacture the parts from materials processed by third parties. But the machine was just the last piece of the process—it created the parts from the already-processed material. He would need seven other pieces of equipment if he also wanted to process the raw materials in-house.

If Diseclar could acquire the machinery needed to complete the entire production process in-house, it could reduce its costs by 35–40%—enough to compete with Asian imports. This equipment came with a steep price tag, which Juan Nicolás estimated at roughly USD350,000.

By 2015, securing a way to process the raw materials wasn't just a matter of reducing costs and becoming more competitive; SENA, which had thus far allowed Diseclar to produce the material in its facilities, had warned Juan Nicolás that they could not continue to support the company in this way. It had been two years since the first prototypes of the raw material, and SENA felt it was time for Diseclar to find a way to produce the material on its own.

Assurance of Raw Material

Plant, coffee, and sugarcane fibers were not difficult to find, given the volume of agriculture around Cali and throughout Colombia. Plastics, on the other hand, were different. Although the amount of materials recovered was improving in several Colombian cities, high fragmentation between individual collectors and the nearly monopolistic collection centers made the availability and price of large volumes of plastics uncertain. Diseclar was able to negotiate the supply of plastics with one local company, and though the needed quantities remained small, Juan Nicolás was uncomfortable with relying on just one supplier.

Infrastructure and Assets

Diseclar had 14,000 kg of raw material, worth roughly USD20,000. The material was processed externally and was not intended to be a final product, but used for the construction of furniture, pergolas, and flooring.

The 350 m^2 warehouse in which it operated cost Diseclar USD280/month. Thanks to the award funds, the enterprise had just acquired an extruder machine for USD100,000. Juan Nicolás wondered if it would be a better idea to first acquire land on which to build a factory while he gathered the funds needed for the remaining machinery.

Finances

As of mid-2015, Diseclar had raised USD85,000 through awards from organizations such as the Emprender Fund, the Stephan Schmidheiny Awards for Innovation in Sustainability, The Venture competition, and the United Nations. Juan Nicolás had also contributed nearly USD15,000 of his own funds during the company's early stages.

Though nothing had been decided yet, Juan Nicolás was exploring possible financing from angel investors, both local and foreign. The goal was to

Table 3.2 Projected profit and loss statement, in USD, years 1–5[a]

Income statement (in thousands of USD)	Year 1	Year 2	Year 3	Year 4	Year 5
Sales	321	456	678	897	1034
Raw materials, labor	111 (6 of which are labor costs)	159 (6 of which are labor costs)	194 (18 of which are labor costs)	236 (36 of which are labor costs)	272 (42 of which are labor costs)
Depreciation	81	114	114	114	114
Other costs	8	21	33	39	61
Gross income	**121**	**162**	**337**	**508**	**587**
Sales expenses	61	86	132	178	195
Administration expenses	98	129	185	249	273
Operating income	**−38**	**−53**	**20**	**81**	**119**

aThis income statement is hypothetical and does not disclose Diseclar's true financial projections obtain USD500,000 to purchase the machinery needed to conduct all production stages in-house, from the processing of materials to the manufacture of the final product.

Based on his projections, Diseclar could generate sales of more than USD300,000, yielding slightly more than a USD50,000 net profit in its first year (Table 3.2).

Organization and Work Team

By 2015, the company had hired its first operator, Ever Guzmán, whose extensive carpentry experience would provide invaluable insight into how to adapt the new material to the manufacture of products that were traditionally made of wood. Assisting Ever was Sebastián Ramírez, who by then had become a full-time employee. In addition, Olga Bonilla was hired as part-time support in sales management. Other external collaborators included Carlos Gustavo Orozco, in charge of accounting services, and Monica Nieto, who collaborated with advertising and media campaigns.

Sustainability as a Competitive Advantage for Negotiating Impact for Resources

From the very beginning, the issue of environmental/social impact was at the core of Diseclar's mission and its communication strategy. However, as Juan Nicolás interacted with customers in the Colombian market, he realized that the eco-friendly aspect of his business was viewed by customers as a nice detail, but was not a differentiating factor that they would be willing to pay for. Unlike consumers in more developed markets, Colombians were much more concerned about price, durability, and aesthetics than they were about sustainability.

In terms of the value chain, Diseclar had an opportunity to create a notable environmental and social impact. So far, Juan Nicolás and every supporter that he had found along the way agreed that the company's "secret sauce" was the material that he and the SENA engineers had come up with: a combination of recycled plastics and organic waste from coffee and sugarcane. To secure the plastic needed for production, he had so far relied on the only plastic collection center in town, which guaranteed neither future availability nor price stability. Juan Nicolás knew that if Diseclar began to manufacture larger volumes, this sole supplier would be insufficient. But, even if he somehow managed to meet the company's needs by importing waste plastic during shortages, he would be completely exposed to price fluctuations that could eat away his margins.

The organic component of his material, a by-product of sugarcane and coffee production, was less worrisome. Cali was known for its sugarcane plantations, and there were more than enough potential providers to deliver any amount of materials needed. However, the company had not yet tried to collaborate with stakeholders higher up in the value chain, such as small farmers. Until then, Diseclar had simply viewed these actors as providers of its raw material. Now, Juan Nicolás wondered if it might make sense to resort to backward vertical integration, particularly given the success that the company's sustainability story had had in competitions and initial rounds of funding.

Environmental and social impact was precisely what the organizations providing financial support were interested in. With each competition, the case for social and environmental impact became more central to Diseclar's story, turning it into a powerful tool to convince these stakeholders. The company's market-facing selling point was a durable, affordable alternative to wood furniture. For donors and organizations, however, the selling point was the social/environmental impact of using recycled plastic and reducing deforestation.

If Diseclar managed to "close the loop" by integrating both low-income recyclers and low-income farmers into its value chain, it would have a much stronger case in terms of its social and environmental impact (Exhibit 9). On the recycling end, Diseclar could play a valuable role precisely where the inefficiencies of the market were hurting small collectors—by providing an alternative to the monopolistic practices of the very few collection centers. By doing this, the company could, in turn, loosen its dependency on one or two providers and reduce its potential exposure to the price fluctuations that this dependency created. To conceptualize and implement this project, Juan Nicolás expected an additional one-time cost of USD30,000 for an external consultant (spread out over one year), and the subsequent operational cost of maintaining the recyclers (USD15,000 per year for one additional employee).

With this scenario, Diseclar could "walk the talk," and could very tangibly create social and environmental value by including base of the pyramid stakeholders in its business model. This could move its sustainability discourse far beyond a mere selling point for organizations and potential funders, and turn it into a stronger, more defensible competitive advantage. This would, of course, make the company's operation more complex and challenging to manage, since it would incorporate processes that, up until that point, had been outside its scope of action.

It would also mean that Juan Nicolás would have to start measuring impact, both social and environmental. If he was to take this route, he knew he couldn't simply say that Diseclar was "helping" individual recyclers and farmers. He would have to show *how*—with numbers. After some online research, he came up with a list of key performance indicators that, if properly implemented, could help him measure and build Diseclar's sustainability case. These included:

- Number of individual recyclers formally employed. (As Diseclar purchases raw material from intermediaries, the social enterprise had not yet employed recyclers.)
- Average income (and % increase) of individual recyclers. (Hopethetically, 150 USD per month can make up to 250 USD with the help of Diseclar.)
- Tons of plastic recovered per year. (Hypothetical recovery rates, according to the income statement [Table 3.2]: year 1, 31 tons; year 2, 45 tons; year 3, 52 tons; year 4, 60 tons; year 5, 69 tons.)
- Number of individual farmers incorporated as suppliers of raw materials. (As Diseclar buys raw material from intermediaries, the social enterprise does not yet incorporate suppliers.)
- Tons of natural fiber waste (coffee and sugarcane) recovered per year. (Hypothetical calculation according income statement [Table 3.2]: year 1, 21 tons; year 2, 30 tons; year 3, 35 tons; year 4, 40 tons; year 5, 46 tons.)

In terms of customers, the decision had different implications depending on who Diseclar planned to serve. By now, it was clear that sustainability was not a main value driver for Diseclar's products in the Colombian market; it was a nice addition, but significantly less important than price, durability, or looks. However, if Juan Nicolás ever wished to explore other markets, such as the United States and Europe, the sustainability factor would be a much more important selling point. In these markets, his socially and environmentally responsible products could even command a premium price that customers would be willing to pay, potentially converting what had been thus far conceived as a value product in Colombia into a premium one in more developed markets.

Defining the Company's Future

Three years after resigning from his job as a business manager, and after experimenting with various types of customers and different applications for his material, Juan Nicolás wondered where he should next take his enterprise. By 2015, he had acquired an extruder machine valued at USD100,000, depleting nearly all the funds that he had raised. Now, he believed that the company needed an additional USD500,000 to reach the next stage.

Grants and awards are essentially aid that aligns with a social enterprise's goals; however, the investor's motivations can often be completely different from those of the enterprise. Depending on an investor's profile and

Table 3.3 Expected conditions for negotiation of Options 1 and 2[a]

Elements of a possible deal	Option 1: for-profit investor	Option 2: impact investor
Amount of investment	USD500,000 More investment possible	Maximum USD500,000
Strategic intend	Scaling sales Indifferent in respect to Diseclar's social mission	Scaling impact In line with Diseclar's social mission
Knowledge of investor	Support entering into US market No knowledge on recycling	Knowledge of social/environmental impact
Expected changes in operations	Shop in Mexico	Reporting on impact and possible inclusion of poor recyclers
Costs for execution of expected changes in operation	USD150,000 One-time investment paid by investor	USD10,000 for hiring expert on impact assessment Inclusion of poor recyclers: annual costs of USD60,000 for salaries
Production of raw material	Insourcing	Insourcing
Annual operating costs with new machines	USD110,000 in México	USD80,000 in Colombia
Influence on strategic decisions	Investor intends to be included in strategic decisions	Investor does not intend to be included in strategic decisions
Expected return on investment	10% of annual earnings before interests, taxes, and amortization	5% of annual earnings before interests, taxes, and amortization

[a]These numbers are hypothetical and do not show Diseclar's actual financial projections

personal preferences, the environmental or social impact (which had helped Diseclar so much in the past) may not even be a negotiation factor. It is possible that factors such as a path to profitability, the ability to scale the business, key partnerships, or a proven track record would be more deciding factors. Facing what Juan Nicolás perceived as an urgent need for capital, the question was whether or not he should seek to negotiate with a traditional for-profit investor or an impact investor (Table 3.3).

Option 1: Negotiating with a For-Profit Investor

Through one of the competitions, Juan Nicolás had met an angel investor from Mexico called Rubén Herrera (pseudonym), an experienced business person who owned and managed large companies in the agave industry. The leaves of the agave plant yield a fiber called henequen, which is traditionally used for rope due to its durability, and the investor was now curious if they could do with henequen what Diseclar had done with coffee and sugarcane fibers.

Herrera thought that this could be an opportunity to find alternative uses for his crops, and although the recycling argument made for good PR, he made it clear that he was not in the recycling business. If Juan Nicolás could prove that he could make furniture out of this raw material, which Herrera controlled in large quantities, then he would consider this a spin-off business and invest in it. This would require Diseclar to set up a shop in Mexico— an idea Juan Nicolás wasn't thrilled about. On one hand, he was struggling to establish full manufacturing capabilities in Colombia, so expanding into another country seemed far-fetched. On the other hand, he thought that partnering up with someone this big could be a game-changer for Diseclar. He would no longer have to struggle for funding and would be closer to the US market. With Herrera's connections, expanding to other markets would be significantly easier.

Juan Nicolás didn't know Herrera very well, but from their conversations he could tell that he wouldn't enter a partnership without thorough scrutiny. "I have to do my homework, and I'll put you to the test," he had told him, meaning that he took due diligence very seriously. It was clear to Juan Nicolás that he would need to create an excellent pitch with market-driven arguments if he wanted to convince Herrera. He was also convinced that any pitch linked too heavily to social or environmental impact could potentially create a negative impression on Herrera.

Option 2: Negotiating with an Impact Investor

Another potential investor was an impact fund manager, also from Mexico, who had learned about Diseclar from Viva Idea during the Stephan Schmidheiny Awards. Rodrigo Benavidez (pseudonym) ran a fund that supported companies that were trying to solve environmental and social problems. Their mission read:

> Our mission is to promote sustainable economic development through strategic services to companies that address environmental and social challenges, contributing to the strengthening of a startup culture and responsible consumption in Latin America.

For Rodrigo, Diseclar was an attractive investment—not only because of the environmental impact generated through the use of materials that would otherwise end up in landfills, but also because of the social component; the model had opportunities to improve the livelihoods of the many low-income families of the disenfranchised individual collectors. The fund, although operating in Mexico, did not require that Diseclar move its operations.

Juan Nicolás had had two conversations with Rodrigo, and found him to be very approachable. "Maybe this time I won't have to deal with the aggressiveness I've encountered with traditional investors…but it's really too soon to tell," thought Juan Nicolás. One thing was clear: no matter how nice of a guy Rodrigo was, this was going to be different from the competitions that had awarded him seed capital. Although his focus wasn't financial returns, it was clear that Rodrigo expected something in return for his money. Juan Nicolás knew that he would have to demonstrate—with quantitative data—the social and environmental impact he had been talking about. The key performance indicators that he had researched were a good first step, but he was nowhere near implementing them, and it would take a lot of work to do so.

The Decision

Juan Nicolás knew that Diseclar needed capital in order to go to its next stage of development, but he was torn about where to search for this money. Pursuing the opportunity with Rubén Herrera would mean showing that his business model had a clear path to profitability and a reasonable expectation of return; it would also mean negotiating with powerful traditional investors that could scale Diseclar's business significantly, but that perhaps would prioritize profits over its social and environmental mission. So far, his enterprise had won many awards and gained supporters without having to face detailed scrutiny of his business model. He knew that, if he were to go after these more traditional sources of capital, his business would have to become much more profit-oriented.

On the other hand, pursuing the opportunity to enter the negotiation with impact investor Rodrigo would allow Juan Nicolás to keep the environmental and social mission at the core of his business. However, he would have to professionalize the way that Diseclar approached these aspects by measuring its impact much more concretely. This would also involve eventually integrating backward to include collectors and farmers in Diseclar's value chain, which not only implied a lot of work but would also add complexity to his operations (Figs. 3.2 and 3.3).

Precisely because of the work involved in pursuing either of these options, Juan Nicolás felt that he couldn't have it both ways. So far, Diseclar had managed to get by without committing to one single strategy and, as many startups, had had the luxury of trying out different things. But now, he

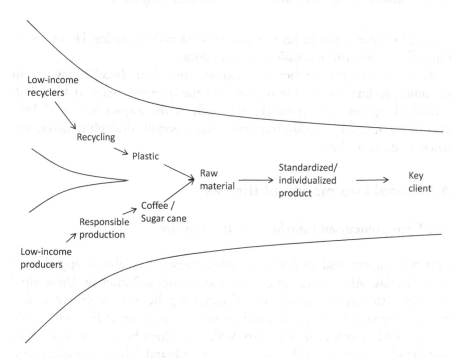

Fig. 3.2 Diseclar's value chain

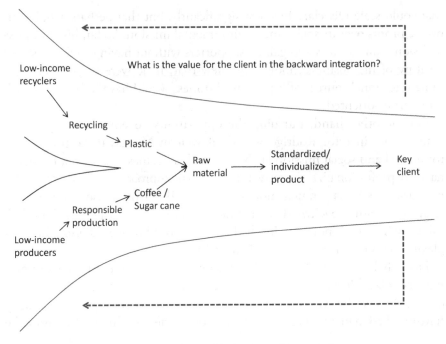

Fig. 3.3 Diseclar's value chain with possible backward integration

wanted to expand, and he knew that he had to make a choice. He smiled to himself, thinking this was easier said than done.

At the end of yet another long day at work, Juan Nicolás was still in his office, feeling uneasy. He turned over the question again in his mind: "Should I prepare a pitch for the for-profit or the impact investor?" Juan Nicolás often faced tradeoffs, but here it was especially difficult to determine where to draw the line.

Additional Information of the Case

The Entrepreneur and the Start of His Venture

Entrepreneurship and professional independence had always appealed to Juan Nicolás. After graduating from the Pontifical Xavierian University[vi] in 2009 with a degree in Industrial Engineering, he first sought stable, formal employment with several different companies. One of his earliest jobs was an eight-month project at SAB Miller, in which he oversaw campaigns and brand activations for the Bavaria beverage brand. There, he noticed two things that would mark the fate of his future undertaking. First, he witnessed the tremendous volume of plastic waste that was being generated by the beverage industry. Second, he saw how many distributors, such as small bars and restaurants, needed low-cost furniture for their establishments.

After the project with Bavaria, he was then hired by Corbeta, a local Procter & Gamble distributor, to manage its chain of stores. He was responsible for overseeing the region's sales force (24 staff members). Through this experience, Juan Nicolás learned how to manage and train personnel, and how to lead efficient work teams.

Finally, in 2012—at 26 years of age—he got a job with Carvajal as a commercial manager. After five months, however, he decided to resign from the position (which had provided him with a decent salary and a solid sense of stability) in order to found Diseclar. Juan Nicolás reflected on his reasons for the decision. "My cousin had just been fired from a company and was unemployed," he said. "I told myself that I did not want to be 30 years old, suddenly fired from my job and unable to cope with responsibilities such as a house and a family. I remember feeling that if I was going to start a business venture, this was the time to do it."

He recalled that the other circumstance that drove him to make the leap from employee to entrepreneur was that after having worked for some time with the SENA on an application for a government contest called "Fondo Emprender," he learned that he had been awarded a large sum of money to launch his project.

Diseclar's Value Proposition[vii]

Diseclar manufactures and designs furniture (chairs, tables, desks, bookcases, etc.) using plastic waste and plant fibers, thus contributing to the reutilization of plastics that otherwise pollute the environment. It provides customers with a 100% eco-friendly product, offered in five different colors, depending on their preference. Three of these colors imitate natural wood, and have a rustic look. Diseclar's leading products are chairs and tables, sold as a kit that includes four chairs and one table. The products are innovative in the following ways:

- They are manufactured with recycled plastic and agro-industrial waste, and are eco-friendly products that will not rot, splinter, or chip.
- They are resistant to rodents, pests, fungi, bacteria, and mold.
- They are weather-resistant (rain, snow, cold, heat).
- They can be used both outdoors and indoors.
- They are highly durable, even under extreme conditions.

Table 3.4 Diseclar's main product line

Garden lounge set	Ideal for outdoor use on terraces and balconies, in gardens, and at poolsides. Made from recycled plastic and plant fibers that are resistant to water, light, mold, and external agents, the garden lounge set will never rot
Coffee break set	Ideal for outdoor use because it is impermeable, resistant to high-temperature areas, easily maintained, and has a modern design that provides elegance and style to any space. Great for terraces, balconies, gardens, and poolsides
Benches	Ideal for outdoor spaces and hallways, with a modern, decorative, and eco-friendly design. Today's decor emphasizes open-home designs and the use of eco-friendly products that are resistant to extreme weather and are easy to maintain. Our recycled materials create beautiful, comfortable products that are also highly durable
Terrace	A modern, yet comfortable design that turns your terrace or garden into the perfect place to share the outdoors with family and friends. Its comfortable, practical, and eco-friendly finish makes it ideal for country homes and enjoying nature
Absenta set	Bar-type tables and chairs with backrests for additional comfort and a modern, functional design. This is an ecological product that can be used in various environments. Easy to handle and maintain, this set is ideal for both inside and outside homes, farms, and similar spaces
Tayrona foldable chair	A foldable chair for outdoor use. Its comfortable design and easy assembly make it ideal to bring camping and fishing, or carry to the beach, the riverside, or other recreational areas

- The furniture is wood-like.
- Logging and deforestation is decreased.
- The environment is preserved and protected.
- No maintenance is needed; there is no need to apply oil, glaze, wax, and/or paint.
- The product is 100% recyclable.

With Diseclar's advantages, customers acquire a more durable, easy-to-maintain product (Table 3.4). A market study revealed several advantages over competing products, which could represent opportunities for Diseclar (e.g., wood chairs and tables can deteriorate and rot, thus constant cleaning can decrease their life span).

Initial Target Market Segment[viii]

Diseclar's target market is restaurants and recreational centers in the region that have a rustic or "country" feel, and that identify with environmental conservation and the improvement of society's quality of life. When he approached these actors, it became evident that the importance of the environmental component is gaining traction. Designer Trino Sánchez is the CEO at Arquint, a company dedicated to the conceptualization and design of spaces for the hospitality industry. In his article entitled "Everything you need to know about the design and decoration of a restaurant," published in *La Barra* magazine (issue 50), Trino explains that a restaurant's interior design is vital to attracting and maintaining customers who sit at tables while eating. Two of his "10 commandments to avoid mistakes" stand out here: (1) Materials: this is the "interface" between the restaurant and its customers, and should reflect warmth, comfort, energy, tranquility, immediacy, suggestiveness, and branding; and (2) environment and sustainability at the forefront. The designer explains that "environmental awareness is growing, and there are multiple ways to be environmental supporters and energy savers. Thus, all 276,180 of the restaurants and recreational centers registered in Colombia have been identified as customers. Diseclar's market study identified that purchasing budgets are geared toward full sets in order to ensure aesthetics and a fluid business concept. Therefore, the proposal is to sell a kit comprised of four chairs and one table. Diseclar is capable of selling 53,945 sets to restaurants and recreational centers.

Teaching Note on the Diseclar Case

The case facilitates a discussion of the challenges associated with negotiating impact for resources, and suggests several key questions that will help entrepreneurs to systematically consider different options for presenting their business model in a sales pitch.

Learning Objectives

Readers can begin by reflecting on Phase I of the market approach to scaling introduced in this book. First, the environmental impact of using recycled materials and the potential inclusion of informal recyclers into Diseclar's value chain illustrates the element of *impact*. Second, the case shows that the enterprise has two distinct options for sources of funding, depending on how it positions itself, illustrating the element of *resources*. On the one hand, Juan Nicolás can choose a traditional for-profit focus, making it easier to raise funds from sources such as for-profit investors that emphasize financial return. On the other hand, focusing on impact would attract impact investors. Third, the case illustrates the element of *standards* by highlighting the norms for navigating relations with traditional investors versus impact investors. Traditional investors seek financial return, while impact investors are interested in a more personalized relationship that focuses on impact. Fourth, if Juan Nicolás chooses to access funds through impact investors, this opens the possibility to negotiating impact for resources.

After having analyzed and discussed the case, readers should be able to:

a. characterize the challenges of exploring opportunities to negotiate impact for the resources needed to scale; and
b. systematically analyze various options for accessing financing based on the four elements of Phase I of the market approach to scaling: *impact*, *resources*, *standards*, and *negotiation*.

Reflection on the Market Approach to Scaling Diseclar's Impact

Juan Nicolás's investment options imply two different ways of conceptualizing the market.

The first option focuses on investors who expect a financial return only. In this case, Diseclar intends to pitch its business model based on benefits of the raw material it uses and the benefits of its product for its customers (Fig. 3.4).

In contrast, the second option focuses on accessing investments from impact investors (Fig. 3.5). In this case, Juan Nicolás must emphasize the

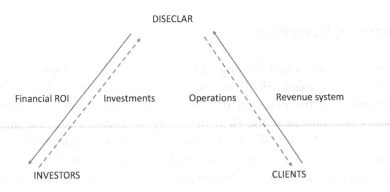

Fig. 3.4 Option 1: market approach to accessing the for-profit investor

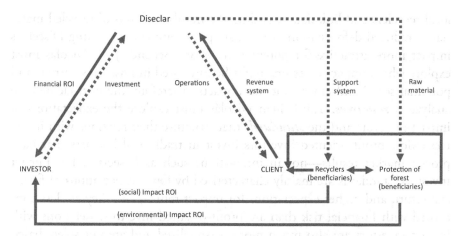

Fig. 3.5 Option 2: market approach to accessing the impact investor

social and environmental impact the enterprise creates through both its operations and its products and services. In the case of Diseclar, this return is social, in that it includes impoverished, informal recyclers in its value chain, and environmental, in that it uses recycled material. To pitch its social impact to potential impact investors, Juan Nicolás must highlight the steps of his downstream value chain. He needs to show how Diseclar has positively impacted the quality of life of low-income recyclers and coffee and sugarcane producers. To pitch his environmental impact, he needs to highlight Diseclar's sales plan and the impact that spurring customers to replace wood with recycled plastic has had on protecting forested areas. Finally, as impact investors still expect a financial return, highlighting the company's revenue processes establishes a potential financial return on investment. This is very important, as Juan Nicolás initially founded the company with a clear for-profit aim, and wants to keep it attractive to impact investors who expect a financial return on their investment—even if this return might be lower than what is expected by for-profit investors.

Tying the Diseclar Case to Phase I of the Market Approach to Scaling

If Juan Nicolás chooses to access resources from impact investors, he will need to calculate and pitch Diseclar's previous and potential social and environmental impact. Therefore, the first element to analyze is ***impact***. The impact analysis must be based on data regarding the increased welfare of local recyclers and link data regarding the number of tons of recycled material to reduced deforestation. These data points are key to making Diseclar's impact more attractive for potential investors. Second, Juan Nicolás must explore which impact investors might be interested in Diseclar's current and potential social and environmental impacts. Therefore, the next element to analyze is *resources*. Third, Juan Nicolás must explore the expectations of impact investors and the *standards* that structure their relations with investees. Most profit-oriented investors invest in traditional business that have proven market results—not in innovations such as Diseclar's. For impact investors, standards are mainly characterized by lower expectations of financial return and higher expectations for impact return, and they are less concerned with financial risk than are profit-oriented investors. Relations with impact investors are also much more personalized and are not solely based on economic criteria. Finally, Juan Nicolás must analyze how he intends to pitch his financial and impact return to investors in order to *negotiate* Diseclar's impact for the resources it needs to scale.

Discussion Questions

The following questions can help readers reflect on the case in preparation for group discussions, or can be used during the discussion sessions.

1. *Do you consider Juan Nicolás to be a social entrepreneur?* This question stimulates reflection on how to define a social entrepreneur. This is a relevant reflection because Juan Nicolás perhaps shows a stronger emphasis on market motivation than on compassion with the beneficiaries included in his business model. Discussion surrounding this question can reflect on the importance of that social motivation has on defining the boundaries of what can be considered a social enterprise. In this book, we argue that the existence of an impact strategy—regardless of motivation—is what defines a social enterprise.
2. *If you were in Juan Nicolás's position, would you choose Option 1 (the for-profit investor) or Option 2 (the impact investor)?* This question reflects on negotiating impact for resources and the four elements included in Phase I of the market-based scaling model.
3. *How would you need to change Diseclar's operations and revenue processes when opting for Option 1 or Option 2, respectively?* This question helps readers generate ideas for how to create operations and revenue processes that appeal to each option. This reflection can be aided by Figs. 3.3 and 3.4.

4. *Prepare and present Juan Nicolás's scaling strategy to hypothetical investor.* This final task helps readers become as concrete as possible in their reflections on the case study. This is an opportunity for a role-playing activity, in which some participants act as investors and others work in teams to present the appropriate sales pitch. Participants should define their position based on what they consider to be the best options for Juan Nicolás to scale his impact.

Notes

i. Based on exchange rates as of April 2011, when fieldwork was completed for the study. At this time, the Colombian peso was at 1772 pesos per USD, and the maximum monthly income of a collector in the recycling industry ranged from USD38 to USD400.

ii. See https://www.javerianacali.edu.co/vicerrectoria-academica/oficina-de-emprendimiento/modelo-campus-nova.

iii. See http://www.sena.edu.co/es-co/Paginas/default.aspx.

iv. See http://www.vivaidea.org/premios.

v. See https://www.chivas.com/the-venture.

vi. See https://www.javeriana.edu.co/home.

vii. Extracted from the company's business plan, May 2014.

viii. Extracted from the company's business plan, May 2014.

References

1. Goldsmith, A. A. (2011). Profits and alms: Cross-sector partnerships for global poverty reduction. *Public Administration & Development, 31*(1), 15–24.

2. Schneider, F. (2012). *The shadow economy and work in the shadow: What do we (not) know?* (Discussion Paper 6423). Bonn, Germany: IZA.

3. Chen, M. A. (2006). Rethinking the informal economy: Linkages with the formal economy and the formal regulatory environment. In B. Guha-khasnobis, R. Kanbur, & E. Ostrom (Eds.), *Linking the formal and informal economy: Concepts and policies* (pp. 75–92). Oxford, UK: Oxford University Press.

4. Kistruck, G. M., Webb, J. W., Sutter, C. J., & Ireland, R. D. (2011). Microfranchising in base-of-the-pyramid markets: Institutional challenges and adaptations to the Franchise model. *Entrepreneurship Theory and Practice, 35,* 503–531.

5. Jäger, U. (2010). *Managing social businesses: Mission, governance, strategy and accountability.* Houndsmills and New York: Palgrave Macmillan.

6. Jäger, U., & Schröer, A. (2013). Integrated organizational identity: A definition of hybrid organizations and a research agenda. *Voluntas, 25,* 1281–1306 (Published online: 3 July 2013).
7. Martínez, C. (2018). *Entrepreneurial decisions in strong institutional voids: Opportunity recognition and exploitation, access to financing, and venture capital decision-making* (Dissertation). University of St. Gallen, St. Gallen.
8. Leme, A., Martins, F., & Hornberger, K. (2014). *The state of impact investing in Latin America.* B. Company.
9. Banco Interamericano de Desarrollo. (2011). *Resumen Ejecutivo, Estudio Nacional de Reciclaje.* Bogotá, Colombia: Organismo Ejecutor AAsociación de Recicladores de Bogotá.

4

Phase II: Designing Operations

Negotiating impact for the resources needed to scale can influence a social enterprise's supply (how to move inputs from suppliers to the social enterprise in order to produce products and services), distribution (how the products and services reach the customer/beneficiary), and revenue processes (how the customer/beneficiary pays for them) [1].[i] This is mainly due to investor expectations regarding impact and financial return. Investors will potentially demand that the social enterprise design more efficient and effective operations [2]. For example, they might ask the enterprise to rent out a segment of land it owns in order to increase cash flow. Or they might request that its products or services be standardized in order to reduce production costs and better serve its target groups, ask the enterprise to design a distribution process that reduces transaction costs, or ask it to implement revenue processes that make it easier for customers to pay, thus ensuring the intended impact and financial return on investment. These expectations all focus on adjusting the enterprise's operations to more efficient or effective models in order to create scalable solutions.

Operations for Scaling

Three elements must be considered in Phase II: *supply and assets*, *products and services*, and *distribution and revenue* (Fig. 4.1).

© The Author(s) 2020
U. Jäger et al., *Scaling Strategies for Social Entrepreneurs*,
https://doi.org/10.1007/978-3-030-31160-5_4

Fig. 4.1 Phase II: designing operations

Mamut provides one useful illustration of this phase. Mamut is a Bolivian company that uses recycled rubber from discarded tires to build safe recreational spaces for public entities and private organizations. Its founders, Manuel and Antonio Laredo, recognized they had an opportunity to create a new market in Bolivia by changing the standards of the construction industry. In this market-creation approach, they designed their business model to include informal recyclers in the enterprise's supply chain and measured its environmental impact by the number of tons recycled and its social impact by the improved quality of life of impoverished recyclers.

Supply and Assets

Supply operations refer to the way in which social enterprises link products, services, capital and information to produce products and services [1]. Social enterprises are interested in generating efficient and effective supply operations in order to achieve high quality at a low cost, and therefore face the decision of internalizing or externalizing them [3]. Whatever the case, effective social enterprises leverage its existing assets. Assets are the holdings, possessions, and economic and human capital a social enterprise has at its disposal to generate efficient operations. Examples of assets include possessions (e.g., furniture, buildings, vehicles), capabilities (e.g., employee knowledge, skills, competencies), rights (e.g., copyrights, patents), etc.

Assets do not require negotiation, as they are already at the enterprise's disposal. In the case of Mamut, the Laredo brothers' key assets were their own possessions, as they came from an entrepreneurial family that gave them access to assets such as juridical advice, which could be used to scale the enterprise and build its initial infrastructure. They had also developed a skilled entrepreneurial team of employees. Scaling the organization's impact implied using this team's knowledge and experience effectively and organizing it toward the enterprise's impact goals.

Guiding questions:
What **assets** do we have? What assets do we need to scale impact? How do we organize the supply of raw material and other inputs into our production in a manner that is both cost-effective and impact-generating?

Products and Services

To scale their impact successfully, social enterprises must find ways to produce their **products and services** in a more effective and efficient manner. This often leads to standardization and specialization [4]. To standardize production means to create operations that repeatedly give the same result. To routinize activities helps social enterprises create this result in less time and at a lower cost, yet in many cases with increased quality [5]. This is much like driving a car. The more you drive, the less you need to think about breaking or steering, and the quicker you can maneuver into a parking spot. Specializing means reducing the amount of products and services a social enterprise provides. This, in turn, reduces the assets and the processes needed to produce and distribute these products and services.

Operations become less complex, and the social enterprise can reduce its costs and increase the quality of its products and services. Specialization means, for instance, that rather than try to provide a wide range of healthcare services to a community, an enterprise focuses on emergency services only. The enterprise can then increase the standardization of this service—for example, by fine-tuning ambulance logistics. In the case of Mamut, the enterprise's leaders decided to specialize in just two types of products. First, they sold shock-absorbent rubber tiles to any customer who was interested. Second, they sold projects to public entities and private organizations so that they could build safe recreational spaces such as children's play parks.

Guiding questions:
What **products and services** should we specialize in to increase the value we create for our customers or beneficiaries? What practices do we need to have in place in order to standardize our products and services to successfully scale impact?

Distribution and Revenue

Distribution refers to how a social enterprise delivers its products and services to distinct target groups. To scale its impact, successful social enterprises are cost-effective in how they distribute their products and services to their customers and beneficiaries. They also develop efficient pricing models that help customers pay for these products or services. In car sales, for instance, the advent of leasing contracts changed the payment landscape, making expensive cars accessible to customers that lack the funds to buy the vehicle outright. The leasing contract allows them to lease the car on a monthly basis. Innovative *revenue* processes like these can help customers gain access to the social enterprises' products and services, and therefore increase its financial return. Social enterprises typically have two options for integrating impact and financial sustainability through distribution and revenue processes.

The first option is to sell products and services to traditional paying customers (those with the capacity to pay market-driven prices), while at the same time providing an impact-related service to beneficiaries along their supply or distribution chain. The second option is to provide products and services to customers who can only pay minimal prices, but do so in exchange for products that create a positive impact on their lives. Mamut is modeled after the first option; it sells urban innovation projects to public entities and private organizations (traditional paying customers) on one hand, and incorporates informal recyclers in its supply chain on the other (beneficiaries).

Guiding questions:
What processes do we use and should we use to *distribute* our products and services in a manner that is both cost-effective and impact-generating? What *revenue processes* can we use to support our customer's capacity to pay? What processes will increase our revenues while also keeping our products and services financially accessible for our customers?

Phase II of creating a market-based scaling strategy is to design the enterprise's operations. The aim is to create value for the customers and beneficiaries and establish a revenue system that supports their capacity to pay for the products and/or services the enterprise offers (Table 4.1).

Table 4.1 Examples of operations and revenues processes

Elements	Examples
Supply and assets	• *Volunteers*: MINKA, an inclusive Argentine business school, includes a network of successful local entrepreneurs in its board of directors. These entrepreneurs assist the school on a voluntary basis • *Machines*: Warmi, an Argentine llama wool producer, incorporates an old machine from the early twentieth century that had not been used by its previous owners in decades to start producing clothing made from llama fibers
Products and services	• *Clean water*: Enrique Lomnitz one of the founders of the Mexican social enterprise Isla Urbana, produces water systems that capture and filter rainwater • *Housing*: Oscar Méndez, a Colombian architect, founded Conceptos Plásticos, which sells bricks and other materials that poor people can use to easily build their own homes • *Guide for dangerous cities*: David Chang founded Dromos, a Chilean social enterprise that created an app to help people stay safe in dangerous cities
Distribution and revenue	• *Site visits and education*: Ilumexico, a Mexican social enterprise, sells solar energy to rural communities by sending in energy experts and educating the communities on how to maintain the newly installed systems • *Online information and postal distribution*: Wakami markets its handicraft products online and mails the purchased products to customers • *Online distribution*: Linguoo created an online radio program to present articles, books and other written resources to people with disabilities, and distributes the content online in ten Latin American countries

The Kingo Case

The case of Kingo in Guatemala illustrates Phase II. Social entrepreneur Juan Fermín Rodríguez establishes operations that respond to the specific circumstances of the low-income contexts in which his enterprise works. Kingo provides solar energy services to isolated and impoverished communities in Guatemala. The enterprise has an information technology-based analytics system that permits its leaders to track each customer's power usage. This allows Juan Fermín and his team to identify in real time which customers are profitable, and which are not. This software, designed in-house after having leveraged the appropriate resources, was an important step in developing efficient and effective operations. However, Juan Fermín was struggling to decide how to best utilize Kingo's assets, such as its human resources—specifically its field staff—in response to the data provided in order to increase its customer base. Juan Fermín and his team were clear that they wanted to further scale Kingo's impact and increase revenues, but were unsure whether outsourcing the management of their distribution channels was the way to go.

The Case: Scaling a Solar Energy Business at the Base of the Pyramid[1]

Juan Fermín Rodríguez, the founder of Kingo, a Guatemalan social enterprise focused on providing solar energy to low-income customers, was struggling with an important decision. It had been five years since the enterprise was founded, and Kingo was ready to scale. Juan Fermín saw two ways to approach this. He could either continue to manage Kingo's distribution in-house and focus on increasing consumption among existing customers, or could outsource its operations to a third party in order to expand his customer base geographically. This was an important decision, as one of Kingo's success drivers was its in-depth knowledge of its customers based on its distribution and through its direct contact to end customers, who live in extremely impoverished areas with minimal infrastructure.

With more than 1.2 billion people in the world lacking electricity, Kingo's vision of "turning lives ON" through solar energy services for low-income customers reflects its commitment to one of humanity's greatest modern challenges: energy access for impoverished and isolated individuals and communities. Kingo's distribution is based on customers who purchase codes from their neighborhood shops (which have a commercial relationship with Kingo technical sales representatives), or directly from Kingo service sales representatives. Kingo technicians install a unit (called a "Kingo") in the customer's home, and the customer then uses the activated codes purchased from the shops or service reps to access electricity. Kingo's vision had attracted investors who were willing to provide the resources it needed to begin scaling its impact, even piquing the interest of public figures such as actor Leonardo DiCaprio, who invested USD10 million dollars in the enterprise.

---

[1]Authors: Derick Barrios, Researcher INCAE Business School; María Lasa, Researcher VIVA Idea; Felipe Symmes, Senior Researcher VIVA Idea and PHD Candidate University of St. Gallen; and Urs Jäger, Professor INCAE Business School and Research Director VIVA Idea.

Juan Fermín knew that economic resources were an important component of scaling. But he also knew that effective operations would be needed to prepare Kingo for the future and ensure that the enterprise could achieve the financial and impact returns that he had promised its investors. He had already decided that technology would be a key element of Kingo's operations. He and his team had developed an information management software that allowed them to track the usage of the units installed in the customers' homes. This software, called "Ant," gathered important information about the factors that influenced Kingo's business—namely, users, devices, agents, and neighborhood shopkeepers. With Ant, Kingo was able to keep a detailed registry that included current customers, new customers, information from the daily reports produced by the sales agents, and sales flows from the neighborhood shops. This recorded an enormous amount of data each day, allowing the company to output up-to-date information for decision-making (via personnel specialized in data management). It also allowed Kingo's leadership to view the progress of its operations in real time, which was through pre-established indicators. The software even helped management staff plan the sales team's visits to the various households that were using Kingo units. Thus, the primordial purpose of the enterprise's data management strategy was to provide the information needed to guide operational and strategic decisions. This was a significant advancement in Kingo's history, as it helped establish a revenue system that supported the company's financial sustainability, defining profitable and unprofitable customer segments and establishing immediate actions to increase sales.

While its model was quite successful, Kingo's main problem was how to develop efficient and effective operations that aligned with its technology, particularly in terms of distribution. Juan Fermín knew that developing operations was a complex endeavor. Kingo sold codes for power usage through its units via (a) direct sales to end users and (b) retail sales to neighborhood stores (called *pulperías*), who then sold the codes to the end users. The latter was managed by Kingo's technical sales representatives, who comprised a field team solely dedicated to shopkeeper relations. These agents made regular visits to the shopkeepers to refill their balances, provide technical support, and collect useful information about the community, similar to how the prepaid cell phone industry operates. In this regard, the function of the sales team was to provide consistent service to shopkeepers so that they could, in turn, have the information they needed to effectively exercise their sales. The technical sales reps were usually local community members, which made it easy to establish personal and trusting relationships with the shopkeepers. However, the cost to maintain these relationships with the shops was getting extremely high, and was significantly reducing the company's profits. Juan Fermín became acutely aware of this fact when Estrella Digital, one of Guatemala's top companies for managing shopkeeper sales channels, offered its services for a price that represented a 20% savings comparing to what it was currently spending. Estrella Digital's managers had already met with Juan Fermín and agreed to adapt Kingo's guidelines—namely, that staff hired by Estrella Digital adhere to Kingo's operational requirements. Juan Fermín was struggling with this offer, however, as the shopkeeper sales channel was the enterprise's strongest source of revenue. In addition, managing this channel provided a valuable source of information about Kingo's end users and their communities. One of the enterprise's main strengths was its proximity to end customers and their communities, which created an in-depth knowledge of the market. As market knowledge was a key success driver, Juan Fermín felt that managing the shop channel in-house, even with a 20% higher cost than outsourcing to Estrella Digital, was perhaps a viable investment.

Juan Fermín was unsure which path of Kingo's operations to take. Should he manage the shopkeeper sales channel in-house to maintain Kingo's market knowledge, despite the high cost (Option 1) or outsource this distribution channel to Estrella Digital due to its low costs (Option 2)?

Guatemala's Solar Energy Industry at the Base of the Pyramid

Kingo was the first and only business in Guatemala to provide isolated, impoverished communities in Guatemala with solar-powered electricity and was working in two different regions of the country.

Alta Verapaz

Alta Verapaz is located approximately 200 km north of Guatemala City. It comprises 17 municipalities and over 1.2 million inhabitants, 76.9% of which are rural. Santo Domingo de Cobán, commonly called Cobán, is the department capital. Data indicates that 89.7% of the residents of Alta Verapaz are of Mayan descent. In 2016, the percentage of residents lacking access to electricity climbed to 66%—the highest in the country (Fig. 4.2).

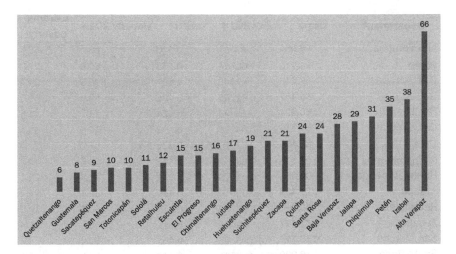

Fig. 4.2 Guatemalans living in homes that lack electricity (percent per department)

According to the latest United Nations Development Report [6], Alta Verapaz also has the lowest Human Development Index (HDI) in the country, with a score of 0.38 (compared with 0.62 for the department of Guatemala [6] (Fig. 4.3) and in 2016, the illiteracy rate in Alta Verapaz was one of the country's highest, at 25.9% [7].

With extremely varied topography that includes mountains and hills, low, cavernous terrain, and rivers and lakes, the department's infrastructure comprises a total of 84 km of paved roads connecting the capital city of Cobán to the municipalities of Carchá, Chamelco, and Chisec. Its urban areas are characterized by roads that are mainly paved, in decent condition, and drivable—though with limited ease in certain stretches. Rural areas are mainly accessed via footpaths[ii] and dirt roads[iii] (60 and 34%, respectively). The remaining 6% are located less than one kilometer from the department's main, paved roads. The overall condition of Alta Verapaz's roadway system makes access to rural areas difficult [8].

Petén

With 35,824 square kilometers of land, Petén comprises nearly a third of Guatemala, making it the largest department in the country and the most extensive sub-national entity in Central America. It is north of Alta Verapaz, bordered to the north and west by Mexico, to the east by Belize, and to the

Department	Users	ECI 2013	HDI	Poverty 2014	Extreme poverty
Alta Verapaz	88.954	0.43491	0.370	83.1	53.6
Petén	86.220	0.63424	0.458	60.8	20.2
Baja Verapaz	47.043	0.7746	0.457	66.3	24.6
Izabal	80.482	0.81709	0.481	59.9	35.2
Quiche	150.724	0.83474	0.424	74.7	41.8
Chiquimula	67.114	0.84896	0.408	70.6	41.1
Jalapa	60.161	0.87966	0.426	67.2	22.3
Suchitepéquez	102.235	0.89682	0.471	63.8	19.8
Huehuetenango	200.051	0.91029	0.399	73.8	28.6
Jutiapa	97.439	0.92954	0.455	62.7	24.2
Retalhuleu	60.196	0.93702	0.476	56.1	15.3
Zacapa	47.437	0.9402	0.511	55.9	21.4
San Marcos	188.714	0.95308	0.451	60.2	22
Santa Rosa	76.980	0.95828	0.470	54.3	12.9
Escuintla	158.198	0.96045	0.516	52.9	11.2
Totonicapán	91.815	0.97246	0.432	77.5	41.1
Sololá	79.152	0.97404	0.455	80.9	39.9
Chimaltenango	118.158	0.97825	0.487	66.1	23.4
Quetzaltenango	163.906	0.98307	0.529	56	16.7
El Progreso	37.343	0.9875	0.518	53.2	13.2
Sacatepéquez	66.267	0.99316	0.567	41.1	8.4
Guatemala	741.159	0.99531	0.614	33.3	5.4

Fig. 4.3 Key data for market potential (*Source* Mentzer et al. [1]. NHDR-UNDP Guatemala, based on Ministry of Energy and Mines [2013] and National Survey of Living Conditions [2014])

southwest by the department of Izabel. Petén has 14 municipalities. The department capital is Flores, situated roughly 488 km from Guatemala City.

In 2016, Petén's total population registered 736,010 inhabitants, 32.4% of which were of Mayan descent. In addition, 31.3% of the department's population was rural, and its illiteracy rate had risen to 93.1%—making Petén one of the departments with the highest illiteracy rates in the country [8]. The percentage of Petén residents with electrical access was at 67%,[vi] and the Human Development Index was at 0.458, ranking it in the top 11 Guatemalan departments with the lowest Human Development Index. Due to its vast territorial extension and low government impetus to improve the department's roadway system, in 2014 Petén registered 1635 km of official roads, 59.5% of which were unpaved and 40.5% of which were asphalt. Also present were many unofficial, unpaved roads that today continue to connect remote communities and villages to these main throughways.

The solar energy market is complex, mainly due to substitute services that are already available in most communities. Many homes are connected to the electrical grid via utility poles and power lines owned by national power companies. Many of these households pay expensive rates for this service despite interruptions to its availability, while others pay an organized group that illegally connects to the grid and offers its energy at extremely low prices. Likewise, the homes of some potential customers already contain solar equipment purchased from informal businesses or individuals. Some of these devices are sold at extremely high prices, in some cases with the possibility of monthly financing. In addition, a large percentage of clients prefer to continue using candles and charging their cell phones at the closest neighborhood shop. These are often households in which few to no members work, or whose family members are primarily elderly.

Development Stages of Kingo

Stage 1: The Advent of an Idea and the Selling of Solar Energy Kits via the Quetsol Model

In 2010, together with his partner Antonio Aguilar, Juan Fermín created a business model that consisted of the sale of kits that included a battery, a solar panel, and two LED lightbulbs to rural Guatemalan residents who lacked electricity in their homes.[v] Juan Fermín and Antonio offered financing to their customers via partnerships with banks and microfinance institutions. They called their enterprise Quetsol.

Because of these partnerships, Quetsol was able to offer its devices at a lower monthly rate than what households would normally spend on other alternatives. These families were spending an average of USD20 per month to burn two candles a day (or the corresponding amount of kerosene) as well as a weekly expense to charge their cell phones at the neighborhood shop. In contrast, the monthly cost of obtaining solar energy through a Quetsol kit was USD15 per day, which provided enough light via the two LED bulbs to illuminate a home and included an outlet to charge cell phones as needed. Thus, users not only saved money but experienced a notable difference in their quality of life—in turn increasing the number of hours that children could study at home, and mitigating cooking-related burn accidents.

Juan Fermín and Antonio worked with this business model for three years, installing equipment in approximately 5000 Guatemalan households and succeeding in raising a small amount of capital. After this time, however, the two founders noticed that their business was not scaling at the rate they had hoped for. They sensed that this was in part because the sales operation for the kits was slow, requiring at least five visits to each community just to start providing them to potential consumers. In addition, the microfinance institutions offered fixed monthly payment schemes, which wasn't ideal for their customers, who primarily worked seasonal or otherwise temporary jobs in agriculture and often had unstable incomes. The partners concluded that in their revenue processes they were not offering customers the payment flexibility they needed. This meant the company was only selling an average of 15 systems per 100 families interested. Juan Fermín felt that the enterprise should be able to grow more rapidly. His vision differed from that of Antonio, and the two parted ways, dissolving Quetsol.[vi]

Stage 2: Selling Solar Energy Services via the Kingo Model

When he first launched Kingo in 2013, Juan Fermín had little capital but was convinced there was significant market opportunity. The three years of previous work with the Quetsol model had shown him that a large segment of the Guatemalan population represented a potential demand for solar-powered electricity. However, these initial years of trial and error had also taught him that successfully launching innovative ideas required a closer relationship with customers. Depending on third parties—in this case, banks and microfinance institutions—and selling solar energy units as a mere one-time transaction drastically diminished the possibility of the business model succeeding in contexts of informality and poverty.

Based on this conclusion, Juan Fermín and his new Kingo team agreed that they needed to approach the problem from a different angle. They decided to replicate the prepaid service model used by cell phone companies, in which customers purchase a card and enter its respective code into their phone device. The idea would be the same, but instead of a phone, the customers would be entering the code into a unit that provided energy. This new model resolved the need to (a) create a closer connection with customers (by offering them an ongoing service instead of just a one-time purchase) and (b) provide them with a flexible payment scheme.

With limited funds, Juan Fermín conducted an initial pilot in 50 homes to evaluate customer receptivity to the new business model. However, he was certain that a larger sample would be needed to ensure the model's success and, in turn, to access more capital. He decided to seek USD50,000 to expand the pilot to 500 homes. To do this, he created a crowdfunding campaign during which he closed himself into a darkened room for 23 days to transmit his experience via crowdfunding tools until he got the money he needed. His effort piqued many people's attention, including international media outlets such as Forbes, CNN, and the BBC, and raised enough funding to test his pilot in all 500 homes.

In fact, mainly thanks to the campaign's media coverage, Kingo raised a total of USD1.1 million in seed money. The funds came from various sources—from family and friends to financial intuitions such as E10, a Guatemala-based boutique venture capital firm that invested in companies that tackle energy challenges in emerging markets in low-income contexts. At this point, Juan Fermín brought Juan José Estrada, Luis del Cid, Matías de Tezanos, and Peter Kasprowicz on board.[vii] Juan José had more than seven years of experience with financial investment in the energy sector. He had also led fundraising strategies and campaigns for more than ten other companies, which meant that he possessed the knowledge and skills needed to raise large amounts of capital. Luis had worked in sales and marketing for L'Oréal corporation for ten years and had served as general manager with the telecommunications company Claro in Honduras and Costa Rica, where he focused on the prepaid phone segment, so had ample experience in mass-consumption industries. Matías was internationally recognized as one of Latin America's most successful entrepreneurs, and his inclusion inspired an important shift in Kingo's vision. He established a culture of joint participation, proposing a new venture capital financing model that would replace the enterprise's outdated notion of Juan Fermín owning 100% of the company. While this change was initially disruptive, it proved a helpful contribution to Kingo and its subsequent exponential growth. Finally, Peter was, according to Juan Fermín, the missing link to creating an innovative, high quality, durable, and trustworthy service. Peter had a Ph.D. in Physics from the University of Oxford and worked with Credit Suisse in the United States. He accepted Juan Fermín's offer to join Kingo in Guatemala, and his technical know-how in many cases proved a perfect complement to his commercial skills.

Stage 3: Raising Economic Funds for Initial Growth

In the period from 2013 to 2018, Juan Fermín spent approximately 60% of his time raising funds in order to rapidly grow his business. In 2013, the enterprise issued a total of USD250,000 in convertible bonds and received a loan from the Inter-American Development Bank. In 2015 it conducted its

Fig. 4.4 Rounds of financing conducted by Kingo

first round of Series A financing[8].[viii] By 2016 it had begun to receive funding from international institutions via convertible bonds, totaling USD5.3 million. In the same year, it received its first debt capital in the amount of USD4 million, and in 2017 it began Series B financing [9], through which it raised a total of USD8 million (Fig. 4.4).[ix]

Just like its capital, the company's customer base of households with installed units also increased over time. At the start of 2016, Kingo had installed 12,000 units; by early 2017 it had tripled this amount, reaching a total of 56,286 units by the first quarter of 2018. This expansion was largely achieved because the company had succeeded in increasing its installation rate by six times in just three years, going from 1100 installations per month to 6000. It also significantly reduced the cost of installation per unit, going from USD94 per unit in the second quarter of 2017 to USD35 per unit in May of 2018 (Fig. 4.5).

With respect to staff growth, Kingo went from being run entirely by Juan Fermín and his partners, who carried out all of the company's necessary tasks, to having a total of 150 employees in 2016, just three years later. By mid-2018 the company was employing 350 people, with plans to hire an additional 600 by the end of the year.

Kingo's Distribution Channel

The Kingo Unit and Its Related Services

Initially, Kingo had purchased standardized units from suppliers in China. But its leadership eventually recognized the need for reliable hardware and

11,200% Growth over last 39 months

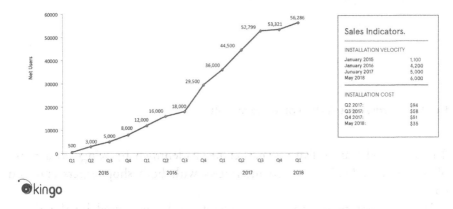

Fig. 4.5 Percentage growth and sales indicators

software that could respond to the needs of the established business model. To meet the demands of the services Kingo provided, these elements would need to be designed in-house.

They shifted to obtaining Kingo hardware from an intermediary (i.e., a broker) in China who managed the entire supply chain; when Kingo contacted the broker with a predetermined prototype for a given Kingo unit, the broker would seek out options for certified local providers that met certain requirements and could guarantee the quality of the device. Based on this design, the broker would present a list of possible suppliers for each component, after which Kingo would conduct testing and determine which companies to contract. It's worth noting that, because the Kingo units were designed in-house, the company owns 100% of its intellectual property.

The Kingo units included an unlimited service guarantee, as well as free battery exchanges and system updates. Any failure in the device was visible to Kingo via its management information software, described below. These issues were reported, at no cost per call, to a call center that could attend customers in any of the indigenous languages used by the communities Kingo served. The call center assigned a ticket to each issue to ensure follow-up, and they were given a specific time and sales person to respond to them.

Kingo had four types of units, each with distinct functions, and was planning to launch two additional models in the third quarter of 2018. The units provided certain standard services, for example, powering LED light bulbs and charging cell phones, and included an array of supplementary electronic devices such as televisions, tablets, and refrigerators (Fig. 4.6).

Kingo Basic	Kingo Light	Kingo TV/Tablet	Kingo Home	*Kingo Plus	*Kingo Production
~1 Light Bulb	~3 Light Bulbs	~2 Light Bulbs	~4 Light Bulbs	~4 Light Bulbs	~4 Light Bulbs
~1 Cellphone	~1 Cellphone	~1 Cellphone	~1 Cellphone	~1 Cellphone	~1 Cellphone
		~TV/Tablet	~ TV 24"	~TV 24"	~TV 24"
				~Refrigeration	~Refrigeration
					~Motors

*Will be launched in Q3 2018

Fig. 4.6 Hardware: selection of Kingo models

This last model arose from a market need identified by Kingo as a result of its constant field visits and interviews with both shopkeepers and end customers.

With respect to software, the prepaid mechanism used by the Kingo sales teams was based on algorithms that were also the company's intellectual property. These codes consisted of 16 digits and could be acquired by users from the neighborhood shops as needed. Consumers could purchase codes per hour, day, week, or month. These algorithms were exclusively generated for each team, were catalogued by a unique identification number, and could only be used once—again, much like how prepaid phone cards work.

Hiring, Development, Culture, and Results-Focused Hierarchy

From an organizational perspective, the company focused on hiring the best available talent in the market for each position, ensuring that it recruited candidates who could most effectively complete the tasks. To this end, Kingo generally offered higher-than-average salaries (regardless of the position level) and fostered an innovative work environment that promoted mutual growth for both the enterprise and the employee. Generally, the people who worked in rural areas (regional supervisors, coordinators, and sales staff) had previously held jobs with below-minimum-wage salaries. In addition, the enterprise's hierarchical leadership levels worked particularly close with one another, such that each level received significant support from the levels above (both directly and indirectly). Regular planning and reporting meetings were held between, for example, managers and regional supervisors, regional supervisors and coordinators, and coordinators and sales staff. Meetings with the entire sales team (supervisors, coordinators, and sales representatives) and their respective operational managers were held roughly once a month. It was common to find Juan Fermín or other members of the leadership team in the rural offices, conducting visits to the communities, or accompanying the sales team.

All employees had to complete a one-week onboarding process, during which they learned about the company culture, devices, sales techniques, etc. This introductory training included field visits in which the new staff members interacted with customers and observed equipment installation or maintenance. After the general training, the staff completed more specific trainings, depending on the respective requirements of each role. In addition, all personnel had access to Kingo University, the company's interactive educational platform that announced updates to the Kingo units and other useful information.

Functional positions, such as human resource managers, were decentralized. Both the Petén and Alta Verapaz offices included all functions, with their respective managers reporting to the main headquarters in Guatemala City. For example, the two human resources managers in Petén and in Alta Verapaz reported to the human resources director in Guatemala City. This decentralized model allowed Kingo to be more strongly imbedded in the market.

The company's information management software played a primordial role in its effective governance. Using efficient software and the up-to-date information it provided made it easy for decision-makers throughout the organization to properly carry out their tasks. For example, the data gathered by Ant helped coordinators efficiently schedule their sales team's routes. In addition, the company's results-focused culture ensured that all levels aligned with this strategy. All employees received clear job descriptions, performance indicators with concrete goals, and the resources needed to achieve these. The sales staff had daily, weekly, and monthly objectives related to acquiring new customers, repairing devices, and selling recharge codes to existing customers.

Kingo's results-focused culture was further reinforced in each of its three headquarter offices. For example, the walls of the Petén headquarters featured messages such as, "An audacious goal: 2 million homes turned ON by 2010." Team activities were held each month to bring employees together in such a way that they felt part of a family. In short, there was a strong culture of belonging that easily compared to that of a large multinational corporation.

The Importance of Community Training and Customer-Relations in Accessing New Areas of Service

One of Kingo's success factors was the close relationships it had with the communities in which it operated, from the first visit to the daily follow-up on operations provided by the sales team. This team made initial contact with community leaders,[x] and would introduce the company's intention to boost community development through an attractive renewable energy service. Once contact had been made with community leaders, Kingo staff then organized events with a group of potential customers, during which the staff would demonstrate the company's various devices in order to generate an initial positive expectancy. After obtaining approval from the community leaders and having secured its first customers, Kingo employed local residents to maintain a close, constant relationship with the community. These individuals were appropriate candidates to sustain customer relations, as they spoke the same language, shared the same culture, and had a more complete understanding of how these homes operated.

Distribution Through Neighborhood Shops

For its business model to work, Kingo needed a local distribution network willing to sell its devices to end users. This meant starting conversations with the communities' main shopkeepers, who owned small neighborhood stores (*pulperías or tienditas*). In these conversations, Kingo sales staff pitched a business agreement that included a per-sale commission. The shopkeepers required consistent attention in order to maintain and increase sales. This was accomplished through technical sales representatives solely dedicated to shopkeeper relations. This distribution channel represented approximatively 75% of the enterprise's revenues.

The sales representatives (see Router Service Agent in Fig. 4.7) were responsible for approximately 200 shops each and reported directly to their respective coordinators. Each coordinator oversaw 1000–2000 shops and reported to the regional supervisor, who in turn oversaw all 4000 shops through which Kingo operated throughout the country (Fig. 4.7). The annual expenditure of sales representatives was USD250,000.[xi]

With respect to income generated from sales, Kingo offered its shopkeeper partners a 6% commission on sales as an incentive to become distributors (this commission was higher than that offered by other businesses that provided similar device and services, such as Tigo).[xii] The shopkeepers would receive this commission once they had sold all of the codes they had previously purchased from Kingo.

Kingo leadership recognized that the shopkeepers played a key role in the sales of the prepaid service and was conscious that the success of the business largely depended on them. Replicating the business model used by cell phone companies, which featured a close relationship with shopkeepers,

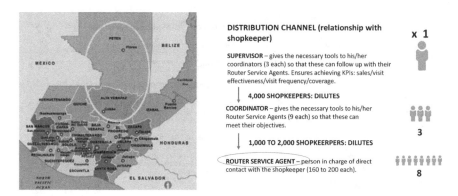

Fig. 4.7 Kingo distribution channel through shopkeepers

facilitated a functional sales model in which the company did not need to invest in fixed assets (such as its own stores or kiosks) to facilitate operations.

Assistance to End Users

Kingo's service sales representatives attended the end users. This team, typically comprising employees from the areas in which the company operated, was responsible for presale tasks,[xiii] the sales of Kingo services directly to households, and equipment installation and maintenance. Much like a loan provision, selling a service implies a risk, as the Kingo units can be stolen or poorly used by the customer. This risk was mitigated through a process of identifying favorable customers. To detect "favorable customers," Kingo's service representatives were trained to evaluate customers based on (a) their capacity to pay for the service, (b) their economic situation and household habits, (c) the number of people living in the home, (d) their place of work, (e) the number of candles or amount of kerosene they used each month, (f) and how often they charged their cell phones at the neighborhood shop. In each of the two markets, Kingo's service distribution channel included roughly 70 sales representatives (see Service Agent in Fig. 4.8) (140 total), seven coordinators (14 total), and one supervisor (2 total) (Fig. 4.8). The distribution channel's annual expenditures totaled USD250,000.[xiv]

Flexibility on Revenue Process Based on Payment and Energy Use Options

Over the years, Kingo's leadership team learned that its customers require a high level of flexibility in how they pay for their electric energy

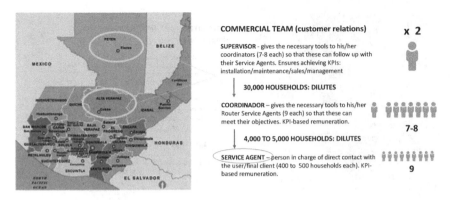

Fig. 4.8   Kingo sales and assistance to end users

consumption. While the direct sale of equipment via financing provided by microfinance institutions in the Quetsol model had worked, it didn't allow the company to grow at the rate its leadership team had hoped. Low-income customers needed to be able to decide how much energy they could buy, and when they could buy it. Thus, from the start, Kingo offered services—not devices—as only services enable this type of flexibility. For instance, a client that already had a Kingo model and wished to update to a superior model with new features could do so. The sales staff would simply exchange the devices at no additional charge. Based on the lesson that it was nearly impossible to implement a scalable business model based on devices sales rather than service sales, Kingo's leadership had implemented a prepaid model that provided customers with a high degree of flexibility that would not have been possible with the one-time sale of a single device.

To ensure profitability, Kingo used a metric called the "utilization rate," which the Ant information management system consistently monitored. A household's utilization rate corresponded to its monthly expenses as a percentage of the cost of a monthly recharge code. The minimum utilization rate was 70%. Maintaining as high a utilization rate as possible not only guaranteed Kingo a return on investment, but also increased its cost-effectiveness. Thus, the sales staff were tasked with obtaining the most accurate possible information about their respective customers. This was achieved through face-to-face interviews and home visits, during which they observed the conditions of the home and determined whether installing a Kingo unit (regardless of the model) would meet the minimum monthly utilization rate. If a customer ran into financial difficulties and was unable to acquire the recharge codes needed to meet the minimum utilization rate, the sales staff was required to pressure the customer to continue consumption so that they would not have to remove the device. After various attempts were made to maintain the customer's patronage (in the form of personal visits from sales staff, who would offer them recharge codes or suggest other options, such as simpler Kingo models), the sales person was obligated to uninstall the device. In such cases, the customer would sign a document canceling the service, and would be removed from the system.

Because it provided an integrated, flexible service, Kingo's customer loyalty was extremely high. This allowed the company to generate regular income from an established customer base, achieving USD2.5 million in sales in 2018. In addition, its in-house sales supported an in-depth understanding of the customers' needs, and monitoring the "utilization rate" for each unit allowed Kingo staff to quickly and efficiently respond to customer requests and make effective decisions that supported its revenue stream.

The Challenge of Scaling

While Kingo's business model had proved to be scalable, Juan Fermín and the enterprise's investors wanted to further grow the business. For one of the first times since he founded the enterprise, Juan Fermín was unsure what to do. Should he focus on managing the shopkeeper sales channel in-house, or outsource the distribution to Estrella Digital?

Option 1: Manage the Shopkeeper Sales Channel In-House

The first option was to continue to manage Kingo's sales channel in-house, despite the high cost, focusing on increasing the consumption rates of the existing client base rather than expanding the number of customers. The cost of reaching new customers was extremely high considering the logistics and sales efforts needed to obtain new customers (which often included training customers, a task that was carried out by the sales team, and didn't always yield results). This was due to the implicit costs of travel: fuel, tires, depreciation, labor hours, etc. To scale by increasing the consumption rate of existing customers would require changes to Kingo's operations. "It's all about operations," Juan Fermín thought to himself. "It's just a question of what works best for our operations, and how to develop an efficient and effective distribution." Keeping the operations up with the expected growth rate, however, was a challenge, particularly with respect to the distribution, as the control process had become quite complex. While the distribution worked, it was extremely costly. Juan Fermín felt these high costs were legitimized by the proximity it allowed his company to have with its customers, which was essential to obtaining market knowledge. "You have to be attuned to what's going on in the trenches," Juan Fermín had often said. "It's precisely this awareness that provides the information that deepens the relationship with your customers; it helps you progressively improve and offer them additional value. The more value you give your customers the more friction you eliminate from the sales channel."

Option 2: Outsource the Distribution Channel to Estrella Digital

The second option was to outsource distribution. Juan Fermín considered companies such as Tigo that had decades of experience in distributing prepaid phone cards to rural communities in Guatemala. They knew how to maintain relationships with customers and intermediaries such as shopkeepers. Recently, however, he had received an offer from Estrella Digital, a company that specialized in managing shopkeeper relations. Estrella Digital had ample knowledge and experience in the cell phone industry and was a leader in its field. As mentioned above, the company had agreed to adapt Kingo's guidelines, such that Kingo sales staff be hired by Estrella Digital but adhere to Kingo's operational requirements. Furthermore, it offered a cost of 20% less than Kingo's current expenditures.

Juan Fermín knew that Kingo's sales teams had been key to developing profitable distribution channels. Outsourcing to a third party was risky. What worried him most was handing over control of his most important distribution channel to another company. Kingo's success had been built through close relationships with customers in low-income contexts. But he also knew that Kingo's operation had become too complex to scale any further as the investor expected. What should Juan Fermín do? Should he scale by increasing the consumption rates of existing customers within his own distribution channels (Option 1) or should he outsource the management of the distribution channel to Estrella Digital (Option 2)?

Additional Information on the Case

Kingo Case Photographs

See Photos 4.1, 4.2, 4.3, 4.4, 4.5, 4.6, 4.7, 4.8, and 4.9.

Photo 4.1   Coordinator explaining how a Kingo unit works to a new customer

Photo 4.2   Phrase on the wall of the regional headquarters in Petén

Photo 4.3 Customer visit from a coordinator and a service sales representative (not visible) to maintenance a Kingo unit

Teaching Note on the Kingo Case

The Kingo case facilitates a discussion regarding the challenges of establishing efficient operations that respond to the scaling expectations of the social entrepreneur and the investors. It puts special attention on the importance of having an in-depth knowledge of the customer or beneficiary in order to develop operations that ensure a financial and impact return on investment.

Photo 4.4   Sign at a local shop advertising the various plans that Kingo offered, with respective prices per day, week, and month

Learning Objectives

Readers can begin by reflecting on this case in the context of the three elements of operations described in Phase II of the market approach to scaling. The first, ***supply*** and assets, includes the production of Kingo units in China and Juan Fermín's capacity to develop a corporate culture that is focused on results. The second, ***products and services***, is reflected in the provision of solar energy to isolated, impoverished customers. The third, ***distribution***

Photo 4.5   Storeroom at the Petén headquarters with new Kingo units

Photo 4.6   Kingo coordinator working on his laptop while the service sales representative maintenances the customer's Kingo unit

Photo 4.7 Conversation between a coordinator and a customer who contacted the call center to say that he was interested in Kingo's service (he later paid for his first recharge code by giving the sales representative a chicken)

and revenue, is illustrated by the fact that the distribution of Kingo units and associated services is at the core of the enterprise's business model. As distribution is central to Kingo's business model, determining whether to outsource this component in order to further scale the business was proving to be a challenging decision for its founder, Juan Fermín.

After having analyzed and discussed the case, readers should be able to:

a. characterize the challenges of establishing operations to meet social entrepreneurs and investors scaling expectations; and
b. systematically analyze the costs and benefits of managing distributions within the company or outsourcing those channels.

Reflection on Kingo in the Context of the Market Approach to Scaling

Phases I and II of the market-based approach to scaling are illustrated in this case (Figs. 4.9 and 4.10). Juan Fermín and his team have successfully

Photo 4.8 Sign in front of a local shop, notifying residents that it offers Kingo recharge codes. Utility poles and power lines owned by a power company can be seen in the background

leveraged resources through the participation of impact investors. They have used these resources to develop an information management system that allows them to remotely monitor the enterprises' sales and distribution operations. They complement this with the work of the sales team, which directly serves the end users and establish personal and commercial relations with shopkeepers in the field. Kingo's revenue system is based on prepaid services, much like that used by the cell phone industry.

The advantage of outsourcing the shopkeeper sales channel to Estrella Digital is that it could manage this channel for 20% less of what Kingo is currently spending. Juan Fermín felt that if Estrella Digital was willing to adapt to Kingo's guidelines, then Kingo would be able to preserve its corporate culture. In any case, Juan Fermín decided that, if he chose this route, he would track any potential change in sales through this distribution to see if it was being affected by this change.

Photo 4.9 Service sales representative conducting a customer visit for equipment maintenance

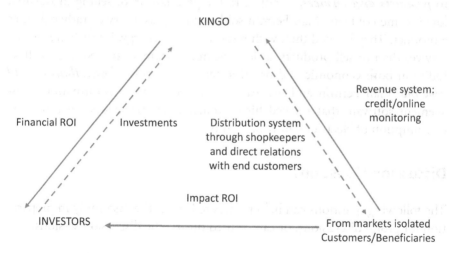

Fig. 4.9 Option 1: manage the shopkeeper sales channel in-house and focus on increasing consumption among existing customers

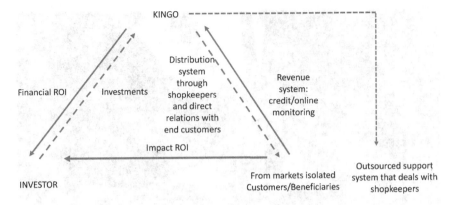

Fig. 4.10 Option 2: outsource management of the shopkeeper sales channel

Tying the Kingo Case to Phase II of the Market Approach to Scaling

In order to establish efficient operations, Juan Fermín and his team began by reflecting on *supply* and assets. To develop efficiency and efficacy in their operations they outsourced the production of Kingo units to China. Also, they knew that a corporate culture focused on results was key. With respect to *products and services*, to adjust to the peculiarities of selling in isolated, low-income contexts, Juan Fermín sold electricity as a service rather than as a product. They learned that, with respect to solar energy, it was better to sell services than to sell products, as low-income customers are looking for flexibility in both economic and practical terms. In terms of *distribution and revenue*, Juan Fermín and his team developed a robust information management software that tracked his customer base's behaviors regarding the consumption of electricity in Kingo units.

Discussion Questions

The following questions can help readers reflect on the case study in preparation for group discussions, or can be used during the discussion sessions.

1. *Do you consider Juan Fermín to be a social entrepreneur?* This question stimulates reflection on how to define a social entrepreneur. Juan Fermín shows a strong for-profit motivation. Discussion surrounding this

question can reflect on the importance of that social motivation has on defining the boundaries of what can be considered a social enterprise. In this book, we argue that the existence of an impact strategy—regardless of motivation—is what defines a social enterprise.

2. *If you were in Juan Fermín's position, would you choose Option 1 (managing the shopkeeper channel in-house) or Option 2 (outsourcing to Estrella Digital)?* (Figs. 4.9 and 4.10). This question helps readers reflect on the creation of efficient operations and its associated elements of *supply and assets, products and services,* and *distribution and revenue.*

3. *How does Juan Fermín use advanced technology to improve his operations processes in low-income contexts?* This final question helps readers reflect on the opportunities that technology provides to help the enterprise establish a more in-depth knowledge of low-income contexts and, therefore, to become more successfully embedded in these contexts. Entrepreneurs often assume that the only way to embed their business in these contexts is to be both socially and emotionally attached to the customer or beneficiary and the social mission it aims to accomplish; however, Kingo demonstrates that technology can add great value in terms of gaining a deep contextual understanding and developing efficient operations and revenue processes.

Notes

i. Although researchers define supply chain more broadly as "a group of at least three entities (enterprises or individuals) directly implicated in the flows (downstream and upstream) of products, services, capital and/or information that go from a source to a client" [1], we define supply as the way how the social enterprise creates the input of products, services, capital and information that they need for their operations.

ii. Dirt paths; typically narrow.

iii. Unpaved roads or paths that are wide enough for a vehicle.

iv. The electrical coverage index indicates the number of households (users that have electrical service) in relation to the total number of households in a given department, expressed as a percentage.

v At that moment, the organization name was "Quetsol".

vi. At that point, Kingo was legally founded and spearheaded by Juan Fermín.

vii. See www.grupooeg.com.

viii. Series A financing is the first opportunity a startup company offers to private investment groups or those wishing to serve as external angel investors.

ix. Series B financing is the round of financing that occurs once the business has proved profitable and requires additional capital to grow.

x. Community leadership typically refers to COCODEs, or Community Development Councils, which pertain to Guatemala's National System of Development Councils (*Sistema Nacional de Consejos de Desarrollo*). Created according to Guatemalan law, they are "…the principal means of participation on the part of the Mayan, Xinca, Garifuna, and non-indigenous populations in public governance and the execution of democratic development planning processes, taking into account the principles of national, multi-ethnic, pluricultural, and multilingual unity of the Guatemalan nation" (Decree 11-2002, Chapter 1, Article 1; translated from the Spanish).

xi. The amount of USD250,000 is hypothetical, and does not reflect Kingo's actual annual expenditure for this distribution channel.

xii. Nevertheless, Kingo recently discovered that many shopkeepers discretely modify the final sales price of their recharge codes to match that of other operators (e.g., Tigo) in order to earn more money, without consulting to Kingo's sales team. Upon learning this, Kingo decided to increase its commission and propose a new scaling model in which the more the shopkeepers sell the greater their commission percentage.

xiii. Once Kingo had an established customer base in a given community, the presale work via COCODEs or local leaders was no longer needed; rather, the work of explanation, "convincing," and sales was carried out directly by technical sales representatives. Working through COCODEs is only necessary when first approaching a new community.

xiv. The annual expenses in this distribution channel were not disclosed by Kingo. Therefore, the amount of USD250,000 is not a real data on the expenses on this distribution channel.

References

1. Mentzer, J. T., Dewitt, W., Keebler, J. S., Min, S., Nix, N. W., Smith, C., et al. (2001). Defining supply chain management. *Journal of Business Logistics, 22,* 1–25.
2. Hockerts, K., & Agrawal, A. (2018). Impact investing: Review and research agenda. *Journal of Small Business & Entrepreneurship.* Published online 31 January 2019.
3. Son, H., Lee, J., & Chung, Y. (2017). Value creation mechanism of social enterprises in manufacturing industry: Empirical evidence from Korea. *Sustainability, 10*(46), 1–24.
4. Seelos, C., & Mair, J. (2019). *Innovation and scaling for impact: How effective social enterprises do it* (256 pp.). Stanford, CA: Stanford University Press.

5. Pentland, B. T., & Reuter, H. H. (1994). Organizational routines as grammars of action. *Administrative Science Quarterly, 39*(3), 484–510.
6. United Nations Development Program. (2015–2016). *Más allá del conflicto, luchas por el bienestar* (Chapter 9, p. 259). National Human Development Report, Guatemala.
7. Guatemalan Ministry of Economy. http://dae.mineco.gob.gt/mapainteractivo/index.php?controller=crm&action=Detalles&id=1. Accessed 1 August 2018.
8. Guatemalan Ministry of Economy. http://dae.mineco.gob.gt/mapainteractivo/index.php?controller=crm&action=detalles&id=1#Infraestructura%20Vial. Accessed 1 August 2018.
9. *Startups Españolas.* (2015). https://www.startups-espanolas.es/2015/08/31/que-significa-series-a-y-series-b-en-la-financiacion-de-startups/.

5

Phase III: Integrating Financing and Impact Logics

Social enterprises that intend to scale through a market approach incorporate both an impact logic and a financing logic into their organizational culture. A "logic," in this sense, is a lens through which the enterprise and its context are viewed [1]. The social entrepreneur's challenge is to balance the social and/or environmental logic that drives the enterprise's mission with the financing logic that enables it to scale [2].

Achieving this balance is no simple task. Often, the enterprise's employees, and even the entrepreneurs themselves, tend toward one logic or the other. More difficult still is that these perspectives can reflect contrasting worldviews, resulting in conflicts between deeply rooted belief systems. For example, some stakeholders may view the financing logic as egoistical and profit-oriented, while others may view the impact logic as altruistic and idealistic [3]. Thus, in Phase III of the market approach to scaling, social entrepreneurs reflect on the tensions that scaling creates between these two logics, impact logic on the one hand, and financing logic on the other.

Exploring How to Integrate Financing and Impact Logics

An organizational culture that encompasses two different logics can affect internal communications, resulting in a two-sided rhetoric that dominates meetings and other interactions, with one side using finance-oriented business language and the other using people-oriented humanitarian language.

© The Author(s) 2020
U. Jäger et al., *Scaling Strategies for Social Entrepreneurs*,
https://doi.org/10.1007/978-3-030-31160-5_5

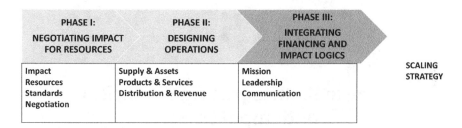

Fig. 5.1 Phase III: integrating financing and impact logics

These conflicting perspectives can be further intensified by new incomers such as impact investors, especially if they strongly emphasize financial return on investment. Striking a proper balance between the enterprise's social or environmental goals and its financing requires a solid sense of *mission*, *leadership*, and *communication* (Fig. 5.1).

Mission

The *mission* is a social enterprise's reason for being; it reflects its basic values, what it is trying to accomplish, and how [4]. When social entrepreneurs discuss scaling strategies with their teams, potential investors, and other stakeholders, challenging conversations about the mission can occur. These can even result in a change in the mission statement—for example, shifting from a regional focus to a global one. In any case, a critical reflection of all elements of the mission with respect to the scaling strategy is necessary. FUNDES illustrates the challenge of aligning a market-based scaling strategy with a pre-established social or environmental mission. FUNDES is a nonprofit organization that helps micro, small, and medium enterprises (MSMEs) in Latin America to grow, in turn reducing poverty. After 20 years in operation, FUNDES's main donor announced that it would be progressively reducing its funding to zero in the next three years, prompting the organization to search for new sources of funding. In response to the withdrawal of support from its main donor, FUNDES eventually shifted its nonprofit model to that of a social enterprise, deciding that it would market its services to large firms. While its mission of helping Latin American MSMEs grow remained unchanged, its customer base shifted to multinational companies and other large firms that included MSMEs in their value chains and were interested in developing these MSMEs' capabilities. Thus, FUNDES adapted to appeal to multinational companies, many of which were unwilling to partner with a nonprofit organization that was solely focused on poverty alleviation. The transition spurred difficult discussions about FUNDES's mission, and the organization ultimately decided that, rather than changing its mission statement, it would present itself as a consulting firm to gain credibility in the corporate world.

Guiding questions:
Where in our ***mission*** do the financing and impact logics unite? What elements can we add to our mission to increase the overlap between these two logics?

Leadership

When scaling a social enterprise, ***leadership*** plays an important role in mediating between a financing orientation and an impact one [5]. Effective leadership helps balance the financing and impact logics and ensures that both are a consistent part of the enterprise's internal discussions, spurring coherent decisions that lead to a successful scaling strategy [6]. In the FUNDES case, leadership had to play an active role during the transition from a nonprofit model to a social enterprise model (which FUNDES calls "a business with a purpose"). FUNDES leadership, for example, adjusted its staff's priorities by setting financing-oriented incentives, turned over more than half of the enterprise's top-level leaders, and reorganized its organizational structure by centralizing its more than 12 autonomous country offices under a single headquarter office in Costa Rica. These actions enabled the enterprise to successfully balance the financing and impact logics and successfully scale its impact from 6000 annually supported MSMEs in 2010 to more than 40,000 in 2016.

Guiding questions:
How is our ***leadership*** structured, and what types of interactions does it promote inside and outside the organization? What kind of leadership structure and interactions would support the overlap between the financing and impact logics?

Communication

When discussing scaling strategies, tensions between financing and impact logics may emerge within the organization [5]. If unattended, these can lead to rifts between colleagues and can reduce organizational efficiency. The stronger these tensions, the more important it is to foster a common

Table 5.1 Examples of using mission, leadership, and communication

Elements	Examples
Mission	• *Balanced mission*: Daniel Buchbinder founded ALTERNA in Guatemala with the following mission: "We identify entrepreneurs and businesses (financing logic) that are creating social and environmental value (impact logic) in their communities, and providing them with hands-on mentorship and accompaniment to help them achieve their goals and maximize their impact" • *Balanced mission*: Nicolás Suárez founded Diseclar with the mission "to produce exclusively designed furniture for outdoor use (financing logic) using recycled plastic materials (impact logic)
Leadership	• *Shared leadership*: Maria Pacheco (leader with an impact focus) and Ligia Chinchilla (leader with a financing focus) founded Kiej de los Bosques and Wakami with the mission of supporting women in poor communities. Their joint leadership made it possible to create the well-known brand, Wakami (financing logic), and a trust-based network within poor communities (impact logic) • *Inspiration*: Alexandra Kissling founded Unidas para Crecer in Costa Rica. Her inspiring leadership motivated many professional women to become volunteer mentors for women in poor communities (impact logic), in turn helping them to create their own business (financing logic)
Communication	• *Systemic language*: Armando Moguel, the head of strategy for FUNDES, a Latin American consulting firm with a social mission, replaced language surrounding impact goals and shared value with a systemic language that integrated impact goals and financing ones • *Pilot projects to showcase balanced impact*: Thiago Pinto founded New Hope, which helps poor recyclers (impact logic) report their recycled garbage supply to companies using a specially designed app (financing logic). They created a pilot project to showcase both the social/environmental and financial results of their solution

language that can bridge these differences both internally and in relations with external stakeholders. External communication is also key to effectively integrating this balance with both new and established stakeholders, and encouraging them to continue to support the organization despite strategic changes. In the FUNDES case, its leaders discussed the new strategy in terms of the broadly viewed concept of "systems," in which large companies see business opportunities to work with MSMEs along their value chains. This new business concept prepared the enterprise's leaders to communicate that FUNDES, formerly a nonprofit, could create economic value for companies by focusing on the common link of strengthening MSMEs. It also helped shift discussions within FUNDES from helping MSMEs to creating value for both MSMEs and companies, and how to adjust FUNDES's business model to enable this.

Guiding questions:
What are our **communication** practices? What practices do we use to foster internal and external communication in a way that unites the financing and impact logics?

Table 5.1 presents additional examples of mission, leadership, and communication to balance financing and impact logics.

The FUNDES Case

Social enterprises that intend to scale through a market approach typically have employees that either (1) defend the impact logic, arguing that it is the enterprise's reason for existence, or (2) defend the financing logic, arguing that profits and financial sustainability are vital to the enterprise's continued existence. For example, employees that view their social enterprise through an impact lens might make statements such as, "All that matters are our beneficiaries. We need to help make the world a better place," while those that favor a financing logic might say, "At the end of the day, we need to be able to pay our bills." Depending on the team members' values, norms, and previous experience, they are either motivated to work at the social enterprise out of interest in the impact they make by working there or in the salary they earn, as well as in the economic success of the organization. The task of the social entrepreneur is to integrate both logics into the structure and identity of their enterprise.

The following case is an example of a nonprofit organization that became a social enterprise in order to take a more market approach to scaling its impact. While many nonprofits include market-oriented activities, these projects are often marginal and are not part of the nonprofit's core mission. Sales, for example, may provide a small amount of additional income to supplement donations or government subsidies. FUNDES, in contrast, decided to put the market approach at the core of its activities. The following case details its transition from a nonprofit model to a social enterprise model, particularly with respect to the challenges of balancing the financing and impact logics.

FUNDES was created in 1984 with the mission of serving MSMEs in Latin America with the goal of reducing poverty—a mission that has remained constant throughout its more than twenty years of operation. During this period, FUNDES made two major adjustments to its strategy in order to more effectively serve its MSME beneficiaries (from the initial mission of helping MSMEs access micro loans, to providing them with training and business development services, to consulting). However, an announcement that its main donor, Fundación Avina (Avina Foundation), would be progressively withdrawing its funding, caused the organization to question its approach and propose a radical change. Such a substantial cut in funding meant that, for the first time in its history, the nonprofit was under pressure to identify a strategy that would enable it to fulfill its social mission while also generating a significant amount of income.

The case highlights two options that FUNDES entertained to solve this problem in order to create a sustainable financing model. The first was to replace Fundación Avina with another donor, an option that would require no changes to its current model. The second was to sell its services to multinational companies (MNCs) and other large firms, which would mean that it would need to find a way to incorporate a financing logic without losing the organization's core social mission.

The Case: Managing Change at FUNDES[1]

It was shortly before Christmas when Ulrich Frei, the Chief Executive Officer (CEO) of the Latin American nonprofit, FUNDES International, entered his office in San Jose, Costa Rica on a Monday morning in December 2010. A large map on the wall highlighted the organization's ten country offices throughout Latin America, through which the organization had supported the competitive development of MSMEs over the last 20 years. As usual, Ulrich poured himself a cup of freshly brewed coffee and turned on his computer. An email titled "Annual Meeting," however, immediately put an end to his relaxed weekend mood. His thoughts turned to the current challenge.

He knew that the annual meeting, scheduled to take place in February 2011 in El Salvador, and including the presidents and managers of all of FUNDES's country organizations, would be critical to the organization's

---

[1]Authors: Urs Jäger, Associate Professor INCAE Business School and Academic Director VIVA Idea; and Silke Bucher, Assistant Professor INCAE Business School.

further development. He also knew that he needed to prove that he could achieve what FUNDES's board of directors expected of him. One of the reasons the board had hired him as CEO was to lead FUNDES toward a future in which the organization could be financially independent from its main donor, Fundación Avina.

As soon as he had become the FUNDES director, Ulrich came up with two options for achieving a financial sustainability. The first was to replace Fundación Avina with another donor, an option that many of FUNDES's country managers supported. The second option was to increase sales by systematically relying on MNCs and other large firms as FUNDES's main customer segment. In this model, FUNDES would offer to help the MNCs and other large firms to efficiently work with the MSMEs in their value chains. While there had always been some discussion surrounding these two options, the situation was now urgent: Fundación Avina had announced that its funding would be gone within the next three years. A concrete decision was imminent—should FUNDES find a new donor, or shift its focus to serving MSMEs through MNCs and other large firms? At the February meeting, Ulrich would need to present both strategies, and argue for one or the other.

MSMEs in Latin America

The Role of MSMEs in the Socioeconomic Development of Latin America

MSMEs play an important role in the socioeconomic development of Latin America. FUNDES considers micro-enterprises as those with less than 10 employees, small enterprises as those with 10–50 employees, and medium enterprises as those with 50–150 employees. Companies employing more than 150 people are generally classified as large.

In 2010, of the more than 18 million MSMEs in Latin America, 48% operated in the service sector, 28% in trade, and 19% in manufacturing [7]. They were contributing some 60% of available jobs, 50% of which were formal and 10% of which were informal [8]. FUNDES characterizes jobs in the informal sector as those in which the hiring MSMEs are not registered, largely disregard labor, fiscal, and environmental legislation, and have no legalized ownership of their assets. MSMEs operating in the informal sector face a variety of limitations to their businesses in terms of capacity for growth, access to capital, employee benefits, and a workforce training.

Differences Between the Countries in Which FUNDES Operated

In 2010, there were large differences between individual Latin American countries in terms of the importance, dynamics, and qualities of MSMEs. For instance, with respect to job creation, micro-enterprises in Colombia were responsible for 51% of employment, whereas in Honduras the percentage was 98%. The density of MSMEs in 2010 ranged from 17 firms per 1000 inhabitants in Costa Rica to 44 per 1000 in Chile, and while informality was a problem throughout all Latin American countries, it was especially high in Bolivia, Peru, Guatemala, and Argentina.

MSMEs' Need for Business Development Services

Latin American MSMEs faced several challenges. Many MSME teams had never received business training or consultancies, although these types of business development services (sometimes referred to as BDS) had proven to be fundamental in increasing their competitiveness. As to external conditions, Latin American MSMEs faced socioeconomic challenges such as a heavy dependency on local and national markets with limited access to international markets; weak links to MNC supply chains (largely due to a lack of competitiveness in terms of volume, quality, and price); difficulty accessing financing; and regulations that impeded effective operations in a variety of ways (Table 5.2). The world economic crisis of 2008, originating in the United States, worsened the situation by reducing the overall demand, delaying payments by clients, and increasing the difficulty in acquiring credit from financial institutions. As a result of these limitations, only 45% of Latin American MSMEs were able to survive the first three years of operation. Against this background, MSMEs needed help increasing their market access, reducing productivity gaps between them and large firms, formalizing their businesses, establishing adequate working conditions, and creating more dynamic business environments [5].

Business Development Service Providers

When it was founded in 1984, FUNDES was one of the first private organizations to promote the competitive development of MSMEs in Latin America. More than 20 years later, it still held a strong market position. In 2010, however, experts expected a rising number of competitors, particularly among the more than 80 members of the Aspen Network for Development Entrepreneurs (ANDE). ANDE was a global network of academic

Table 5.2 FUNDES's principal customers and competitors in four countries

Country	Competitors	Customers			
		Government	Large enterprises	Boards	Development organizations
Panama	IDCE	INDEH MITRADEL SENACYT AMPYME	Alimentos Pascual Gulf Oil	APEX SIP SumaRSE	COSPAE
Costa Rica	CLACDS-INCAE CEGESTI CINPE Grupo KAISEN SGE Consultores	MEIC/DIGEPYME SBD INA	DOS PINOS FLORIDA BEBIDAS METALCO PIPASA	CICR Consejo Mipyme	Instituto Excelencia CEDEMIPYME
El Salvador	FEPADE CHEMONICS ESEN	CENPROMYPE CONAMYPE INSAFOR EXPORTA	Alimentos DIANA	ANEP Chamber of Industry and Commerce	CENTROMYPE Independent consultants GTZ
Guatemala	CRECER Rain forest Alliance	Ministry of the Economy	Cervecería Centroamericana Grupo Solid Ingenio Pantaleón Banco Industrial	AGEXPORT Chamber of industry Chamber of commerce CentraRSE	

Source Based on CLACDS, 2010, Dimensión y caracterización del mercado de Servicios de Desarrollo Empresarial (SDE) en Centroamérica, Market study, p. 10 (own translation)

institutions, corporations, development finance institutions, and investment funds dedicated to promoting entrepreneurship in emerging markets. FUNDES was part of this network.

What is more, in 2010, a market study on business development services had revealed more than 40 potential competitors that were providing services similar FUNDES's (Table 5.3). Regarding service capacity, the study showed that some potential FUNDES clients did not perceive significant differences when comparing FUNDES's services with those offered by similar consulting companies, research institutions, government entities, or local branches of international organizations. Finally, the market study drew attention to the fact that FUNDES had to face very diverse conditions in the business development service market due to the differences between Latin American countries with respect to the role of MSMEs.

Table 5.3 FUNDES's potential market and non-market competitors in four countries (regional and international)

Competitor	Service	PN	CR	ES	GT
AED	CSR training and assessment services		■		
Ahues-Vásques Consultores	Business efficiency consultancy	■			
Aporta Solutions	Customized trainings	■			
Asociación Salvadorena de Industriales (ASI)	Services to strengthen productivity and economic development			■	
ASORIN Desarrollo empresarial	Consultancy and assessment in human resources and organizational development			■	
Cámara de Comercio de Guatemala	Training and assessment in commerce for businesses				■
Cámera de Comercio e Industria de El Salvador (CAMARASAL)	Business assessment services			■	
Cámara de Industria de Guatemala	Training and assessment for businesses in diverse topics				■
CEDEMIPYME	Training and administrative management for MSMEs		■		
Cegesti	Improved competitivity and sustainable development		■		
CentraRSE	CSR training and assessment services				■
CIETEC	Creation, strengthening, and development of new businesses		■		
CNPE-UNA	Research center	■			
CLACDS-INCAE	Research center		■		
COEXPORT	Assessment and business services for exporters			■	
CONCYT	National policy in science and technology				■
COSPAE	Business development	■			
CRECER	Business development, management, organizational performance, etc.		■		
Eco Global	Agro-tourism; development of local entrepreneurial endeavors		■		
FEPADE	Business services			■	
Fundación CENTROMYPE	Training and management support for small and medium enterprises			■	

(continued)

Table 5.3   (continued)

Competitor	Service	PN	CR	ES	GT
FUNDEA	Financing and support for MSME business services				X
FUNDEMAS	CSR training, entrepreneurship, and education quality improvement			X	
FUSADES	Research center			X	
Grupo APORTA	Customized business services	X			
Grupo CELAC	Business strategies	X			
Grupo FASI	Group of businesses that provide business training and assessment			X	
Grupo Kaisen	Strategic planning, BSC, ISO 9001	X		X	X
IEE-CICR	Non-financial business development services for the national productive sector			X	
INA	Professional training and development in various topics			X	
INADEH	Job training and development programs	X			
INSAFORP	Job training and development programs			X	
Instituto Desarrollo de la Cultura Empresarial (IDCE)	Training and consultancy services in business and entrepreneurial culture	X			
INTECAP	Professional development for human resources staff				X
JB Capacitación Empresarial	Business training and education services	X			
KPMG	Professional assessment services	X			
LATCERT	Technical consultancy and assessment for small, medium and large enterprises			X	
MITRADEL	Job training programs	X			
Price Waterhouse Coopers	Businesses auditing and assessment services			X	
REDNOMYPEM	Training and assessment for micro-enterprises	X			
REYSA Consulting Group	Business development services	X			
SGE Consultores	Technology transfer processes, consultancy, pre-audit and training for the industrial sector			X	
SumaRSE	CSR training and consultancy	X			

Inclusion of MSMEs in Large Firms' Value Chain

An increasingly popular approach among business development service providers was to support MSMEs by fostering their connection to national and international markets. At the same time, a growing number of MNCs and other large firms were pursuing strategies to more effectively include MSMEs in their value chains.

This approach could be observed in the work of MNCs like Nespresso. Several years earlier, Nespresso's leaders had recognized that their future success was intimately tied to the success of the small coffee farmers from whom they purchased. Their need for consistent supply of top-quality Arabica beans meant that they needed to find a way to partner in the development of these rural farming families. Through the company's sustainability program, which operated in partnership with the Rainforest Alliance and the World Bank Group's International Finance Firm, Nespresso sought to secure "Real Farmer Income"™ through significant enhancements in quality, sustainability, and productivity among the farmers from which they sourced coffee in Latin America. Through efforts such as the development of community-based production infrastructure, providing farmers with financial training, and sponsoring productivity-enhancing research at leading institutions, Nespresso was able to impact over 50,000 small farmers in five countries across the region.

Development Stages of FUNDES

Stage 1: Using Donations to Provide Access to Micro Loans (1984–1996)

FUNDES began as a pilot project in Panama. Operating as a foundation, it helped MSMEs access capital by providing guarantees. Its founders considered the absence of micro loans to be one of the main obstacles to the growth and success of small businesses. It thus functioned like a financial institution, and was often referred to as "the small firm's bank." At the start of the 1990s, FUNDES had 160 employees.

In these early days, FUNDES was financed primarily through donations from its founder, Stephan Schmidheiny. But as its network grew larger and larger over the years, its country managers, employees, trainers, and consultants needed new sources of funding (Table 5.4). Soon, country managers were asked to acquire private co-financing from local sources. The financial concept was again modified in 1994, when Schmidheiny created Fundación Avina, a financial trust, as part of his philanthropic network. From that time forward, nearly 100% of FUNDES's budget was financed by Avina. One of the FUNDES's managers characterized the financial situation by saying, "Resources were no problem—we had no real need to generate income. The central office paid the salaries; we just had to carry out the mission."

Stage 2: Acquiring Financial Resources for a Training and Business Environment Development Program (1996–2002)

In 1996, a research study commissioned by FUNDES confirmed that, in addition to financing, MSMEs were in great need of business training and education [7]. FUNDES's leaders decided that, while they would maintain

Table 5.4 Characteristics of four selected FUNDES countries

Country	Market	Demand	Payment capacity	Summary
Panama	Large market with available resources. Ample business development service (BDS) providers and independent consultancies. Insufficient local supply to meet demand	"Incipient" market with significant government participation. Demand is generic, irregular, and lacks sophistication	Elevated capacity to pay, particularly the government sector, due to a high level of urgency and a relative lack of knowledge regarding market prices, which impedes favorable transactions; moderate payment capacity with respect to businesses partners	Panama is in a period of expansion, and shows the greatest growth in demand for BDS providers
Costa Rica	Moderate market with reduced space for new participants. Sufficient local supply to meet the demand	"Mature" market with a high demand for medium and large enterprises. Government demand is moderate and largely self-sufficient. Sophisticated demand	Moderate capacity to pay in all segments; the cost-benefit relation of BDS requires that payments not be excessive and that results be tangible	In comparison to other Latin American countries Costa Rica provides stable market environment
El Salvador	Moderate market. Many BDS providers and independent consultancies. Supply matches demand	Market is in transition. The evolution of the demand is related to cooperative resources and government demand. Generic demand, small enterprise segment	Very low payment capacity. The smallest enterprises are accustomed to receiving subsidized BDS. For cooperants and larger enterprise segments, payment capacity increases to moderate	El Salvador's BDS market is transitioning toward a more sophisticated market
Guatemala	Large market. Many BDS providers and independent consultancies	Moderate, growing market, with low government demand and high dependency on cooperative resources. High-quality demand from business and cooperant sector	Very low payment capacity on the part of the government and small enterprises. Payment capacity of cooperant sector is moderate. Larger enterprises have a high payment capacity, but this is closely tied to the cost-benefit relation	Guatemala is in a phase of maturation toward a more specialized demand

the original service of facilitating access to capital, the service portfolio needed to be broadened. It added courses in basic management operations such as finance, marketing, sales, trade, and human resources, which ran from a few hours to several weeks. In addition, FUNDES started a "Business-Enabling Environment" program, which helped to create infrastructures such as micro loan banks that could provide MSMEs with the financial resources they needed.

Stage 3: Acquiring Financial Resources for Coaching and Consulting (2002–2009)

After having focused on training for several years, FUNDES managers realized that once people had completed the training, FUNDES never learned what challenges they faced when trying to implement what they had learned. For this reason, in 2004 FUNDES participated in an impact evaluation of its training and business environment services, performed by the United Nations Economic Commission for Latin America and the Caribbean (ECLAC). "Through the ECLAC study, we learned that MSMEs were facing concrete problems that needed specific solutions," said René Bronsil, who had become FUNDES's CEO in 2000. "We needed to help putting the lessons learned during the trainings into SME's business practices."

By 2004, FUNDES was supplementing its income from Avina donations with the sale of products and services, as well as contributions from international organizations and strategic allies who financed specific projects. By 2008, it had also successfully tested an additional funding option: by supporting cooperation between MSMEs and over 50 large firms in different countries, the organization had begun to receive income from large firms in exchange for its business development projects, which focused on efficiently including MSMEs in their value chains. This was an important development, as Fundación Avina had further reduced its funding—dropping from more than USD8 million in 2001 to USD3 million in 2005. For René this meant that, apart from restructuring its service portfolio, FUNDES also needed to find ways to strengthen its financial independence.

FUNDES's Mission and Vision

FUNDES's mission is to promote the competitive development of MSMEs in Latin America in an effort to reduce poverty. Its vision is to be committed, with the help of its team of collaborators, to the mission and sustainability of the organization. It focuses on driving competitiveness and sustainable development among MSMEs in Latin America with innovative, customized solutions, the latest technology, and a global network of offices and allies. FUNDES's objective is for MSMEs in Latin America to grow and become more competitive and sustainable so as to generate greater wealth, employment, and wellbeing [8].

FUNDES's Organizational Structure

In 2010, FUNDES had 10 country offices in Latin America: Argentina, Bolivia, Chile, Colombia, Costa Rica, El Salvador, Guatemala, Mexico, Panama, and Venezuela. Its central office, FUNDES International, was located in Costa Rica and also represented the Costa Rica country office. The central office and each of the country offices had an international management team, which reported to the CEO. Each team included a research and development manager, a business development manager, and a finance and administration manager. FUNDES's projects were supported by 170 permanent employees and a pool of more than 500 external consultants (Tables 5.5 and 5.6). All of the country offices were franchises, autonomous units that each paid a regular fee to FUNDES International. In exchange, they were able to offer their services under the FUNDES brand. Within this network of independent franchises were two different legal statuses: FUNDES International and the country office in Chile were firms and, as such, were required to pay taxes. All other country offices, including the Costa Rica office, were foundations.

FUNDES's Income and Cooperation

A typical FUNDES project lasted from two to three years. Depending on the type of service, the country and region served, and the scope, a project budget could range from USD10,000 to USD2 million. FUNDES had conducted several larger projects in partnership with large firms, international organizations, and local governments. More than 14 institutions—among them the ECLAC and the Development Bank of Latin America (CAF)—had supported projects by providing expertise, access to resources, and additional cooperation partners. Additionally, they played an important role in financing (or, in some cases, co-financing) the projects. Actively opening up new sources of funding had become increasingly important over the years, and from 2008 forward FUNDES had been increasingly seeking more opportunities to collaborate with MNCs and other large firms.

Table 5.5 Number of FUNDES employees and external consultants (2000–2009)

	2000	2001	2002	2003	2004	2005	2006	2007	2008	2009
Number of employees total	400	402	270	229	176	173	190	202	184	147
Mexico	30	32	25	15	13	19	17	21	18	18
Guatemala	20	16	15	15	14	15	18	13	13	11
El Salvador	5	16	24	18	16	18	19	21	19	20
Costa Rica	21	23	25	25	24	23	23	27	30	20
Panama	25	25	33	34	20	15	18	21	18	14
Colombia	26	16	16	13	13	12	17	16	17	12
Venezuela	13	14	10	10	11	9	9	10	8	6
Bolivia	26	22	13	11	12	11	20	20	11	11
Chile	17	21	31	28	29	21	20	21	20	12
Argentina	6	11	10	11	6	8	6	7	8	4
FUNDES International	71	68	68	49	18	22	23	25	22	19

Source FUNDES International financial report

Table 5.6 Revenue per country in thousands of USD (2000–2009)

	2000	2001	2002	2003	2004	2005	2006	2007	2008	2009
Income total	3192	5505	4654	4897	5601	6955	9242	8411	8450	7145
Mexico	266	1238	1013	990	989	1312	3380	2207	1775	1676
Guatemala	339	118	117	150	223	141	109	232	325	163
El Salvador	2	704	851	967	1447	2177	2606	1428	1415	1512
Costa Rica	342	526	543	701	601	571	583	758	718	553
Panama	112	295	797	561	255	226	185	399	511	322
Colombia	404	229	239	329	514	679	536	959	554	583
Venezuela	452	612	300	130	344	238	333	570	737	254
Bolivia	265	518	84	175	347	501	366	392	763	653
Chile	891	936	692	785	847	1049	978	1098	1244	1117
Argentina	120	329	17	108	34	60	166	367	408	312

Source FUNDES International financial report

FUNDES Cooperation Partners

As of 2010, FUNDES had more than 14 cooperation partners supporting its projects:

- *The Economic Commission for Latin America and the Caribbean (ECLAC)*: A technical cooperation partnership in which ECLAC supports FUNDES with various assessments of its services and a Business Procedure Simplification program.
- *Andean Development Corporation (CAF)*: FUNDES shares CAF's objective of promoting MSME development in the region. With CAF's collaboration, FUNDES has carried out one of its most emblematic projects, the Camelid Chain Development in the Bolivian Highlands.

- *State Secretariat for Economic Affairs in Switzerland (SECO)*: SECO was a key donor in the development of FUNDES's Business Procedure Simplification Program.
- *Aspen Network of Development Entrepreneurs (ANDE)*: FUNDES is a member of ANDE, an international organization composed of leading intermediaries (of financial services and business development services) that share the dream of starting a movement to unfurl the potential of small businesses in emerging markets.

The Challenge of Balancing FUNDES's Historically Nonprofit Model with Its Newly Emerging Market Orientation

In 2008, Ulrich succeeded René Bronsil, becoming FUNDES's fourth CEO. Coming from a large firm in the pharmaceutical industry, Ulrich had no experience managing a nonprofit organization—but he knew the business world.

In 2009, FUNDES offered four types of services: (a) *Business-level development*: helping MSMEs improve their performance, acquire international certifications, and plan new initiatives; (b) *Value chain development*: establishing strategic long-term relations between MSMEs—often grouped together to form a larger business entity (cluster)—and large firms to the benefit of both parties; (c) *Sectorial/territorial development*: designing and implementing interventions that would transform key business sectors and create jobs in the long term; (d) *Improvement of the business environment*: reducing public sector obstacles to initiating, operating, developing, and closing businesses.

Ulrich was convinced that grouping MSMEs from a certain sector and/or regional context together and connecting these "clusters" to one key player in the market—a large "anchor firm"—as part of this player's supply chain was the way to go. FUNDES had already had experiences in this field. On his visits to different Latin American countries, Ulrich had personally verified a number of projects in which FUNDES had successfully supported collaborations between large local firms and local MSMEs. These projects had had both an economic and a social/environmental impact. The large firms had been willing to pay for the service and, in some cases, even the MSMEs had contributed a symbolic per-month amount to the project. Ulrich was particularly impressed with two projects he visited, described below.

Project I: COPROCA

COPROCA emerged in 1991, originating from the Association of Llama and Alpaca Breeders of the High Andes (AIGACAA) to satisfy an international demand for raw materials and finished products made from alpaca and llama fibers. The firm worked with 1200 alpaca and llama breeders—all family farms—in the Bolivian highlands. Camalids represented one of Bolivia's most important agriculture sectors, and involved approximately 54,000 families. Bolivia's GDP per capita was a mere USD1000, and llama and alpaca breeders represented one of the lowest-paying sectors. The impoverished conditions of these llama and alpaca breeders was evident in unsustainable rural development, significant losses in herds, a lack of proper nutrition, and a lack of motivation toward their work. The consequence for COPROCA was an unsatisfactory supply of llama and alpaca wool in terms of both quality and quantity. COPROCA asked for FUNDES's help. Its solution was to provide COPROCA's suppliers with strategic development support using an associative, sectorial approach to strengthen the supply chain, decrease the cost of logistics and transportation, and work toward higher quality standards. COPROCA set standards for the production of both raw materials and final products. Because of the efforts to strengthen the suppliers in its value chain, these standards could be achieved. Additionally, COPROCA analyzed and improved its internal supply chain management processes. In the end, COPROCA was able to increase the quality and quantity of its raw material.

Project II: CSH

In 2009, the largest steel manufacturer in Chile, Corporación Siderúrgica de Huachipato (CSH), was serving 70% of the national market. CSH had reached an annual production rate of roughly 1.5 million barrels using natural primary materials such as iron, coal, and chalk. A total of 2400 people worked directly for the company, with another 3000 affiliated via sub-contracts, and over 500 small and medium enterprises provided various products and services. Starting in 2002, however, CSH was forced to become even more competitive. The company started developing better-quality products, acquired international certifications, expanded its operations, and began exporting. It had just one major obstacle to navigate: finding a solution to the high costs of importing spare parts caused by a lack of local suppliers and service providers for the mechanical and electrical maintenance of steelwork equipment. At that time, Chile had just decided to foster its development in specific sectors.

One rather large project developed by the Corporation for Strengthening Production (CORFO), the public institution in charge of promoting economic development, was specifically focused on the development of MSME suppliers. CORFO organized the program, together with a specialized operator and a consulting company. FUNDES was involved as a CSH consultant. The goal of the project was to build up a high-quality national provider network, which could replace a large portion of the imports that CSH currently relied on for its steelwork. This development program helped CSH save costs and be more competitive; the suppliers, in turn, were able to grow and improve their businesses.

These projects, Ulrich thought, could serve as examples for how FUNDES could develop a financial strategy based on selling consulting services to large firms. However, he also considered the internal challenges of changing FUNDES's strategy. "When I first started at FUNDES, I felt like I was entering a philanthropic organization," he said. "Six of the ten country managers wanted to continue with the old model of being largely funded by donations."

Ulrich knew that recent developments had created conditions in which deciding on a new financial strategy for FUNDES had become pressing. The economic crises that had begun in 2008 was still having resonating effects, which had resulted in reduced income from trainings because companies had begun to cut their employee training budgets. Consequently, in 2009 the revenue per country, which had been rising consistently each year, began to drop. In addition, many foundations and international organizations were struggling to stay afloat, and were reducing their donations and/or shifting their attention to regions other than Latin America. Likewise, in early 2009, Fundación Avina announced that it would reduce its funds to zero over the next three years (Fig. 5.2 and Table 5.7).

These external pressures, coupled with the fact that FUNDES had historically operated as a nonprofit—which implied significant resistance to transforming its business model into one that solely sells services to large firms—drove Ulrich to search for a donor that could replace Fundación Avina. After meeting with several different organizations, he piqued the attention of one potential large donor, the American Bold Foundation (pseudonym). A visit to New York strengthened the trust between Ulrich and the head of the foundation, and he was convinced that its strategy of funding 100% of FUNDES's budget would sufficiently support his organization's social mission. The Bold Foundation wanted to leverage its impact on MSMEs in Latin America; however, it didn't aim to accomplish this through its own projects, but by investing in a successful organization such as FUNDES.

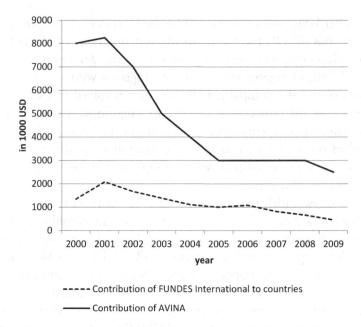

Fig. 5.2 Origin and allocation of funds in thousands of USDs (*Source* FUNDES International financial report)

Table 5.7 Sources of income

Income streams	USD (million)				
	2009	2010	2011	2012	2013 (budget)
Projects (with large firms or/and government)	2753	5096	7401	11,025	15,054
Consulting of SMEs	2630	483	269	123	86
Education of SMEs	1160	1820	879	779	–
Total income	**6543**	**7400**	**8548**	**11,927**	**15,140**
Income	*Large firms*	*Government*	*Donors*	*SMEs*	*2012*
Mexico	102	1841	1399		3342
Guatemala	533				533
El Salvador	200	779	1494	19	2492
Costa Rica	724				724
Panama	175	596			771
Colombia	1374				1374
Venezuela	149				149
Bolivia	22		437	89	548
Chile	626	602	48	97	1373
Argentina	600			21	621
Total	**4506**	**3818**	**3378**	**226**	**11927**

Source FUNDES International financial report

The foundation felt that FUNDES was a unique option for several reasons:

a. It had more than 25 years of experience in supporting MSMEs.
b. It was present in ten countries.
c. Its own research activities had not only allowed it to repeatedly adapt its services to the real and current needs of MSMEs, but had also proved extremely valuable to international organizations such as the World Bank.
d. FUNDES was well known for its implementation capacity, its measurable and verifiable results, its intellectual property, and the value of its brand.

The American Bold Foundation was interested in further strengthening the path that FUNDES was already on in supporting MSMEs. However, the majority of FUNDES's team was highly skeptical when it came to large enterprises, and believed in working directly with MSMEs.

In addition to replacing Fundación Avina with the American Bold Foundation, Ulrich saw a second option. He could strengthen FUNDES's market orientation by selling business development services to large firms—such as Nespresso—in turn linking MSMEs to their supply chains. When working with MSMEs, these large firms were already following strategies similar to FUNDES's, albeit with different goals.

"Large firms need help building effective local supply chains, and have the money to do so," thought Ulrich. "They're not necessarily interested in poverty alleviation, as such. But they know they must take social and environmental issues into account in order to guarantee their own long-term growth." Hence, gaining these companies as customers of FUNDES's business development services seemed an intriguing funding option.

The Decision

Ulrich sat in his office thinking of the changes ahead and the upcoming annual meeting. Working with FUNDES over the last few years had taught him a key lesson: "We are mission driven, but we need to become more and more profit oriented," he thought. "We strive for financial results, but also for a positive social and environmental impact. This isn't an easy thing to balance." For several years, FUNDES had begun to move between the worlds of profit-oriented firms and mission-oriented nonprofits. This had positioned it as a unique organization. "But this is no longer enough," thought Ulrich.

Ulrich was strongly drawn to the option of shifting FUNDES's business model toward a market-oriented strategy based on the sale of business development services to large firms. Thus, he was unsure if he should accept the American Bold Foundation's offer to finance 100% of FUNDES's activities. However, he also knew that many country managers were vehemently opposed to the idea of becoming more market oriented. He recalled one manager saying, "This sounds completely like a business—is FUNDES planning to focus only on customers who can pay? What about the many other MSMEs that need our help, but can't afford to pay for it?"

"Comments such as this one might mean that we need to accept the Bold Foundation's offer," Ulrich said to himself. Many of FUNDES's country managers and employees strongly identified with the nonprofit sector, so shifting to a market-oriented model would imply a major shift in leadership and communications. What should Ulrich do? Should he accept the Bold Foundation's offer to fund 100% of FUNDES's operations (Option 1)? Or should he shift to a market-oriented strategy, and sell FUNDES's services to large firms (Option 2)?

Teaching Note on the FUNDES Case

The FUNDES case can be taught as part of a course on a market approach to scaling, to illustrate Phase III of this approach: "Integrating financing and impact logics." It can also be used in a course on business strategy or organizational change to discuss how a nonprofit can implement a fully market-oriented business model without losing its social or environmental mission, or in a course on nonprofit management to discuss issues such as revenue diversification, mission drift (see Chapter 2), or change management with respect to strengthening market orientation without having to shift the core mission. The case is also suitable for a corporate social responsibility (CSR) course, with respect to integrating social and/or environmental bottom lines into the core business, or in a business ethics course to illustrate how business models can be used as a means to support social or environmental goals.

Learning Objectives

The FUNDES case illustrates the challenges of shifting from a nonprofit service model to a market approach. It allows students to discuss the challenges and tensions that arise when a nonprofit organization attempts to become more market driven.

After having analyzed and discussed the case, readers should be able to:

a. understand the actors with whom FUNDES can negotiate impact for resources;
b. be able to use the elements of Phase III of the market approach to scaling (*mission*, *leadership*, and *communication*) to reflect on FUNDES's challenges of transitioning from a nonprofit organization to a market-oriented social enterprise; and
c. systematically analyze various alternatives for managing change with respect to the three elements of Phase III.

Reflection on FUNDES's Market Approach to Scaling

Each of the two options described in the case implies a different conceptualization of the market. FUNDES had historically followed a very simple model, with Fundación Avina supplying nearly 100% of its budget and its consulting work entirely focused on helping MSMEs to grow. In other words, it worked almost entirely within impact logic.

Then, a fundamental shift occurred when Fundación Avina announced that it would be progressively withdrawing its funding. FUNDES's then CEO, Ulrich Frei, saw two options. Option 1 was to replace Fundación Avina with the American Bold Foundation, which required no change to FUNDES's existing model (Fig. 5.3).

Option 2 was to sell FUNDES's products and services to multinational companies (MNCs) and other large firms that wished to more effectively include MSMEs in their value chains (Fig. 5.4). With this option, the MNCs would pay FUNDES for business development services that would help them efficiently integrate MSMEs into their value chains. Theoretically, this option not only supports the multinational, but also the MSMEs by enabling them to access new markets.

Option 2 would allow FUNDES to transition into a social enterprise model, as it uses a market approach to achieve its social mission of supporting MSMEs throughout the Latin American region. FUNDES could then become attractive to potential impact investors with an interest in supporting MSMEs. The products and services that it provides are in the form of professional development service consultancies to MNCs that want to more efficiently include MSMEs in their value chains. By improving their access

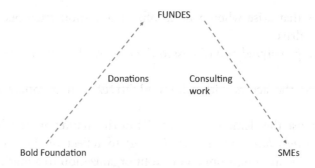

Fig. 5.3   Option 1: the American Bold Foundation

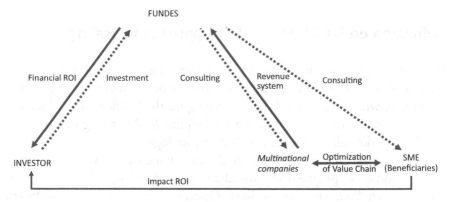

Fig. 5.4   Option 2: market approach through selling services to MNCs

to MNC markets, these products and services in turn generate a positive impact on the MSMEs.

Tying the FUNDES Case to Phase III of the Market Approach to Scaling

Option 2 challenges FUNDES's core values, as it requires the enterprise to incorporate a market approach into its business model. Phase III of the market approach to scaling provides students with a framework through which to reflect on Ulrich's options, highlighting the three essential elements of *mission*, *leadership*, and *communication*.

FUNDES is a nonprofit organization that changed its products and services strategies over time. The first changes—from providing MSMEs with access to microfinancing, to providing them with training and business development services, to providing them with consulting services—were mainly service-focused. During that time, FUNDES's mission remained stable. In the face of overarching developments, and based on what it was learning about its beneficiaries, FUNDES then adapted its portfolio so that it could continue to fulfill this mission under changing conditions. The new challenge was different from the previous ones, as the driver of change was abrupt resource scarcity; thus, the organization was confronted with the question of how to generate significant and sustainable income. At the same time, however, many of FUNDES's country managers had already demonstrated the perception that selling services to MNCs would threaten the organization's core mission. Sales to large enterprises had occurred in some fifty projects over the years, and the expansion of which now represented Option 2 for creating a sustainable financing strategy. The question is, would this option require Ulrich to change FUNDES's *mission*? After a significant reflection, he decided that it wouldn't. Selling FUNDES's business development services to MNCs was a different strategy of obtaining economic resources, but the organization's core mission of supporting MSMEs remained. The only difference was that shifting to a stronger market-orientation meant that MNCs and large enterprises would become increasingly important to this mission, as they would be the organization's main customer. This, in turn, might lead to situations in which the MNCs would want to dictate which MSMEs FUNDES could support. Thus, an additional question arises in the case: How can FUNDES prevent mission drift?

With respect to *leadership*, the market approach was not new to FUNDES. It had emerged over the years by necessity, and its staff had developed the skills to sell certain products and services to MSMEs. However, the announcement of a withdrawal of funding from Fundación Avina created an extreme and immediate situation, making a market approach more necessary than ever. Fundación Avina hired Ulrich to help FUNDES respond to this change. Over time, FUNDES had already adapted and expanded its products and services to effectively address the various needs of its key beneficiaries—Latin American MSMEs. It had also begun to draw from a wider array of funding sources over the years, including the generation of income through sales to large firms. For Ulrich, the only valid and long-term alternative was a systematic, market approach, which was already being expressed in some of FUNDES's projects. His idea was to convince the country managers, employees, and leadership that this was the best option. He would do this at the February 2011 annual meeting in El Salvador. FUNDES's future development could focus on creating a structure that balanced a clear market orientation with a core social mission in both the organization's processes and capabilities as well as in its relations with customers, partners, and competitors—in other words, it could become a social enterprise that successfully balanced financing and impact logics. Ulrich knew the importance of involving key stakeholders in this transition, as it would help him determine how a market approach might affect the organization's various internal and external stakeholders, particularly in terms of their relative importance and how the transition might in turn affect FUNDES's social mission.

Discussions of the FUNDES case could also explore the fact that the country managers, which are autonomous leaders of their country organizations, are key to transitioning to a market-based strategy. One possible way to gain their support is to highlight FUNDES's recent history. Ulrich could, for example, show that selling FUNDES's services was not a new idea; in fact, it was already common practice in some country offices. He could present the managers with specific cases as examples of best practices. Another possibility would be to train those FUNDES managers who were skeptical to the change, and in extreme cases to replace those that could not support the change with professionals who supported the market approach. At the time of this case, many country managers decided to leave in light of the possibility that FUNDES would implement a market approach, a strategy they neither understood nor supported. However, Ulrich realized that these leaders were strongly in line with FUNDES' social mission and loosing them could have a negative effect on the social enterprise's social orientation. He knew the need to reinforce FUNDES's mission with leaders who could potentially develop a market approach to creating impact—not just a traditional for-profit one.

In addition to country managers, FUNDES's staff was also key to leading this new strategy forward. Thus, FUNDES had to turn over a significant percentage of its staff, many of which steadfastly identified the organization as a nonprofit. Ulrich envisaged that many of them could develop the necessary skills to work within FUNDES market approach, but also knew that many would not be capable of navigating this transition due to their strong identification with the nonprofit sector and, thus, resistance to the change at hand. Additionally, Ulrich wanted to hire people that had experience working in MNC value chains. This could prove invaluable in navigating sales to MNCs and developing effective consultancy services for them. Thus, Ulrich would need to change the FUNDES's staff profile from a nonprofit to a much more market-oriented one. In other words, he needed staff that did not see a financing logic as a barrier to impact.

FUNDES also faced challenges in terms of both internal and external *communication*. With respect to internal communication, the key issue was related to organizational structure. Like many nonprofits (and in contrast to most for-profit organizations), FUNDES's country offices were not hierarchically subordinated to its central office. The country offices operated autonomously and viewed the central office as operating in service to them, not vice versa. In this model, the central office cannot implement its decisions by formal authority. The main issue then becomes how to lead change without having formal authority over all aspects of the organization. At FUNDES International, a few leaders who had worked with for-profit companies in the past proposed a market approach by launching communication forums, such as traditional strategy meetings, or by arguments that assumed a strong hierarchy. These ideas faced significant resistance. Most of the country managers who worked at FUNDES had joined the organization because they deeply supported its social mission. For most of these people, a market orientation was the opposite of fulfilling this mission, and thus provoked a significant amount of fear. In such cases, managing change requires clear communication that takes the employees' fear of mission drift into account and explains that a strategy change does not necessarily cause a mission drift.

With respect to external communication, it was important for FUNDES to develop a new concept that would allow it to sell its products and services to MNCs and other large firms. In the past, the projects that FUNDES sold to MNCs were typically assigned to the CSR department, as it was considered a philanthropic endeavor and therefore not part of the MNC's core interest. FUNDES, therefore, needed to develop a concept that would appeal to MNC's core business. They created an understanding of value chains as a social system where different supply chain actors relate to one another in circular and multidimensional ways. In this way, FUNDES tried to highlight the importance of MSMEs for the economic success of the MNCs' core business.

Discussion Questions

The following questions can help readers reflect on the case in preparation for group discussions, or can be used during the discussion sessions.

1. *Is FUNDES an example of an organization that tries to reach financial sustainability in order to execute its social mission, or one that risks mission drift?* This question allows participants to explore their basic values. As the case focuses on two options—preserving an impact logic through a nonprofit approach, or balancing an impact logic with a market

approach—participants might, for example, discuss their basic assumptions regarding the definition of a social enterprise. The objective of this discussion is to highlight that the market approach is a strategy for securing sustainable financing and scaling an enterprise, and is not meant to be a replacement of the social mission.

2. *To what degree is Ulrich the original driver of the new market orientation, and to what degree did the market orientation simply emerge over time?* This question allows participants to explore their basic assumptions regarding leadership. Some might highlight the leadership role that Ulrich played in the transition, while others might highlight the strategy's gradual and inevitable emergence. This discussion aims to explore the importance of leadership in such a complex situation as Ulrich's, and the fact that highlighting the emergence of change over time can both combat staff resistance and avoid the solution being presented as the idea of a single leader.

3. *What kind of resistance to change is Ulrich likely to face when implementing the new market strategy?* This question guides the discussion toward the transition process, and explores the challenges of implementing a market-based strategy in what has largely been a nonprofit context. Some participants might find Option 1 to be favorable, as it does not require any change.

4. *Which stakeholders should Ulrich involve and what kind of communication concept should he develop in the upcoming transition in order to successfully implement the market-based strategy?* This question leads participants to reflect on stakeholder expectations, such as those of FUNDES's country managers, its customers, and other nonprofits.

5. *What concepts and discourses can FUNDES develop to appeal to large firms?* This question reflects on the necessary shift in how FUNDES communicates with its customers. As explained above, FUNDES needs to emphasize a market approach to impact using concepts that MNCs and other large firms identify with, such as shared value and value chain systems.

References

1. Chia, R. (1996). *Organizational analysis as deconstructive practice.* Berlin and New York: Walter de Gruyter.
2. Friedman, A., & Phillips, M. (2004). Balancing strategy and accountability: A model for the governance of professional associations. *Nonprofit Management and Leadership, 15*(2), 187–204.

3. Kreutzer, K., & Jäger, U. (2010). Volunteering versus managerialism: Conflict over organizational identity in voluntary associations. *Nonprofit and Voluntary Sector Quarterly, 40,* 634–661.

4. Jäger, U. (2010). *Managing social businesses. Mission, governance, strategy and accountability.* Houndsmills and New York: Palgrave Macmillan.

5. Speckbacher, G. (2008). Nonprofit versus corporate governance: An economic approach. *Nonprofit Management and Leadership, 18*(3), 295–320.

6. Schröer, A., & Jäger, U. (2015). Beyond balancing? A research agenda on leadership in hybrid organizations. *International Studies of Management and Organization, 45*(3), 1–22.

7. Jäger, U., & Beyes, T. (2010). Strategizing in NPOs. A case study on the practice of organizational change between social mission and economic rationale. *Voluntas, 21*(1), 82–100.

8. FUNDES International. (2005). *20 years promoting SME development in Latin America.* San Antonio de Belén: Stocker Group SA. www.fundes.org. October 2011.

6

Examples of Scaling Strategies

After having analyzed each of the elements included in Phases I, II, and III, social entrepreneurs have gathered a significant amount of information about the business model they will use to design the scaling strategy. In this chapter we provide examples of established scaling strategies that social entrepreneurs might use when developing their strategy. This list is not exhaustive, but rather is useful to illustrate examples of market-based scaling strategies that can be constructed using our proposed three-phased approach. In this light, we will analyze three different scaling strategies: co-creation in low-income contexts, collective impact, and replicating business models.

Scaling Through Co-creation in Low-Income Contexts: The uSound Case

This strategy consists of identifying, selecting, and leveraging resources that social enterprises use to scale their impact in low-income contexts. Many enterprises—social or otherwise—claim they lack sufficient resources to create a viable business in low-income contexts, much less to be able to scale that business. The market-based view of scaling strategies, thus, is especially relevant for entrepreneurs working in such environments, in which resources are extremely scarce.

Some 4.5 billion people live in low-income contexts worldwide [1]. According to the World Bank, this group has a collective spending power of

© The Author(s) 2020
U. Jäger et al., *Scaling Strategies for Social Entrepreneurs*,
https://doi.org/10.1007/978-3-030-31160-5_6

more than USD5 trillion per year.[i] This is an immense market, and one that is attracting an increasing number of companies that recognize the inherent opportunities and challenges of building a business. While the market opportunities seem immense, however, they come with equally immense challenges. Stakeholders in these contexts live in situations of economic poverty, with an annual income of less than USD3000 per capita [2]. Basic needs are often unmet, and potential customers and other stakeholders lack the resources to maintain a decent quality of life. Formal institutions and physical infrastructure are typically underdeveloped in terms of quality and effectiveness [3]. This means that assets such as land, livestock, businesses, and homes lack legalized documentation [4], and transactions often follow local norms, values, and beliefs rather than formalized laws or rules [5].

Exploring market opportunities in these contexts requires a cognitive leap; business owners must know what resources are available to be able to construct robust, context-appropriate business strategies [6]. In these low-income contexts, resources are subjective, and depend on how actors assign value to them based on their use [7]. For example, impoverished grassroot recyclers view waste as an economic resource, which differs from how stakeholders in other environments might view it. Seen in this light, low-income contexts are filled with untapped opportunities. Social enterprises wanting to scale in low-income contexts need to adjust their lens to see resources where others simply see poverty and informality. This task of identifying, selecting, and exploiting the resources needed to create a viable scaling strategy in low-income contexts requires a strong connection—or embeddedness—in these communities.

Co-creation in low-income markets, a strategy introduced by Ted London and Urs Jäger, provides a useful instrument to explore resources that can be used to scale impact in low-income contexts [8]. In this strategy, social enterprises intending to scale identify and utilize resources that already exist in low-income contexts. These include economic, knowledge, leadership, network, and innovation resources. Thus, this strategy of co-creating in low-income markets consists of identifying, choosing, and exploiting scaling opportunities based on specific needs and/or social problems, which the social enterprise transforms into business opportunities. This could mean, for example, transforming beneficiaries—such as the poor—into paying customers, or into employees, such as social enterprises that hire people with disabilities (e.g., Dinner in the Dark hires visually impaired staff to serve clients in unlit restaurants).

London and Jäger's concept of co-creation argues that social enterprises intending to scale should: (1) recognize and respect members of low-income markets as a valuable source of knowledge and skills, (2) perceive low-income markets not as a context full of problems that need fixing, but as an environment that is rich in resources and potential markets; and (3) seek to identify and utilize resources that already exist in these markets and can facilitate the development of a robust, scalable business model.

These resources include:

1. *Economic resources.* What resources do consumers and producers have that can increase their purchasing power or provide them with greater access to alternative financial resources?
2. *Knowledge resources.* What resources do local experts have that can advise or inform decision-making in the social enterprise?
3. *Leadership resources.* What resources do local leaders have that can influence the decisions of other members from low-income markets?
4. *Network resources.* What resources do low-income markets have that can create platforms to connect individuals and communities?
5. *Innovation resources.* What resources do low-income markets have that can catalyze innovation and change?

The three phases of the market approach to scaling allow social enterprises to integrate the resources found in low-income contexts into their overall scaling strategy. This is highlighted in the **resources** element of Phase I: *Negotiating impact for resources.* In this phase, social entrepreneurs analyze how they can gain access to resources by identifying what low-income markets provide. This means that they do not focus on resources that exist outside of the low-income contexts in which they work, nor do they aim to rely on impact investors alone.

The uSound Case

The uSound case shows how a social enterprise can explore and exploit resources from low-income contexts. uSound is an Argentine company that was founded in 2015 by Ezequiel Escobar and three of his colleagues, all MBA students from the province of Jujuy. Together, they developed an innovative, low-cost hearing aid. In the case, Ezequiel has to decide whether uSound should remain in Jujuy or move to the capital city of Buenos Aires to scale its impact. To make this decision, he must view Jujuy's low-income context through a lens that allows him to understand the advantages of being located in the poorest region of the country.

The Case: Using Co-creation to Bring Technology from Northern Argentina to the World[1]

In November of 2015, Ezequiel Escobar, CEO of the Argentine technology startup, uSound, was returning to Jujuy, Argentina from an entrepreneurship acceleration training in Boston, Massachusetts. In addition to the support that the event had afforded his enterprise, he had also had the opportunity to compare the vast differences between the two cities. In Boston, the internet speed, affordable hardware, access to investors, and political context that supported new ventures differed greatly from what he had experienced at home.

Ezequiel was a young *Qulla*—a member of the indigenous Coya community that resided in Jujuy—with zero computer knowledge, who rose to become an icon of technology in Argentina. His enterprise, uSound, successfully developed an application through which the user could use the headphones of his or her smartphone as a hearing aid. Having developed a technological enterprise that had a strong social mission, significant potential for scalability, and eventually gained a global audience—all of this from a region with scarce resources—Ezequiel was something of a hero to those who understood the difficulties of working in low-income contexts.

uSound had won several competitions and received support from accelerators and other organizations in Buenos Aires, as well as the United States and Europe. These experiences had exposed Ezequiel and his founding partners to the differences between the market in Jujuy versus more developed contexts.

uSound was already a successful startup that employed 14 people and had a headquarter office in Jujuy, and the leadership team wanted to continue to grow the business. The colleagues who co-founded uSound along with Ezequiel were all university classmates from Jujuy. All wanted the enterprise's growth plan to preserve its local "Jujuyan" spirit, characterized by a strong connection to nature, artistic creativity, and indigenous culture. However, to achieve success in the increasingly competitive and globalized world of technology, Ezequiel and his founding partners would need employees that had the technological knowledge needed to develop and improve their product, and they would need financial resources. The need for resources posed a problem: Should uSound remain headquartered in Jujuy (Option 1), or

---

[1]Author: Urs Jäger, Associate Professor INCAE Business School and Academic Director VIVA Idea.

should it reallocate to Buenos Aires, where access to investment and other resources would be available (Option 2)?

The Context of Jujuy

Jujuy is one of the Argentina's northernmost provinces, with a territory of 53,219 km² (roughly 20,548 square miles) and 673,000 inhabitants. It borders Bolivia to the north, Chile to the west, and the province of Salta, Argentina, to the east and south.

Northern Argentina is historically the poorest region in the country, and Jujuy is no exception. With small, aging buildings, a large indigenous population, and a perpetual cycle of migrants and tourists, Jujuy demonstrates the stereotypical features of a developing Latin American town. Slow, unreliable internet service is a testament to its underdevelopment; however, many Jujuyans are able to connect with the rest of the world through basic smartphones and affordable service plans.

When Ezequiel and his partners first launched uSound, the region posed a significant challenge for entrepreneurs. They were socially demonized, as the public held deeply rooted beliefs toward them, such as, "only criminals make money" and "the good people work for the government." Particularly in informal markets, which were estimated to represent roughly 50% of the market, had a strong negative influence on the image of entrepreneurs.[ii] Terms such as "startup," "accelerator," "incubator," and "financing" were not well known. Low incomes (meaning low wages compared to the average Argentine), cultural tensions between indigenous and "white" people— as local media outlets described the situation—presented challenges for any enterprise. Given this complex situation, many companies avoided the region entirely.

uSounds' CEO

Ezequiel was a young Argentine *Qulla* with big dreams. He had a pleasant childhood, surrounded by vegetation, livestock, and wildlife. He was born in Tilcara, a small, rural town North of San Salvador, the capital city of Jujuy.

Ezequiel's mother, a housewife, sold empanadas and lamb with his grandmother, both *Qulla* people. His father was raised in El Chaco by a Canadian missionary, who adopted and educated him after he had lost both parents.

As a missionary, his grandfather traveled extensively to provide support to low-income people in Honduras, Costa Rica, and Argentina. These stories, along with the projects his grandfather had developed in Tilcara, fed Ezequiel's awareness of entrepreneurship and social impact endeavors.

His grandfather also introduced Ezequiel to a computer expert who happened to be traveling in Northern Argentina. The stranger took the time to show the young Ezequiel the infinite possibilities that such a tiny device as a laptop could offer. His face brightened with wonder.

Tilcara had plenty of animals, plants, and mountains, but not a single computer. Nor did it have internet service. Lacking even the most basic computer skills, but motivated by a short presentation, Ezequiel went on to earn a degree in Computer Science, challenging himself to learn how to create programs like the ones the computer expert had showed him.

In 2011, Ezequiel visited his grandfather in Canada. There, he realized that people in Jujuy were not so different from those abroad, and that resolving many of the obstacles faced by Jujuyans was simply a matter of determination.

The Birth of uSound: A Problem Identified, an Opportunity Discovered

In mid-2012, Ezequiel and his classmates received the following assignment in one of their classes: "Identify a market problem, and propose a solution." Identifying the problem was easy. Ariel, one of their Computer Science classmates, suffered from hearing loss. He would arrive to all his classes well before his peers to ensure that he had a front row seat, so as to better hear his teachers.

Ezequiel and his classmates were inspired by Ariel's problem. After discussing several ideas, they decided to propose a smartphone application. The smartphone would serve as a microphone, and their software would improve the audio quality, transforming its headphones into conventional hearing aids. Given the widespread use of smartphones in the region, anyone with a hearing disadvantage—however low their income—would be able to access their product.

After completing the project, Ezequiel and his classmates passed the class and earned their degree. Also Ariel, who lacked the money to purchase a conventional hearing aid (which cost roughly USD2000), was able to finish his studies. Although he didn't always have enough time to arrive to his lessons before his classmates, and few classmates and teachers understood his situation well enough to reserve him a seat in the front row, his new hearing aid from his classmates helped him hear and understand his teachers as well as his fellow students. Ezequiel and his classmates recognized that Ariel was not alone. About 5.3% of the world's population suffers from hearing loss, whereas most of those were not able to buy conventional hearing aids. They realized that their idea had to be put into action, and they decided to launch their enterprise.[iii]

uSound: From Smartphone Application to Social Enterprise

uSound created an innovative system that turned smartphones into hearing aids. By means of a downloadable application, users could perform a basic diagnosis of their hearing level, and the app's logarithm would adjust the sound accordingly. In other words, uSound's customers could use their own smartphone headphones in place of a conventional hearing aid.

The interactive application also integrated clinical and medical knowledge, allowing its developers to learn and improve the product according to the users' needs. The uSound system improved people's quality of life in essential aspects such as communication and education. It also helped prevent future auditory loss by dynamically adjusting the intensity of sound to an optimal level for each user.

By mid-2016, the app had been downloaded more than 250,000 times in 150 countries. Of these, 52,000 users had minor to moderate hearing loss, and 13,000 were using the "Hearing Assistant" mode. uSound had implemented three strategies to deliver the app to its users:

1) *Business-to-consumer* (B2C): Users download uSound from an e-store (Google Play or App Store) and, after a 30-day trial period, can pay a fee to continue use (for USD4.99/month, USD19.00/6 months, or USD29.99/year).[iv]
2) *Business-to-business* (B2B): Partnerships with foundations and institutions that identify people with hearing loss, as well as governments, phone companies, and smartphone manufacturers that sell uSound licenses wholesale.
3) *Consumer-to-consumer* (C2C): Any individual can access the uSound website and donate licenses to other people around the world.

The uSound team was composed of capable professionals, and had the necessary knowledge to develop all of its projects. Ezequiel and some of his classmates had sufficient computer science skills to be part of the uSound team and, when it was necessary to integrate other skills (i.e., graphic design), the enterprise received more than 35 qualified applications within hours after having published the position on Facebook.

uSound became known as a group of innovative local youth who had broken paradigms and understood the context of an emerging market. They had turned a university assignment into an internationally awarded social enterprise, and their business vision had allowed them to build partnerships with public and private institutions both within and outside of Argentina.

New Challenges and Opportunities

The development of a smartphone application provided the uSound team with the opportunity to record user information. Firsthand, real-time data helped them develop a tailor-made hearing aid that worked in conjunction with the smartphone application. This technology became known as "Smart Earphones"—the new generation of uSound headphones. At an estimated price of USD200, these headphones cost one-tenth of a conventional hearing aid.

In 2016, uSound focused its innovations on creating and improving a headset prototype, which it hoped to use in a pilot program called "Jujuy Escucha" (Jujuy Hears), supported by the national government, the Ministry of Health, and other local public institutions. The pilot intended to provide Smart Earphones to 1000 users. Funded by the national government, uSound would provide the headphones free of charge to participants in the pilot program. In return, it would be able to collect useful information from all institutions involved. This coincided with the national government's launch of "Plan Belgrano," the objective of which was to improve living conditions in Northern Argentina.[v] Impact investors had also approached Ezequiel in various public events, expressing interest in investing in the company. Impact investors were particularly attracted by the easily measurable social impact and the enterprise's potential to scale globally.

Despite these innovations, uSound was experiencing problems with respect to the political, social and economic context in which it operated. Duty taxes hindered the import of materials for the hearing aid prototypes, and unreliable internet service limited communication with distributors. The enterprise was also isolated from the tech world, which was quickly and constantly changing, and was key to the company's development and entry into international markets.

Ezequiel, however, was willing to continue to innovate and overcome these difficulties. He and his team wanted to show Argentina that it was possible to undertake an entrepreneurial endeavor despite multiple setbacks.

However, Ezequiel had to make a decision regarding the growth of his enterprise. With the challenges presented by the region and new opportunities arising for uSound, should he remain in Jujuy (Option 1), or should he move to an area that offered better conditions for emerging businesses, such as Buenos Aires (Option 2)?

Additional Information of the Case: *uSound Case Photographs*

See Photos 6.1, 6.2, and 6.3.

Photo 6.1 Ezequiel Escobar (first row, third from the left), founder of uSound, with his co-founders

Photo 6.2 Beneficiaries testing uSound product

Photo 6.3 Headphones and uSound app

Teaching Note on the uSound Case

This case can be taught in a course on scaling social enterprises as a means of introducing the strategy of co-creation in low-income markets, and examining this option through the three phases of the market approach to scaling. It is also suitable for corporate social responsibility courses, particularly with respect to navigating the complexities of low-income markets (broadly known as the "base of the pyramid") as it illustrates an enterprise that developed successful strategies within these markets.

Learning Objectives

The uSound case can be used to problematize the exploration and exploitation of resources in low-income contexts.

After having analyzed and discussed the case, readers should be able to:

a. understand the element of *Resources* (Phase I of the market approach to scaling) when working in low-income contexts;
b. use the co-creation strategy to reflect on uSound's challenges with respect to scaling its impact; and
c. systematically analyze business opportunities based on the resources identified.

Reflection on uSound's Market Approach to Scaling

Although uSound provided its devices online as an app and earphone package at less than 20% of the cost of other hearing aids, its approach was mainly through third-party actors who were interested in beneficiaries gaining access to the technology. The government, for example, expressed interest in subsidizing the app to help citizens access a social service as the product was relatively cheap and easy to access for low-income population that had widespread access to smartphones. As uSound focuses on selling a product in low-income contexts in which consumers have limited economic resources, understanding governments as potential customers that donate the hearing aids to the end customer has been an important part of its revenue processes. Although Ezequiel and his team aim to reduce the costs of their product as far as to make it achievable for low-income customers they are still struggling to sell their products to end customers who live in extreme poverty contexts. However, they were able to quickly distribute their app to thousands of beneficiaries with third-party actors such as governments, NGOs, and private donors subsidizing or covering the cost (Fig. 6.1).

Profit-oriented investors who are interested in financial return on investment (ROI) were attracted to uSound because they perceived its strong competitive advantage associated with selling a product at just 20% of the price of competing hearing aids. The investors perceived a high potential for future financial returns, but also uSound's potential to significantly increase its social impact. They calculated the potential impact ROI based

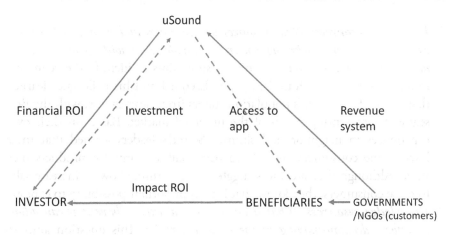

Fig. 6.1 Market approach for scaling of uSound

on uSound's capacity to increase sales within low-income markets. Their doubt was whether or not uSound would be able to reduce its price enough not to have to rely on third parties such as governments to donate the product to their target group. Despite this doubt, the impact ROI was particularly attractive to impact investors, as uSound was able to clearly measure its impact by tracking the number of downloads and, in turn, estimating the number of users. By mid-2016, the app had been downloaded more than 250,000 times in 150 countries.

Reflection on Using the Co-creation Strategy

uSound needs to decide if it should continue to work in Jujuy (Option 1) or relocate its headquarter office to Buenos Aires (Option 2). Based on Jujuy's social and economic data as described in the case, for the sake discussion we can assume that Buenos Aires would provide uSound with a more favorable context in which to scale its impact, including access to capital, knowledge, and human resources. Thus, based on the work of London and Jäger, we propose that the analysis focuses on the five types of available resources in Jujuy (economic, knowledge, leadership, network, and innovation resources). An overarching question for the discussion could be, "What resources can Jujuy provide that can enable uSound to scale its impact globally?"

To answer this overarching question, participants can analyze the uSound case according to the five potential resources and their associated questions (Table 6.1). This allows participants to identify which economic, knowledge, leadership, network, and innovation resources the region has to offer.

1. *Economic resources: What resources do consumers and producers have that can increase their purchasing power or provide them with greater access to alternative financial resources?* This question aims to identify the economic resources that can be found in Jujuy. Ezequiel and his colleagues learned that 5.3% of the world's population suffers from hearing loss, with the BoP segment representing much of the unserved market. Based on their own experiences in neighborhood slums, uSound's leaders learned that these low-income consumers are able to pay small amounts for products they value. Although they are still struggling to determine how to increase sales to these consumers, they know that it is an important possibility to explore.

2. *Knowledge resources: What resources do local experts have that can advise or inform decision-making in the social enterprise?* This question aims to identify the knowledge resource that can be found in Jujuy. While it did face challenges such as unreliable electricity and internet access, uSound

Table 6.1 Five resources identified and utilized in Jujuy by uSound

Economic resources	Knowledge resources	Leadership resources	Network resources	Innovation resources
• 5.3% of the world's population suffers from hearing loss • The BoP segment represents much of the unserved market • Low-income consumers are able to pay small amounts for products they value • Salaries for employees in Jujuy are relatively low	• People from Jujuy are able to strive in difficult situations what resulted in elevated creativity and problem-solving skills • Closeness to end users in BoP segment supports understanding uSound's end users • Accessing online courses to increase programming knowledge is possible	• uSound showcased the fact that it was possible to generate significant, global impact from the poorest region of the country • With their continuing success, Ezequiel and his growing team had become national role models • They were able to influence government institutions (regional and national level) for the benefit of uSound	• uSound had the potential to connect groups that would otherwise have remained separate • They united various Jujuyan organizations and individuals to create an entrepreneurship hub in Jujuy, which attracts talented young professionals and fosters innovations for uSound and other local businesses	• San Salvador de Jujuy has a university that offers programming courses • Graduates from Jujuy live with low-income and need to innovate to survive in their everyday life. That way they have an innovative attitude • Internet access is available

also trusted the knowledge of local people, especially those that live in poverty and isolated indigenous communities. For Ezequiel, it was important to gather human talent from Jujuy, as he considered this staff members' ability to strive in difficult situations resulted in elevated creativity and problem-solving skills. Therefore, these staff members best understood uSound's end users living in poverty.

3. *Leadership resources: What resources do local leaders have that can influence the decisions of other members from low-income markets?* This question aims to identify the leadership resources that can be found in Jujuy. With their continuing success, Ezequiel and his growing team had become local role models, and were able to influence government institutions for the benefit of uSound and the broader business community. Staying in Jujuy was an advantage, as it showcased the fact that it was possible to generate significant, global impact from the poorest region of the country.

4. *Network resources: What resources do low-income markets have that can create platforms to connect individuals and communities?* This question aims to identify the network resources that can be found in Jujuy. Ezequiel understood that uSound had the potential to connect groups that would otherwise have remained separate. Through workshops that united various Jujuyan organizations and individuals, he explored new business ideas, leading to the creation of an entrepreneurship hub in Jujuy, which attracts talented young professionals and fosters innovations for uSound and other local businesses.

5. *Innovation resources: What resources do low-income markets have that can catalyze innovation and change?* This question aims to identify the innovation resources that can be found in Jujuy. San Salvador de Jujuy, the provincial capital where uSound is located, has a university that offers programming courses. Ezequiel felt that professionals from this university easily rival those that graduate from schools in Buenos Aires. Furthermore, their embeddedness in low-income contexts is precisely what makes them valuable to an organization like uSound. According to Ezequiel, staying in Jujuy is important, as the human resources available there are more capable of understanding the contextual complexity and produce an app that can adapt to the needs of the beneficiaries.

Discussion Questions

The following questions can help readers reflect on the case in preparation for group discussions, or can be used during the discussion sessions.

1. *Would you want to build a social enterprise in Jujuy?* This question helps participants to consider the core decision. They must make a decision that both considers their own position and assumes the position of Ezequiel.

2. *What economic, knowledge, leadership, network, and innovation resources have you identified?* This question guides participants to systematically analyze the case according to the five resources of the co-creation strategy presented above.

3. *How would you describe the low-income context in Jujuy?* This question aims to structure the resource analysis into a conceptualization of the market in which uSound operates. The uSound case allows participants to think in terms of what resources exist in a given low-income context. Furthermore, it can drive a discussion on how being embedded in a low-income context better facilitates the participation of impact investors. As these actors are interested in impact, being headquartered in an impoverished region, and showing that using local resources to achieve global impact is possible, can be an advantage for negotiating impact for resources.

4. *What are some important cornerstones of uSound's operations to allow it to scale its business globally?* This question focuses on the element of **distribution and revenue** in Phase III of the market approach to scaling, and aims to highlight the advantages of business such as uSound, which offers a virtual product and operates via an online distribution channel. Although the uSound case is mainly focused on the **resources** element of Phase I of the strategy guide, it also provides an interesting exploration of how technology facilitates scalable distribution and revenue processes for social enterprises located in low-income contexts.

Scaling Through Collective Impact: The Warmi Case

The collective impact strategy, as introduced by Kania and Kramer [9], assumes that impact can only be scaled if the organization collaborates with other actors such as nonprofits and government entities. Coordination between organizations is a complex endeavor, however, as it requires alignment between multiple agendas, interests, capabilities, and worldviews toward a common goal. The three phases of the market approach to scaling helps social entrepreneurs determine whether or not their enterprise is prepared to use a collective impact strategy. In each phase, they examine their business model, then analyze the resulting data with respect to two questions: (a) *How does our current business model support collective impact?* and (b) *What is missing that would help facilitate a collective impact strategy, and how can we fill these gaps?*

To apply Kania and Kramer's collective impact strategy to developing strategies of social enterprises intending to scale through a market approach we focus on four elements: The first, is a common agenda. All participants must have a shared vision for change, a common understanding of the problem, and a joint approach to solving it. A guiding question to analyze the data gathered by the three phases to scale is: *Are there any other actors that share the social enterprise's impact goals?*

The second essential element to a successful collective impact strategy is a shared measurement system. Thus, the social enterprise should have an impact measurement system that is easy to understand for all actors involved, including third parties and the general public. An information management system that provides an immense amount of complex and data is not necessarily sufficient, as the information may not be easily digested by all audiences. The guiding question is, therefore: *Does the social enterprise have an impact measurement system that generates simple and inspiring results?*

Third, collective impact initiatives need mutually reinforcing activities. Success depends on a diverse group of people working together by undertaking the specific activities they excel in a way that is well-coordinated with and supports the actions of others. Each actor must fit into the bigger picture. The social entrepreneur needs to analyze the data gathered in the *Resources* element of Phase I with respect to the question: *Are any of the actors that share our impact goals willing and capable of investing their time in collaborating with the enterprise—and others—in a way that mutually-reinforces our common agenda?*

Fourth, it is essential to develop trust between the actors involved in a collective impact initiative. Regular meetings, familiarity with one another's contexts, and common experiences are key to creating space for constant discussion and integration. To gauge whether their enterprise is prepared to enter into trustful relations with others, social entrepreneurs first need to analyze if the leadership and communication practices they have in place support the continuous communication that is necessary for collective action. The guiding question here is: *What collective leadership and communication practices do we have in place, or need to implement, in order to support trustful relations with our partners?*

The Warmi Case

The Warmi case introduces a social enterprise that began by using the collective impact strategy of coordinating extremely diverse actors such as five for-profit investors, indigenous political leaders, indigenous llama wool producers, and experts from luxury markets. From its beginning, Warmi's common agenda was to produce llama wool and sell it to luxury markets for the benefit of poor indigenous producers (beneficiaries). The challenges of this strategy were (a) creating a shared measurement system, (b) mutually reinforcing activities and (c) developing and maintaining trust relations between the actors involved. To strengthen the collective impact strategy, the actors founded Hilandería Warmi, or the Warmi Spinning Mill. This mill is an Argentine company founded in 2014 by Juan Collado, an influential Argentine businessperson, and Rosario Quispe, an influential indigenous Coya leader. Both were interested in fueling more inclusive development (development that included indigenous Coya communities) in one of Argentina's poorest regions—La Puna, in the province of Jujuy. The Warmi mill had a social business model aimed at transforming communities in a sustainable way by designing, producing, and selling (mainly exporting) excellent-quality products made from llama fibers. In the case, Rosario is pushing to relocate the mill's operations to Puna highlands (where the majority of the indigenous Coya live) in order to increase its impact on the region. Gastón Aróstegui, the mill's general manager, agreed with Rosario's request, but also understood the difficulties of moving out of San Salvador de Jujuy, a larger city that enabled efficient operations and export processes.

The Case: Hilandería Warmi (the Warmi Spinning Mill): Collective Impact Produced by Business Collaborators and Indigenous Communities[2]

It was a cold October morning in 2018 in Jujuy, Argentina. Gastón Aróstegui, general manager of Hilandería Warmi, or the Warmi Spinning Mill, was at his office in San Salvador de Jujuy, taking his last sip of mate before heading to Abra Pampa in the Puna highlands. He was to meet with Helvio Quispe, an entrepreneur from the indigenous Coya community

[2]Authors: José Pablo Valverde Coto, Researcher VIVA Idea and PhD student University of St. Gallen; Felipe Symmes, Senior Researcher Viva Idea Researcher and PhD Candidate University of St. Gallen; and Urs Jäger, Associate Professor INCAE Business School and Academic Director VIVA Idea.

(a millenary culture of the South American Andes), and a representative from the Warmi Sayajsunjo[vi] Women's Association (Warmi), which had been founded by his mother, Rosario Quispe. The reason for the meeting was for Gastón to share his final decision regarding whether or not to move the mill's operations to the Puna in order to increase its impact on the Coya's quality of life (Option 1) or maintain operations in San Salvador de Jujuy (Option 2). This was an important decision, as it would determine the organization's scaling strategy for the coming years.

The Warmi Spinning Mill was founded to complement the work that the Warmi Sayajsunjo Women's Association had been doing for more than twenty years under the leadership of Rosario. The association's trainings helped generate and strengthen productive chains to provide residents of the Puna with decent livelihoods while respecting their culture and lifestyle. The Warmi Spinning Mill, founded in 2014 in a partnership with nine other influential Argentine businesspeople, aimed to complement the association's work by creating llama and alpaca wool clothing and selling it in luxury markets, using an innovative model that integrated fiber producers from indigenous Coya communities with the mill's manufacturing and marketing operations to produce a positive and sustainable impact on socioeconomic development in the Puna region.

Gastón was nervous, as the last meetings he had had with Warmi representatives had revealed that the impact created by the Warmi Spinning Mill was not enough to meet expectations, especially due to the fact that the mill was located in San Salvador de Jujuy, and not in the Puna, a five-hour drive from the location of the Spinning Mill, where the indigenous Coya resided. The Coya leaders claimed that the mill historically belonged in the Puna; thus, would better meet its impact goals if it was located there. Gastón had managed the Warmi Spinning Mill since its foundation four years prior, and he understood these claims. However, he also understood that transferring the mill's operations from San Salvador de Jujuy to the Puna implied significant logistical and financial challenges. He was receiving a lot of pressure from investors—particularly Collado, who was both the mill's founder and the investor closest to its operations processes—to ensure the mill's financial sustainability in the short run.

Gastón and Helvio discussed the option of transferring the mill's operations from San Salvador de Jujuy to the Puna. It would mean moving the spinning process 223 km—a drastic transition with serious logistical implications. Gastón was unsure what to do. Should he transfer the mill's operations to the Puna (Option 1) or maintain operations in San Salvador de Jujuy until the mill's financial situation became more stable (Option 2)?

The Textile Industry in the Jujuy Region

Contextual Reality

Jujuy is a province in northern Argentina with a territorial extension of 53,219 km^2 and 673,000 inhabitants.[vii] It is bordered to the north by Bolivia, to the west by Chile, and to the east and south by the Argentine province of Salta. Jujuy's terrain results in vast biological diversity. Its territory is divided into four agroecological zones: Puna, Quebrada, Valles, and Ramal.

The Puna is home to a particularly hostile natural environment. Sitting 3500–4500 meters above sea level (m.a.s.l.), with summits reaching 6000 m.a.s.l., the region experiences extreme temperature swings, with an average annual temperature of 10 °C and temperatures varying from 25 °C during the day to −15 °C at night. The region has very low precipitation levels (maximum 350 mm annually) during the summer (December to March) and features nearly cloudless skies throughout the year, resulting in dry, desert-like soils that are sensitive to erosion due to winds in the winter and heavy rains in the summer.

The region's unique geography, coupled with its scarcity of resources, which is limited to minerals, llamas, sheep, and goats, has marginalized its population from the economic development enjoyed by the rest of Argentina. More than 70% of the rural population is unable to meet its basic needs, a significant percentage is illiterate, and the region has the highest infant mortality rate in the country. This situation drives inhabitants to migrate to Quebrada and Valles, or to larger population centers such as Abra Pampa, Quiaca, San Salvador de Jujuy, or San Antonio de los Cobres, attracted by the possibility of better jobs (such as harvesting, construction, mill work, or mining), education, and services.

According to the National Agricultural Census [10], two-thirds of the llamas in Argentina are in Jujuy. Of these, 95% are in the Puna. Most farmers who remained in the Puna work in a subsistence economy scheme based on family owned livestock farms.[viii] Due to the region's extreme environment, agriculture is limited to species that have adapted to these conditions over thousands of years and produce limited harvests, such as beans, potatoes, corn, and alfalfa and barley (for animal feed).

Families in the Puna have an average of five to nine children, but nearly half of these commonly migrate to urban centers in search of better opportunities. Thus, widows, single women, older married couples (those whose children have all migrated, often leaving their own children behind), and young married couples with small children are responsible for livestock production. Thus, the average number of active family members is two. However, due to the scarcity of job opportunities, it is also common for men to work at the mines or mills, leaving women in charge of both the children and the livestock. With these men away for up to eight months at a time, 46% of livestock production in the Puna is done by women.[ix]

The Textile Industry

At the time of writing this case, the Puna region's textile industry presented many poor practices, mainly in terms of market and price transparency. Producers received a very low price from the *barracas* or collection centers, for the llama fibers they sheared. The centers collected and sorted fibers, then sold it to spinning mills or artisans to make clothing. Finally, various distributors and retailers sold the products.

The collection centers, in addition to acting as intermediaries between producers and spinning mills, represented a destruction of value in the distribution chain, as they sought to purchase raw materials from producers at the lowest possible price and then increase the sale price to spinning mills to increase their profit margin.

The pressure to lower their prices reinforced the fiber producers' distrust of the collection centers, so they would resort to tricks such as adding stones or lamb leg bones or moistening the fibers to increase the weight of the bags at the time of sale. Because of the turbulent market dynamics in certain locations, it was often impossible for buyers to thoroughly check the bags.

This phenomenon was nothing new, but rather followed a historical process that structurally resembles a Moebius strip, in which community producers have no incentive to improve the quality of their product or to develop products with greater added value.

A Vision for Developing the Puna

Stage 1: The Warmi Suyajsunqo Association

The Warmi Suyajsunqo Association was born under the guidance of Rosario in 1995. Its purpose was to represent a group of Coya women and organize them to overcome poverty and isolation while at the same time safeguarding their culture, which was the foundation of their beliefs (Figs. 6.6 and 6.7). Rosario describes the association's mission as follows: "We are weaving a dream to live with dignity from our work, respecting our culture and lifestyle. According to the Warmi philosophy, living together and in harmony implies knowing and respecting others, participating and cooperating in joint projects that highlight people's interdependence and respect for the values of pluralism, mutual understanding and peace."

The Warmi Suyajsunqo Association established the following values:

- *Solidarity*: Continuous and permanent cooperation in the development of new processes, jobs, and interpersonal relationships.
- *Respect*: Understanding and valuing people's rights, customs, cultural diversity, and freedom of thought.
- *Honesty*: Acting with honesty and integrity in all daily activities. We consider honesty to be a fundamental step to achieving harmonious human relationships.
- *Love to the Earth*: Preserving and caring for Mother Earth, as this is the essence of our culture, livelihoods, and growth.
- *Social Spirit*: Manifesting our principle of solidarity through honesty and trust in people, and in our own efforts to improve the Coya society's situation through labor market integration.
- *Commitment to People*: Valuing and understanding the most determinant factors of social reality and participating in each factor, facing its challenges for the purpose of continuous advancement.

In addition, the Association decided on the following institutional priorities:

1. To have a decent livelihood in the land where we were born and where our ancestors have lived.
2. To be able to make a living with our work and make decisions based on local traditions.
3. To be part of the whole—having equal rights but also accepted as different.
4. To achieve gender equity—to be in harmony with others and nature.

Two years after its creation, the association's hard work earned international recognition and access to financing. Moreover, since 1999, the women in the Association have worked with Fundación Avina to further strengthen their organization through financing.[x] Today, after more than 20 years of hard work, the Warmi Suyajsunqo Association comprises more than 3000 Inter-Andean Puna and Valles families, reaching 84 indigenous communities.

The Warmi Suyajsunqo Association's mission of improving the quality of life of indigenous populations was based on the provision of various training programs, services, and microcredits, available to all community members. Its vision was to become a key driver of growth and development in the Puna. By 2012, the association's programs had benefited 20,000 Coya—a result that reflects several years of ongoing work and struggle.

The following are some of the association's achievements over the last 20 years:

1. **Organization**: It organized a government system that included 70 male and 70 female community leaders and 84 organized member communities. This system reestablished the traditional governance of the Coya that was destroyed by the colonial power.
2. **Microcredits**: It established a communal fund for organized communities. To date, more than 750 loans have been provided, with a low delinquency rate. According to Rosario, "The communities took ownership of the process, which made it easier to collect the repayments." However, the accounting process is carried out with hard copy folders containing the communities' accounts in handwriting, and the fund has not been recapitalized for more than ten years, which has proved problematic.
3. **Health**: It promoted campaigns on sexual and reproductive health, cervical cancer, and other pathologies.

Stage 2: The Creation of Different Projects to Develop the Puna

Although the Warmi Suyajsunqo Association was key to the development of the Puna, its leaders felt it was important to create additional initiatives that could promote a more holistic development of the region. Thus, the University of La Puna, in partnership with Siglo 21 University in Córdoba, was founded in 2012. Thanks to these efforts, 60 young people in the area gained access to education without having to leave their homes. The goal of the university was to educate the future Warmi Suyajsungo leaders that would continue the work of their parents through the association. The university was especially valuable for serving as a bridge to the modernity and knowledge that his parents were unable to access. "In that way, our rights and way of life could be defended more efficiently," said Rosario.

Stage 3: Hilandería Warmi (the Warmi Spinning Mill)

In 2013, Rosario met Juan Collado, a successful local business person who had been pondering for some time how the organizations he led could have a greater social impact. Without hesitation, both decided to find a way to empower and develop Coya communities in the Puna region. Rosario told Juan about a spinning mill they received from the Verzinis, an industrial family that operated the spinning mill for more than thirteen years in San Salvador de Jujuy. The family decided to offer their business to the Warmi Sayasunqo Association. The association's leaders saw this as a great opportunity—the missing piece for the development of the Puna. However, the organization had neither the funds to buy the mill equipment, nor the management capabilities to run its operations. To achieve this, it would need to partner with external actors.

Rosario and Juan were quickly confident that they could collaboratively launch the Warmi Spinning Mill with the support of eight prestigious private investors that Juan had been in touch with. They agreed that the Warmi Suyajsunqo Association would own 10% of the mill. For the first time in Argentina, influential businesspeople intended to create collective impact in collaboration with indigenous communities to develop a project that featured shared capital and horizontal decision-making.

In 2014, the Warmi Spinning Mill was formally founded. Since its inception, the mill has aimed to develop a social business model that helps transform communities in a sustainable way by designing, producing, and selling excellent-quality products made from llama fibers collected by Coya producers. The mill used the equipment that had been imported to Argentina nearly a century earlier; this was a good starting point for the project. The Warmi Spinning Mill became known for its success in coordinating llama fiber producers on a community level, resulting in the creation of high-quality products, distribution, and sales.

Warmi's Organizational Structure

Operations and Structure

The mill's operations had two main locations. The raw material and its respective producers were located in Abra Pampa, in the Puna region. All the productive process took place in San Salvador de Jujuy where 22 people worked (Fig. 6.2). The Warmi Association did not participate directly in the Abra Pampa operations, but served as a link between the mill in San Salvador de Jujuy and the llama fiber producers in the Puna. Gastón, the mill's general manager, played a transversal role. His tasks included everything from strategy building, to helping the team problem solve, to

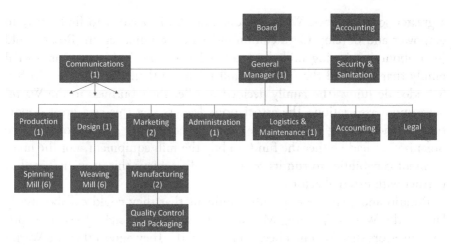

Fig. 6.2 Warmi Spinning Mill organization chart

visiting the Puna two or three times a month, to flying to Buenos Aires to negotiate with potential customers.

The mill had a productive capacity of 2800 kg per month (the equivalent of 2100 m of fabric per month) and a manufacturing cycle of 25–35 days, including storing, sorting, washing, spinning, weaving, manufacturing, and quality control. Roughly 64% of production costs were fixed, including salaries, external salaries, and rent. Variable costs amounted to 36%, and included llama and sheep fibers, packaged gas, dyes, and manufacturing (Figs. 6.3, 6.4, and 6.5).

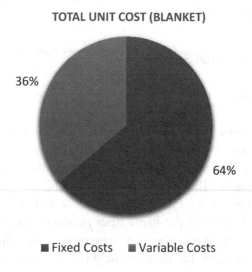

Fig. 6.3 Production costs

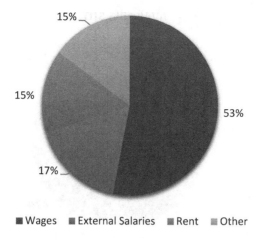

Fig. 6.4 Fixed cost per unit

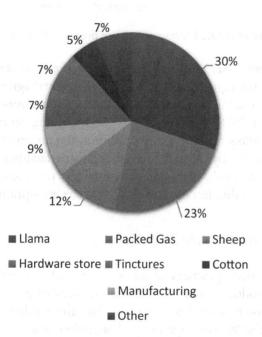

Fig. 6.5 Variable cost per unit

The industry was seasonal, so the second half of the year was key to reaching the break-even point for sales. For this reason, as well as the long manufacturing period, the mill kept a significant inventory of finished products to cope with incoming customer orders (Fig. 6.6).

AVAILABLE STOCK

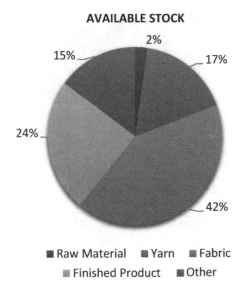

Fig. 6.6 Inventory of finished and semi-finished products (September 2018)

The mill spent USD3000 per month (plus taxes) to rent the 2000 m² property where the equipment was located. The rental agreement expired in July 2018, and Gastón negotiated a three-month extension, which carried them to October 2018. The cost of rent was increasing, so represented a significant cash outflow for the mill. In addition, the property did not offer all the services required by the mill. For example, the facilities lacked access to the natural gas network, so packaged natural gas was used, and there were no government production incentives (such as tax exemptions).

Changing the Practices of the Textile Industry

To break from poor practices of an industry that did not support added value among producers, the mill's leadership decided to pay what community leaders consensually determined as fair. The resulting price was then fixed through the Warmi Suyajsunqo Association. Rosario would talk with producers and establish the price with the mill. The value chain (without any impact of the Warmi Suyajsunqo Association) shows positive (+) and negative (−) impacts for each stakeholder, as outlined in Table 6.2.

The Warmi Suyajsunqo Association profoundly changed the Industry's value chain. Table 6.3 shows the value chain after Warmi's intervention, reflecting positive (+) and negative (−) impacts for each stakeholder.

Table 6.2 Textile industry value chain

Puna producers	Communities in the Puna	Collection centers	Spinning and weaving mills	Marketing	Consumer
Impact	Impact	Impact	Impact	Impact	Impact
(−) Low-priced fiber sales	(−) Producers not organized on a community level	(−) High fiber classification costs	(−) Prices defined by collection centers (collusion)	(−) Low quality-price ratio	(−) Low quality-price ratio
(−) Geographically scattered producers	(−) No active participation within the industry	(−) Lack of adequate infrastructure	(−) Problems with supplier development	(−) Difficulty finding new markets due to lack of differentiation	(−) Lack of product differentiation
(−) Inefficient and infrequent shearing practices		(−) Profit margin implies either reducing the price paid to producers and/or increasing the price charged to the mill	(−) Receipt of fibers with low quality standards	(−) Limited production volume for market expansion	
(−) Lack of infrastructure		(−) Very few collection centers	(−) Development of generic products that hinder competitiveness	(−) Low international positioning of llama fiber	
(−) Obsolete equipment		(−) Receipt of fibers with low quality standards	(−) Difficulty reaching and maintaining an optimal technical scale	(−) Distrust in suppliers	
(−) Lack of ethical animal handling practices		(+) Source of income	(−) Low negotiation power on sale price	(+) Source of income	
(+) Source of complementary income			(+) Source of income	(+) High negotiation power on sale price	
(+) Use of existing resources			(+) Generation of employment in urban areas		

Table 6.3 Impact of the Warmi mill's value chain

Puna producers	Puna communities	Barracas/collection centers	Spinning and weaving mills	Marketing	Consumer
Impact	Impact	Impact	Impact	Impact	Impact
(−) Geographically scattered producers	(−) No active participation within the industry	(−) High fiber classification costs	(+) Lower possibility of collusion by collection centers	(−) Low quality-price ratio	(−) Low quality-price ratio
(−) Inefficient and infrequent shearing practices	(+) Creation of a daily producer communication channel through the Warmi Sayajsunqo Association	(−) Lack of adequate infrastructure	(+) Improved relationship with suppliers to develop them	(−) Difficulty finding new markets due to lack of differentiation	(−) Lack of product differentiation
(−) Lack of infrastructure		(−) Profit margin implies either reducing the price paid to producers and/or increasing the price charged to the mill	(+) Enables conditions to improve fiber quality standards	(−) Limited production volume for market expansion	
(−) Obsolete equipment		(−) Very few collection centers	(+) Friendlier environment in which to achieve a differentiated product	(−) Low international positioning of llama fiber	
(−) Lack of good animal handling practices		(−) Receipt of fibers with low quality standards	(−) Difficulty reaching and maintaining an optimal technical scale	(+) Increased confidence in regional producers	
(+) Source of complementary income		(+) Source of income	(−) Low negotiation power on sale price	(+) Source of income	
(+) Use of resources		(−) Reduction in fiber volume	(+) Source of income	(+) High negotiation power on sale price	
(+) Possibility to forego a link in the chain (barracas/ collection centers)		(−) Increase in purchase price→profit reduction	(+) Generation of employment in urban areas		
(+) Agreements in fixing prices of raw material (2–3 times the market price)		(−) Increased negative perception of producers			

By October 2018, the mill was paying producers USD1.75 per kilo—nearly three times more than what they typically received from the collection centers or other buyers. According to Juan, since the spinning mill had begun to consensually fix the price in collaboration with the Warmi Suyajsunqo Association, the price paid to producers had increased by approximately 15 times, and forced the collection centers to adopt the new break-even price across the market.

The Warmi Suyajsunqo Association fulfilled its role of organizing producers, who had historically been very divided. The association united more than 3000 small producer families from 84 communities in the Puna. Coya producers typically shear llamas for only four months per year, so their work at the spinning mill provides a timely contribution to their income for a specific period of time. Increasing income and working collaboratively with communities has, thus, had a positive impact on their quality of life.

Target Market and Sales

The Warmi Spinning Mill was founded on the idea of selling Coya products from the Puna in national and international luxury markets. Products manufactured by the Warmi Spinning Mill include scarves, shawls, ponchos, blankets, throws, and bedspreads. In the 24 months preceding this case study, sales included 30% blankets, 27% bedspreads, 16% scarves, and 15% shawls. In the same period, a significant corporate sale to Yacimientos Petrolíferos Fiscales (YPF)[xi] raised the percentage of bedspreads to 74%, moving blankets to a second position with 8% (Figs. 6.7 and 6.8).

The Warmi Spinning Mill also sought out commercial partners to distribute its products around the world through an e-commerce platform (Figs. 6.9 and 6.10).

The Challenge: Moving the Mill Operations to the Puna

Financial Situation

Gastón was uncomfortable with saying that the business was sustainable (Table 6.4). In fact, the mill had very high market volatility. Its most relevant channel was corporate sales (40%). A single sale through this channel could significantly impact results. For example, one corporate sale could total USD45,000, which could define whether the mill would reach its equilibrium by the end of the period.

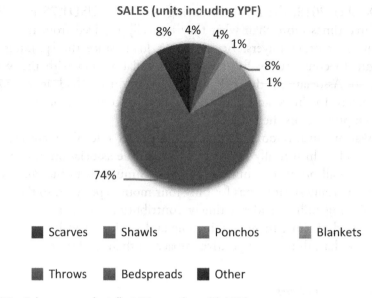

Fig. 6.7 Sales per product (last 24 months, with YPF)

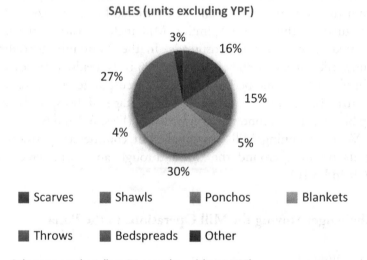

Fig. 6.8 Sales per product (last 24 months, without YPF)

The company had also recently broken into the export market. After analyzing the textile market's volatility, said Gastón, "We just made our first export sale, and I can't imagine a scenario in which we wouldn't have made it. Where would we be?" The sale comprised a total of USD105,000 in throws, sold to T.J. Maxx stores in the United States.

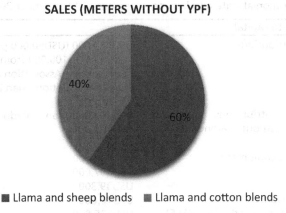

Fig. 6.9 Sales per fabric (last 24 months, without YPF)

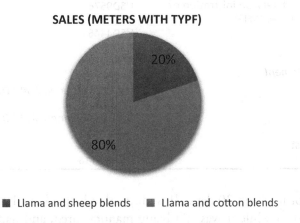

Fig. 6.10 Sales per fabric (last 24 months, with YPF)

While the company had met its break-even point since 2017 (in 2014, 2015, and 2016, the mill required partner contributions to resolve liquidity problems), the path toward stability, growth, and sustainability needed a retail strategy that included strengthening e-commerce via social networks and other tools.

In 2015, 5% of the mill's sales derived from retail. By 2018, its retail sales totaled 25%. Gastón believed that this strategy of reducing dependence on corporate sales would help increase robustness, as well as provide a higher profit margin and lower market volatility.

Besides sales, the Warmi Spinning Mill had problems with working capital. Gastón's constant challenge was being able to purchase raw material and

Table 6.4 Patrimonial state and income statement—21 September 2018

Contributions to capital	
Members contributions	USD400,000 (USD50,000 per partner, except USD100,000 from the Warmi Sayasunquo Association and Juan) Share participation: Juan 22%; 11% per partner
Extraordinary contributions	USD105,000 Juan Collado
Contributions without shareholding	USD100,000
Assets	
Machinery and equipment	USD122,500
Inventory	USD107,000
Cash	USD39,300
Accounts receivable	USD70,000
Sectoral Argentine Fund (FONARSEC)	USD225,000
Total	**USD563,800**
Accounts payable	
Argentine Federal Administration of Public Revenues (AFIP)	USD9576
Suppliers	USD4446
Checks	USD1026
Total	**USD17,100**
Income statement	
Sales	USD268,373 annually/USD22,300 monthly
Fixed cost	USD198,755 annually/USD16,500 monthly
Variable cost	USD45,500
EBITDA	**USD24,118**

then pay for it within 30 days. This means that he paid out 100% of the cost of the product while it was still being manufactured, and had not yet been sold to customers. Furthermore, this was an industry that typically paid for a finished product 90 days after having received the merchandise (Table 6.5).

Gastón considered himself a "strange creature" in the textile industry, since he was unable to maintain this financing scheme. Whenever a new client told him that he or she would pay in 90 days, Gastón had to reply that he needed 50% upfront, and 50% once the product was delivered. This represented a significant challenge for anyone in the textile industry.

Gastón would then analyze the client and determine whether he or she was sensitive enough to understand the mill's objective. "If the client didn't understand or wasn't interested in what we do—if it was nothing more than a business transaction—then we weren't interested in continuing negotiations with them," he said. "But if the client was fully aware, which happened more than 90% of the time, he or she would seek us out. These negotiations were much easier."

Table 6.5 Working capital

Account receivable as of 21 September 2018	Days being sold	Amount (in Argentine pesos)
Consignment	+60	206,400
Current account	30	138,060
Sales (estimated)	0	2,500,000
Total		**2,844,460**
Payments due as of 21 September 2018		
Account	**Days**	**Amount**
Suppliers	30	175,179.28
Checks issued	30	30,715.45
AFIP	30	385,000
Other (loans, trainings, etc.)		85,000
Total		**675,894.73**

Exchange rate as of 21 September 2018: ARS7.29 = USD1

Once a dialogue was established, Gastón would offer different options, such as adapting products to a given topic in exchange for a co-branding opportunity, special discounts for advance payments, etc. Gastón believed in transparency, so would tell his customers, "I need this, but please tell me how I can help you in exchange."

To this regard, the mill was constantly growing its social networks, so communications was one of the non-financial benefits offered to clients in the negotiation process. For example, just one year after launching its profile, the mill's Instagram account had reached more than 22,000 followers. It also participated in international fairs such as *New York Now*, *Wanted Design*, and the *International Contemporary Furniture Fair (ICFF)* in order to strengthen and position its brand. Participation in these fairs was carried out by one of the partners living in New York, who personally managed and presented the products at the fairs.

Scaling Impact in the Puna

Under the current scheme, in which the mill's main operations were located in San Salvador de Jujuy, Gastón believed that the added value for Coya producers was minimal; thus, so was the mill's impact on the Puna region. This created issues when integrating communities, since neither the communities nor the Warmi Suyajsunqo Association were taking ownership of the project. Rosario explained this situation by saying, "It's like someone giving me a car, but not giving me the keys."

Gastón recalled the original project vision in 2014, which included moving the mill to Abra Pampa. "We both want the same thing; I'm just negotiating when it should happen," he said. He knew that 80% of the microenterprises in Argentina did not survive their first five years. He explained to Rosario that consolidating an MSME in Argentina was a significant challenge, particularly from an economic standpoint, but also in terms of the professionalization of human resources. "What you're asking for isn't something we can achieve overnight. Yes; we're on the right track, but in some situations the timing won't be what we'd hope for," Gastón had told them.

To counterbalance the delay in the relocation of some of the mill's operations to the Puna, the company had donated a percentage of its earnings from the latest period to build a roof at the Abra Pampa associations' building, in effort to create a positive impact in the region. Also, Coca-Cola had donated a truck that the mill could use to visit producers and collect the fiber directly from their homes or grazing sites. Although the truck could have potentially been used for other initiatives in the Puna, it remained in disuse for its first six months after having arrived in Abra Pampa due to the lack of a suitable container in which to carry the raw materials.

Gastón felt that moving operations to Abra Pampa was the best path for increasing the mill's impact in the Puna, as initially promised. He could continue to make in-kind or monetary donations on behalf of the company, but this would not be sustainable in the long run. Given the characteristics of the project—particularly its strong component of cultural integration—it was a complex decision. Many aspects depended less on the spinning mill's business unit than they did on the social dynamics and idiosyncrasies of the actors in the Puna region. Moving to Abra Pampa would further increase this dependence.

However, Abra Pampa was improving its infrastructure. By October 2018, the Warmi Suyajsunqo Association had a brand-new, 1200 m² warehouse that could accommodate up to 70% of the industrial processes that occurred in San Salvador de Jujuy. Moving operations to Abra Pampa would increase the quality of the raw material that arrived at the mill for manufacturing. At present one-third of the weight of this material was dirt, since the fibers had just been sheared and were not yet cleaned. Moving the spinning process to the Puna meant that instead of transporting fiber with the dirt still attached, the yarn would be spun directly in the Puna, then transported to San Salvador de Jujuy where the weaving and manufacturing would take place. This would help the mill comply with the high-quality standards demanded by international luxury markets. One of the most significant challenges of having all operations in San Salvador de Jujuy was the producers' low productivity and quality of llama fibers, which made it difficult to access luxury markets. These weekly freights had a monthly cost of approximately USD1500.

A key assumption had been that the freight cost of transporting raw materials would be diluted by the considerable increase in the relative value of the intermediate product—in other words, the wool would be cheaper to transport once it had been spun into yarn. For example, 1 kg of fiber brought in roughly USD1.75, while 1 kg of yarn was valued at USD17. Gastón believed that transporting a clean intermediary product would have a positive impact on transportation costs, due to the more efficient use of space. However, the increase in equipment maintenance costs in a remote area like Abra Pampa also had to be taken into account. Thus, Gastón's analysis resulted in a higher overall cost of 10–20% compared to maintaining all operations in San Salvador de Jujuy.

He also considered purchasing two new machines for the move to Abra Pampa. A grant from the national government, which Warmi had applied for two years earlier, covered the cost of one of the machines. The other could be accessed through a strategic partnership with its owner. This latter collaboration was still being negotiated. Options included renting the machine or negotiating a percentage of the profits from the fiber it processed.

Gastón was also conducting a feasibility study regarding access to electrical services. This represented an additional obstacle, since the Abra Pampa utility company had informed him that they had no prior experience in supplying electricity for industrial use in the area. Their requests had so far been limited to bakeries and warehouses. When referring to situations like these, Gastón would say to his colleagues, "We've broken several paradigms already; we just need to be pioneers again."

Another issue to consider in the mill's eventual transfer was the humidity levels in Abra Pampa. Textile consultants had recently informed Gastón that the relative humidity in Abra Pampa would make production unfeasible. To maintain operations, the mill would require eight dehumidifiers, at a cost of USD3500 each.

Thus in order to transfer the mill to the Puna, the enterprise would have to request its first ever loan from the Development Bank of Investment and Foreign Trade (BICE), in the amount of roughly USD120,000. The terms of the loan were much friendlier than most loans on the market, however, with a subsidized 20% fixed interest rate in Argentine pesos, a grace period of one year, and six years for repayment.

The Decision

Gastón was convinced that transferring the mill's operations would create a favorable context to further its impact in Coya communities in the Puna. He knew that residents of the Puna needed this impact urgently. They depended on a subsistence economy based on a fundamental concern for the present—that is, day-to-day survival. Basic questions such as, "What am I going to eat today?" were resolved, for example, by seeking a lamb that could provide the family with food for a week. What they would eat the following week was irrelevant; they were only concerned with what they would eat today. Understanding this reality had helped Gastón adapt his business to the Puna inhabitants' worldview, in which basic needs were immediate. "One year for the Coya might equal three years for other communities," Gastón and Helvio had agreed. Therefore, a cooperative relationship meant ongoing negotiations.

However, Gastón was also aware that the decision involved major financial challenges. Collado and the other investors had expressed concerns about potentially transferring a major portion of the mill's production to the Puna. Was this the right time? They had finally reached business stability—but it was still fragile. Should they consider other options before considering such a significant transition? Gastón turned these questions over in his mind while completing his daily tasks at the mill. One of the things on his to-do list was to coordinate a partners' visit to Abra Pampa, since so far only Juan had been there.

The decision also implied transactional-operational risks. Currently, all of the mill's production was in one place. In the new model, the production team would be divided, which would present coordination challenges and a 220 km "gap" between the yarn and the fabric. Gastón had spent countless hours determining what the process must look like in order to succeed, since many families depended on the mill. He had many doubts, and was tempted to reconsider the timing of moving the mill to the Puna region. "Maybe the company isn't financially strong enough to weather such a shock," he thought. Perhaps it would be better to delay the relocation, and first focus on strengthening the company in San Salvador de Jujuy. "That would better secure our economic survival," he thought.

He recalled what Juan had said in one of their many conversations: "The mill transcends us as its leaders—it transcends "Juan," "Helvio," "Gastón," and "Rosario"—it moves forward because of everything that's pushing it from behind. The mill is something beyond individual people." Gastón was in a difficult position. Should he continue with plans to relocate the mill's operations to Abra Pampa (Option 1) or should he wait for a better moment and stay in San Salvador de Jujuy (Option 2)?

Additional Information of the Case: *Warmi Case Photographs*

See Photos 6.4 and 6.5.

Teaching Note on the Warmi Case

The Warmi case can be taught as part of a course on scaling social enterprises to introduce the strategy of collective impact described above. It is also suitable for a discussion on the complex issues of low-income markets, as it illustrates how a company has achieved success within these markets.

Learning Objectives

This case can be used to problematize the challenges of creating collective impact in low-income and multicultural contexts.

After having analyzed and discussed the case, readers should be able to:

Photo 6.4   Production process at Warmi Spinning Mill

Photo 6.5 Meeting between Gastón Aróstegui, General Manager at Warmi Spinning Mill, and Rosario and Helvio Quispe and other representatives of Warmi Association

a. understand challenges of negotiating impact for resources in low-income contexts;
b. be able to use the collective impact strategy to reflect on the challenges faced by the Warmi Spinning mill with respect to scaling its impact; and
c. develop a market approach to the collective impact strategy.

Reflection on the Warmi Spinning Mill's Market Approach to Scaling

The Warmi Suyajsunqo Association focuses on increasing quality of life among indigenous Coya communities in the Puna. The association's leader, Rosario, decided to collaborate with five influential businesspeople to collectively create an impact in the Puna. The business collaborators intended to strengthen the Warmi Suyajsunqo Association by facilitating the sale of llama fiber to international luxury markets. The investors provided economic resources and the strategic guidance of Juan; the indigenous communities provided the Warmi brand (which has since been valued at USD50,000) and the work of coordinating the producers scattered throughout the region in order to obtain the raw material (Fig. 6.11). With these

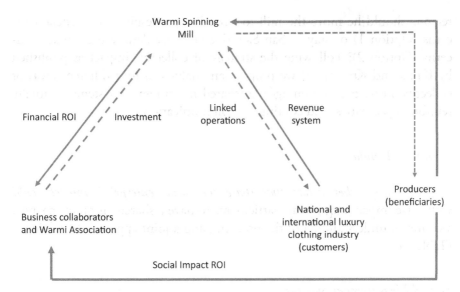

Fig. 6.11 The Warmi Spinning Mill's market approach to scaling

resources, the Warmi Spinning Mill established operations for the production of luxury llama wool products to be sold online and in various high-end stores in Buenos Aires, Europe, and the United States.

The main challenges that Warmi Spinning Mill is facing are in relation to its capacity to generate financial and social impact in the Puna region. On the one hand, the business collaborators perceive their investment as mainly focused on impact and less on financial return. But Juan aims to prove that Warmi can, in fact, become profitable while still generating a social impact. On the other hand, the Coyas communities do not feel that the mill has impacted their quality of life. The higher price paid to producers is not enough to considerably increase quality of life in the Puna, as it is a seasonable activity. Therefore, the Warmi Suyajsunqo Association is advocating to relocate the mill to Abra Pampa in the Puna in order to generate jobs and become an axis of development, alongside other projects.

Reflection on the Warmi Spinning Mill's Collective Impact Strategy

The Warmi Spinning Mill is based on a collective impact strategy. The challenge that Gastón faces in leading the mill is how to strengthen this strategy into its next phase—and in doing so scale the mill's impact in the region. Should he move the mill to Abra Pampa despite the financial concerns (Option 1) or stay in San Salvador de Jujuy despite the impact concerns (Option 2)? Following the strategy of collective impact as published by Kania and Kramer [9] we propose an analysis in four different areas of collective impact: common agenda, shared measurement systems, mutually reinforcing activities, and continuous communication.

Common Agenda

Are there any other actors that share the social enterprise's impact goals? Collective impact requires all participants to have a shared vision for change, a common understanding of the problem, and a joint approach to solving it (Table 6.6).

Shared Measurement Systems

Does the social enterprise have an impact measurement system that generates simple and inspiring results? Developing a shared measurement system is essential to collective impact.

It is important that business collaborators, indigenous communities, and the Warmi Spinning Mill team are aligned in all goals related to the common agenda. It is key that the actors agree on the necessary indicators (Table 6.7).

Mutually Reinforcing Activities

Are any of the actors that share our impact goals willing and capable of investing their time in collaborating with the enterprise—and others—in a way that mutually-reinforces our common agenda?

Success depends on a diverse group of people working together by undertaking the specific activities they excel at in a way that both supports and is well-coordinated with the actions of others. Each actor must fit into the bigger picture (Table 6.8).

Continuous Communication

What collective leadership and communication practices do we have in place, or need to implement, in order to support trustful relations with our partners?

Table 6.6 Common agenda

Common agenda (Status quo)	Common agenda if relocated to Abra Pampa (Option 1)	Common agenda if operations remain in San Salvador de Jujuy (Option 2)
Juan, the business collaborators, Helvio and Rosario, and the members of the Warmi Association need to develop a clear common vision of how to support communities in the Puna. This vision does not include, however, the strategy of how to achieve it	The Warmi Suyajsunqo Association has an overall strategy for developing communities in the Puna, which includes relocating the spinning mill to Abra Pampa. What is not yet clear, is how the mill can impact the community beyond the financial income from the additional jobs it will create • The impact of the spinning mill on the Coya communities needs to be defined	Juan intends to make the business venture economically sustainable The Warmi Suyajsunqo Association does not sympathize with the economic arguments presented by Gastón • Gastón needs to find a better way to explain to the Warmi Suyajsunqo Association why staying in San Salvador de Jujuy would be better for the venture both financially and in terms of its impact on the Puna region

Table 6.7 Shared measurement systems

Shared measurement systems (Status quo)	Shared measurement systems if relocated to Abra Pampa (Option 1)	Shared measurement systems if operations remain in San Salvador de Jujuy (Option 2)
The different parties measure success using different baselines, which are considered more important than concrete impact indicators The business collaborators are mainly focused on philanthropic issues. They measure success according to the mill's impact in the Puna The Warmi Suyajsunqo Association measures success based on the mill's impact in the Puna Collado and Gastón measure success according to both financial sustainability and impact	This option prioritizes impact criteria Financial criteria is put at risk • Gastón might seek another actor (e.g., government or foundation) that could help finance the venture based on the additional impact this option would create in the Puna. This could help Gastón buy time to strengthen the currently fragile financial sustainability make this option more profitable	This option is mainly focused on financial sustainability Impact criteria is secondary. The venture needs to wait to move to the Puna until it becomes a profitable option • Gastón needs to invest in building trust relations between the Spinning Mill and the Warmi Suyajsunqo Association

Table 6.8 Mutually reinforcing activities

Mutually reinforcing activities (Status quo)	Mutually reinforcing activities if relocated to Abra Pampa (Option 1)	Mutually reinforcing activities if operations remain in San Salvador de Jujuy (Option 2)
Gastón acts as a go-between for the Warmi Suyajsunqo Association and the business collaborators The business collaborators only talk to Gastón The Warmi Suyajsunqo Association only talks to Gastón	This option could spark a stronger interaction between the business collaborators and the Warmi Suyajsunqo Association The Warmi Suyajsunqo Association would need to become more active in linking the mill's operations with its impact on the Puna community • Gastón needs to define his management role. For example, he might focus on selling to international clients • He might also opt to strengthen a direct relationship between the mill's buyers in the Puna. This might expand the mill's collective impact strategy to include these buyers, as they might be more willing to pay the 50% up front if they more fully understand the Warmi "story."	This could be risky, as the Warmi Suyajsunqo Association may become less active • Gastón would need to find ways to motivate the Warmi Suyajsunqo Association to continue to be an active collaborator

Table 6.9 Continuous communication

Continuous communication (Status quo)	Continuous communication if relocated to Abra Pampa (Option 1)	Continuous communication if operations remain in San Salvador de Jujuy (Option 2)
The communication between Gastón, the business collaborators and the Warmi Suyajsunqo Association is limited to phone calls and short visits	A collective communication and leadership plan would become urgent, as the mill would need to have a new leadership structure that includes a stronger involvement of the indigenous Coya communities of the Puna • Gastón would need to define a government structure for production decisions, which would need to include the business collaborators, the buyers (which would have to agree to 50% up-front payments), Gastón, and the Warmi Suyajsunqo Association • He would also need to create a communication plan to explain the mill's mission to the outside world, including international buyers and their end customers	This option also needs to have a strong collective communication plan • Gastón would need to define a collective communication plan that strengthens the commitment of all actors involved

Developing trust between the actors involved in a collective impact initiative is a monumental challenge. Regular meetings, understanding one another's contexts, and common experiences are key to creating the space for constant discussion and integration (Table 6.9).

Discussion Questions

The following questions can help readers reflect on the case study in preparation for group discussions, or can be used during the discussion sessions.

1. *Is the Warmi Spinning Mill a collective impact initiative? Why?* This question helps participants closely consider the collective impact strategy. To answer this question, they must reflect on the market approach to collectively scaling impact illustrated by the mill.
2. *What common agenda, shared measurement systems, mutually-reinforcing activities, and continuous communication can the mill develop for its collective impact strategy?* This question helps participants systematically analyze the case according to the four elements of a successful collective impact strategy as presented above.
3. *How would you integrate the business collaborators, the Warmi Suyajsunqo Association, the producers, and the mill's team despite their cultural differences?* This question aims to challenge participants to consider the various cultural differences of the actors involved in this collective impact initiative. Overcoming these cultural differences involves mutual understanding and the development of common experiences.

Scaling Through Replicating Business Models: The Ciudad Saludable Case

This strategy focuses on replicating business models from one context to another. Replication is a demanding task. The business model needs to be capable of being applied to new environments that are suitable for replication. The Five R's model proposed by Dees et al. [11] argues that five critical elements need to be in place before starting a replication process. These include:

1. Readiness. *Has the innovation proved to be successful and not merely dependent on a particular person or a circumstance? Are the key drivers of the innovation's success well understood?*
2. Receptivity. *Is the new target population interested?*
3. Resources. *Do the necessary resources as financial, know-how, and human capital exist to implement the project?*
4. Risk. *What happens if it fails? Will there be losses in credibility or reputation?*
5. Returns. *Will it be possible to serve more people well? Will this be financially sustainable?*

The work carried out in the three phases of the market approach to scaling can help social entrepreneurs as they analyze the five R's and design their replication strategy. First, social entrepreneurs use the information gathered in Phase II (Designing operations and revenues), and Phase III (Balancing financing and impact logics) to analyze their business model and better understand their enterprise's success drivers in its current environment (Readiness). Second, they analyze the new context in respect to Phase I of the market approach to scaling (Negotiating impact for resources)—in other words, analyzing whether the target context is interested in the market approach (Receptivity). Third, they dig deeper into Phase I, particularly the element of resources, in order to, in the words of the five R's model, compose a list of resources available in the environment in which they intend to replicate their business model. The aim here is to determine if the new context has what they need to implement the project. This includes an analysis of whether there are impact investors interested in this new target population and related impact, and whether there are collaborators that can help implement the solution (Resources). Fourth, based on this evaluation of Phase I in the new context, social entrepreneurs can estimate the risk of losing potential investors if the replication project should fail (Risk). Fifth, analyzing the negotiation element of Phase I, they evaluate expectations of potential impact investors in the new context for both financial and impact return (Return).

The Ciudad Saludable Case

The Ciudad Saludable case facilitates reflection on the replication strategy. In 2002, Albina founded the organization as a nonprofit that aimed to tackle environmental problems in Lima, Peru. Its mission was particularly focused on formalizing the work carried out by grassroot recyclers, which it achieved through collaborations with local and national government on environmental plans and strategies for cleaning up the city. After it received a financial award from Fundación Avina (in collaboration with McKinsey & Company), Ciudad Saludable was able to obtain the local and international exposure needed to secure enough donations and other vital resources to finance and staff its initial environmental and social projects. After ten years of success, Albina was thinking about replicating her business model in other parts of the world.

The Case: Replicate a Nonprofit Branch or a Hybrid Organization?[3]

Albina Ruiz was sitting in a coffee house on one of Lima's lively, bustling streets, observing the passersby. It was September 2010. After a long day of work, she reflected on her personal journey in the city. It had begun with Ciudad Saludable, which she founded in 2002 as a nonprofit organization with the objective of creating healthy cities through an inclusive and environmentally minded solid waste management plan that included the participation of households, businesses, local governments, and recycling microenterprises. The initial objectives of Ciudad Saludable, which translates to "Healthy City," were to promote economically and socially inclusive recycling, construct integrated solid waste management systems, and provide environmental education to the public and private sectors.

The organization had been very successful in regularizing the work of many poor recyclers and collaborating with private, public, and civil society actors. Nevertheless, Albina believed in financial self-sustainable organizations that could have a social impact. Therefore, in addition to Ciudad Saludable, which followed a nonprofit model, in 2008 Albina created another organization focused on consulting services, Peru Waste Innovation (PWI). PWI was a for-profit enterprise, and was intended to fund a percentage of Ciudad Saludable's administration costs, activities, and services in order to reduce its dependency on donor dollars.

Albina thought about the numerous awards she had received; she thought about her nomination as an Ashoka Fellow, and Ciudad Saludable's success story. But she was, at heart, a tireless entrepreneur, and she dreamed of achieving an even greater social impact. She knew that to do this, she

---

[3]Authors: Felipe Symmes, Senior researcher VIVA Idea and PHD Candidate University of Saint Gallen; Urs Jäger, Associate Professor INCAE Business School and Academic Director VIVA Idea; and Christina Katsianis, Research consultant VIVA Idea.

needed capital. This had been evident since early 2010, when she wanted to participate in a USD1 million pitch with a Japanese cooperation initiative that consisted of helping municipalities around the world to construct and implement solid waste management systems. To participate, Albina needed USD300,000 to guarantee the organization's liquidity. But she couldn't come up with that amount of case. It was clear to Albina that if she wanted to participate in larger projects, she would need to raise more capital.

As she watched the streets of Lima, she considered accessing impact investors. "If we could use resources from impact investors to strengthen key impact areas—like educating poor recyclers—then scaling our impact would completely be feasible," thought Albina. However, she also knew that accessing resources from impact investors required clear decisions and a long, challenging process. She knew this because a European institutional impact investor, EUVestment (pseudonym), had already started a due diligence process with Ciudad Saludable. Negotiations with EUVestment were slow-going, particularly because they expected Albina to generate financial return and impact return simultaneously. During these conversations, Albina realized that she wasn't entirely prepared to negotiate with EUVestment, as she often didn't understand their expectations, and she had the impression that they didn't always understand hers. Impact investment was new territory for Albina. She found it too profit-driven—at times even indifferent toward her beneficiaries.

EUVestment was mainly interested in the scalable solutions represented by Ciudad Saludable, a nonprofit. Compared with PWI, Ciudad Saludable had more experience with achieving social and environmental impact by working with grassroot recyclers. However, as a nonprofit, Ciudad Saludable couldn't offer a financial ROI. The investor was particularly concerned by the fact that PWI was relatively new and hard to scale, and its social and environmental impact was not as clearly demonstrated as Ciudad Saludable's.

After much reflection, Albina prepared two different scaling strategies. The first option was to replicate the Ciudad Saludable model without PWI in other cities. This was a validated nonprofit model with proven success. What was unclear, however, was how to make this option attractive to impact investors, as it offered no financial return. The second option was to replicate both Ciudad Saludable and PWI—a hybrid model that intended to create income by PWI and social and environmental impact by Ciudad Saludable—in other contexts. With this option, the investor could invest in the for-profit branch, PWI. Albina felt that this option could be attractive to investors, but wasn't yet sure how it would help her scale impact, as PWI was originally created to obtain the internal economic resources needed to fuel Ciudad Saludable's impact.

Albina's path ahead remained unclear. Should she propose a replication strategy for the nonprofit branch only (Option 1) or propose that the investor view the two organizations as a single hybrid organization comprising a nonprofit branch and a for-profit branch, and engage in a replication process that included both (Option 2)?

Peru and the Problem of Solid Waste[xii]

From 2005 to 2010, Peru's Gross Domestic Product (GDP) grew at an annual rate of 6.8%, despite the fact that its GDP growth in 2009 was only 1.09% due to the international crisis.[xiii] This overall growth was the result of the country's macroeconomic and political stability, a favorable environment for local and foreign business investment, the promotion of exports, and the opening of new markets. At the time, Peru's GDP was expected to continue to rise at a similar rate over the next five years, driven by direct foreign and national investments, foreign trade and, increasingly, by internal consumption and tourism. In terms of economic growth, Peru was an example for other Latin American countries.

The economic growth sustained over the past several years had also affected the percentage of people living below the poverty line of USD1.90 per day, which fell 11%—having decreased from 15% in 2002 to 5% in 2010.[xiv] Furthermore, a study by the Inter-American Development Bank (IDB) revealed that the percentage of middle-class households had reached 51% of the total population in 2010, having grown from an estimated 25% of Peruvian households in 2005 [12]. The IDB study indicated that the average middle-class income had grown at a greater rate than the GDP, signifying that the GDP growth had been of particular benefit to this sector. Nevertheless, the IDB study also indicated that the emerging middle class was highly vulnerable, and its edification not only depended on the strength of the domestic product, but also on the continuity of social policies.

These economic growth indicators, however, masked two persistent problems: poverty in rural zones was still above 50% (in some regions estimated at nearly 80%), and the growth experienced by Peru's various regions was extremely unequal. In 2010, the GDP of Cusco, Tacna, Tumbes, Apurímac, and Lima experienced a growth of 10–15%, while Cajamarca and Pasco decreased by 1 and 2% respectively. These differences, coupled with the ineffectiveness of public spending in the highlands and jungle regions, led to social conflicts in rural zones and an increased migration to cities, in turn generating overcrowding and poverty belts in major cities. High economic growth rates also brought other problems: increased solid waste, fossil fuel combustion, air and water pollution, higher deforestation rates due to agricultural and urban expansion, noise pollution, and other issues affecting the health and decreasing the quality of life of Peruvians.

The generation of solid waste, in particular, became a problem for large cities. The per capita generation of waste at the local level in Peru increased by 40% between 2000 and 2010, and many of its districts had no idea how to approach the issue. The eight districts that comprised the northern part of Lima, totaling roughly 2.5 million inhabitants, were generating an average of 1500 tons of waste per day. These municipalities lacked integrated plans to adequately manage waste. Thus, it was common to see improvised dumps in public areas. In addition to lacking an integrated management plan, some districts would deposit waste in dumps that did not have the authorization of DIGESA, the Ministry of Health's Environmental Health Board. The waste issue caused an increase in epidermal and digestive illnesses, as well as incidences of poisoning among some residents of the Carabayllo, Independencia, and Comas districts, according to health reports released in these zones.

Although Lima's solid waste management problem was more evident in some districts than others, the problem had extended across the country. In 2009, just 58 of Peru's 194 provinces[xv] had an Integrated Plan for the Environmental Management of Solid Waste [13]. In 2007, DIGESA conducted a study in 128 districts of various regions in the country. The objective was to analyze the quality of solid waste management services and assign a sanitation and environmental risk rating. The rating was based on four components: collection, reception and transportation, sanitation evaluation of service personnel, and final deposition infrastructure. The study determined that four departments (Cajamarca, Huánuco, Tumbes, and Ucayali) had an extremely high environmental risk indicator, and that another eight, including the department of Lima, also rated relatively high. An exemplary case of environmental risk was the Reque dump site, located in the Chiclayo province, where 127,000 tons of solid waste were deposited and burned each year, causing various illnesses in the surrounding population.

The Emergence of Ciudad Saludable

Stage 1: Founding the Nonprofit

In 2002, Albina founded Ciudad Saludable as a nonprofit organization. Its interventions included: social, economic, and environmental governance; the construction of an "environmental citizenship" through education and communication; economic and social inclusion for recyclers; the use of clean, low-cost technologies; strategic communication between the public and the private sectors; the design of public policies; and the implementation of just and highly competitive recycling chains.

Ciudad Saludable initially worked through a multidisciplinary team of four professionals—one psychologist and three engineers (industrial, agricultural, and chemical)—who shared similar values regarding environmental issues. At first the team worked at Albina's home, using her family computer. They developed a proposal for the environmental impact project that would later become Ciudad Saludable, and Albina submitted it to a contest organized by Fundación AVINA in collaboration with McKinsey & Company. They won second place, receiving USD13,000 and a consultancy from McKinsey. In addition to the award, participation in the contest afforded the Ciudad Saludable team both local and international exposure, through which they were able to obtain donations and volunteers from international organizations such as the Open Society Institute and the Skoll Foundation to finance and staff their initial environmental and social impact projects.[xvi]

Stage 2: Standardization of Services

From 2002 to 2008, Ciudad Saludable was able to standardize most of its services. For instance, when government officials or companies wanted to tackle environmental and social problems in their communities, and contacted Ciudad Saludable help, Albina and her team would gather information from local authorities, grassroots leaders, local businesses, and poor recyclers, and diagnose the situation (Fig. 6.12). They analyzed each recycler and his or her economic and social situation to estimate the level of impact that Ciudad Saludable's training and support could have on their quality of life, particularly with respect to labor and income. Once Albina and her team decided to execute a project, they typically supported the recyclers for

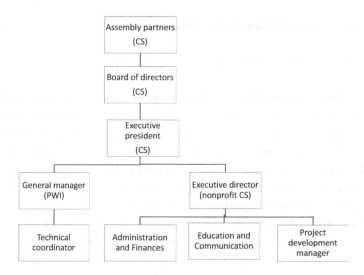

Fig. 6.12 Ciudad Saludable organizational chart

two to four years. Ciudad Saludable also had other projects, such as creating environmental recycling guides and conducting empirical studies on waste and recycling for international nongovernmental organizations, municipalities, and other public bodies.

From the time it was founded in 2008, Ciudad Saludable had covered its costs through income generated from traditional paying customers, such as public institutions and companies, and through donations from public bodies and diverse international organizations. Generating enough financing was difficult. So, Albina proposed the idea of reducing Ciudad Saludable's dependency on donations to become financially self-sustaining in the long run.

Stage 3: The Naissance of PWI

To achieve this objective of financial sustainability, in 2008, Albina founded PWI. The profits earned through PWI would pay for a large percentage of Ciudad Saludable's costs.

PWI provided consulting services on topics related to integrated solid waste management. However, in 2010 the enterprise was still not generating a surplus. One reason for this was that its niche in the market was very small, as its scope was limited to the provision of consulting services to mining businesses. To solve this problem, a PWI executive suggested widening the target market to include consulting services to agricultural and fishing businesses. Additionally, although considered one of the top consulting firms in the region on a technical level, PWI was not winning as many bids as it should have been due to high corruption levels in the consulting industry. Because PWI policies forbid the receipt or provision of bribes, the organization was not only losing bids, but was also losing popularity among government institutions and other consulting firms.

Stage 4: The Social Enterprise "Ciudad Saludable"

Ciudad Saludable's nonprofit arm (nonprofit CS) and PWI together created Ciudad Saludable social enterprise, with Albina as president. With ample social impact success stories of Ciudad Saludable's far-reaching efforts prior to 2010, it is no surprise that Albina gained international recognition.

From 2002 to 2010, Ciudad Saludable regularized 501 recyclers and educated 4.2 million people in solid waste management through educational and communication campaigns. Its work was publicly recognized by specialist networks and in political discourse. As a result, Albina received numerous awards around the globe. Her organization became a role model for approaching the issue of solid waste in various regions of the world, and various government institutions in Peru, including the Ministries of Environment, Health, and Education had a high level of respect for Albina and her approach to resolving solid waste management issues.

One of Ciudad Saludable's greatest achievements was the 2009 approval of Law No. 29419, the first in the world to nationally regulate recycler activities. The law was drafted with input from poor recyclers, the government, and citizen advocates as representatives of Ciudad Saludable, and was backed by ten of Peru's 15 political parties. Law No. 29419 then served as a basis for the creation of like-minded legislations. Brazil, for example, approved a similar law in 2010, and Chile in 2016. Another relevant achievement was the creation of RENAREPE, a national recyclers' network, in 2010. The network is a "second-tier" partnership that unites 55 organizations from across the country under the common goal of ensuring that recyclers have greater support when pressuring political parties. Albina, who has been creating recycler associations since 1998, had learned from experience that, uniting various small-scale associations led to more effective governance than creating a single large one.

In addition to the above achievements, Ciudad Saludable's programs directly impacted grassroots organizations and, therefore, the lives of thousands of Peruvians, providing them with a dignified source of income. One such case was that of Nelly Ticse, one of the organization's thousands of beneficiaries. Nelly was responsible for the social work component of the Rupa Association, a recycling micro-enterprise. Despite having been unable to finish high school, Nelly had become the "go-to" person for many of the women and families in her community. Her hard work and perseverance had allowed her to overcome many difficulties and had given her an inherently entrepreneurial spirit. It wasn't easy—for example, she recalls that the mayor initially didn't want to work with her association—but she persisted. "We requested an audience, and we told him about our project," she recalled. "We offered clean-up services so that we would be allowed to recycle without the "serenazgo" (local authorities) taking away our materials. The mayor accepted the offer, but said that we needed to formalize our business. Ciudad Saludable helped us with the formalization process and connected us with businesses that generate plastic and cardboard waste."[xvii]

Initial Conversations with EUVestment

Ciudad Saludable's impact and approval from the various sectors involved in managing and recycling solid waste convinced Albina that she was on the right path. Ciudad Saludable had enormous potential for impact, but still depended on donations. Albina started to look for alternative sources of income. Her efforts to generate internal financing for Ciudad Saludable through PWI had just been strengthened. This was an emergent endeavor. Albina wondered if she could be patient enough to wait for the additional income from PWI to increase enough to support Ciudad Saludable's work. The urgency grew when Albina decided to participate in a USD1 million pitch with a Japanese cooperation initiative, which required that the bidding organization demonstrate USD300,000 in working capital. Ciudad Saludable didn't have this kind of working capital, so Albina began to consider the various external financing actors and instruments available in the market that could adapt to her situation and her objectives of scaling the organization's impact. Prior to reaching this stage, the majority of Ciudad Saludable funding had been through grants: USD1 million in 2008, USD1.6 million in 2009, and USD1.1 million in 2010 [14]. As PWI had not generated a profit until 2010, the success of the internal financing model was yet to be proven. Albina was determined to become more self-sustaining and less reliant on the somewhat inconsistent donor grants. While PWI was a key first step in this direction, an exploration of external financing instruments was necessary to evaluate the participation in the pitch for the Japanese Cooperation.

To identify potential investors, Albina began by searching for relevant, active investors in the region who might be willing to invest in Peru's solid waste management industry in the form of equity. At this point in Albina's impact investment journey, detailed research proved to be key. This helped Albina identify important details such as the type of funding provided by various investors, the requirements and preconditions for such funding, and the application process involved. She has since stressed to her team that taking the time to find investors that are the best possible financial match while also possessing a social and environmental mission would save Ciudad Saludable significant time and energy that might otherwise have been spent in managing investor expectation the social enterprise could not meet, nor would want to meet.

However, the encounter with EUVestment was more the result of serendipity than preparation. Albina met the managers of this organization at one of Latin America's many social enterprise events. The EUVestment managers casually introduced themselves to Albina, and immediately realized that the two organizations were looking for each other. Albina was impressed to learn that institutional investors also embark on a long, arduous process to find suitable social enterprises in which to invest their resources. The initial email conversations with EUVestment were promising.

Proposing a Scaling Strategy

EUVestment's due diligence and negotiation process, however, was an even bigger surprise to Albina Ruiz, as it went beyond a financial and legal assessment. The process was divided into two parts. First—and, for EUVestment, most important—was to assess the organization's social impact and how it would be scaled through the economic resources injected. At first, the funds provided to Ciudad Saludable would allow it to participate in larger pitches such as that of the Japanese cooperation initiative, but EUVestment was concerned that this focus was only relevant in the initial stages. Their main question was, "What next?" For EUVestment, the scaling strategy was unclear. "How will you scale to other contexts" and "How will you reach a global scale?" were the main questions. Albina was, however, pleasantly surprised to discover that the investor shared her goal of increasing the impact on beneficiaries: recyclers, local communities, and local and national governments. Whenever they met, EUVestment managers were very interested in the progress achieved by Ciudad Saludable in public policy settings—an aspect often overlooked by impact investors who tend to seek more specific, tangible outcomes based on rigid impact assessment models.

The second part was the financial and legal analysis. As mentioned above, the investor was mainly interested in Ciudad Saludable's impact goals. However, their internal policy did not allow them to invest in nonprofit organizations. The fact that Albina felt that equity was the best financial instrument also disqualified the nonprofit arm of Ciudad Saludable as a subject for impact investment. This was a monumental hurdle, as the social impact, which is what most interested the investor, was made by the nonprofit arm of Ciudad Saludable; the intent of PWI was to operate as Ciudad Saludable's donor rather than to focus its consulting services on social impact.

The Decision

Albina's morning reflections were abruptly halted by a roaring street sweeper that had pulled up at the edge of the curb. Based on the process experienced with EUVestment (which was still playing out), particularly the lengthy due diligence and negotiation process, she had learned how to approach impact investors and be able to speak their language. She had also learned to respect them as an opportunity to scale impact and access larger projects. Albina considered her present goal: to participate in the USD1 million pitch organized by the Japanese cooperation initiative "But they expect a USD300,000 working capital, and Ciudad Saludable doesn't have that kind of money," she thought, desperately. "I need to raise the capital somehow, and impact investors are a solid option."

Albina still felt that EUVestment was an excellent candidate. However, their interest in both impact and financial return was perplexing. Its real interest was in the nonprofit organization, Ciudad Saludable, but it would be impossible to provide a financial return if they invested in it. Thus, Albina prepared two different scaling strategies to pitch to EUVestment.

The first was to replicate Ciudad Saludable to other contexts. This was in line with the impact interest. However, it was unclear how EUVestment would implement its investment if Ciudad Saludable was a nonprofit organization. The second option was to replicate Ciudad Saludable and Peru Waste Innovation as a single, united entity. This strategy established the two organizations as a hybrid consortium composed of a for-profit and a non-profit organization.

These were Albina's options. She could either focus her presentation on the need for funds to replicate the nonprofit organization's business model (Option 1) or on replicating both organizations as a single, hybridized entity (Option 2)? Albina reconsidered her options and decided how she would continue to scale her impact in the future.

Additional Information of the Case

Process for working with grassroot recyclers and social impact

Ciudad Saludable case photographs

See Photos 6.6, 6.7, and 6.8.

Teaching Note on the Ciudad Saludable Case

This case study can be taught as part of a course on scaling social enterprises to introduce the replication strategy and the three phases of a market approach to scaling as a tool to help develop this strategy. It is also suitable for a corporate social responsibility course with respect to the discussion of social issues in low-income contexts and a course on hybrid organizations.

Photo 6.6 Typical way of working of grassroot recyclers

Photo 6.7 Recycling process of one of the grassroot recyclers trained by Ciudad Saludable

Photo 6.8 Group of women empowered by Ciudad Saludable working in the field

Learning Objectives

Ciudad Saludable can be used to analyze the complexities of replicating business models in other contexts.

After having analyzed and discussed the case, readers should be able to:

a. understand the market approach for scaling impact of Ciudad Saludable;
b. be able to use the replication strategy to reflect on Ciudad Saludable's challenges regarding scaling its impact; and
c. systematically analyze business opportunities when considering a replication strategy.

Reflection on Ciudad Saludable's Market Approach to Scaling

Ciudad Saludable began as a nonprofit, then later became a social enterprise with the foundation of PWI. It essentially became a hybrid organization. On one hand, was the nonprofit arm of Ciudad Saludable, an impact-oriented nonprofit that aimed to help small recyclers become regularized MSMEs and, in turn, clean up the streets of Lima. On the other hand, was PWI, a consulting company that used Ciudad Saludable's knowledge of recycling and MSME support to sell consulting services to companies and municipalities, which acted as traditional paying customers (Fig. 6.13).

The opportunity to secure impact investments for Ciudad Saludable implied a market approach to scaling. The impact investor was particularly interested in the impact made by Ciudad Saludable, but as a nonprofit it could not offer a financial ROI. Therefore, Albina and the investor eventually agreed that the financial investment would be accomplished by selling projects to traditional paying clients via the for-profit PWI. This branch would receive the EUVestment funds in order to grow and, in turn, fuel more income into Ciudad Saludable. This income would help to scale the social and environmental impact return provided by Ciudad Saludable (Tables 6.10 and 6.11).

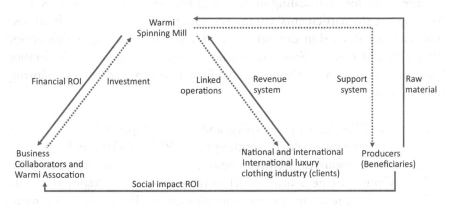

Fig. 6.13 Ciudad Saludable's market approach to scaling

Table 6.10 Ciudad Saludable's social impact work in communities

Steps	Description
1: Petition	Petition received from a local government or company that wants to tackle environmental and social problems in their communities
2: Initial gathering of information	Information gathered from local authorities, grassroots leaders, local businesses, and grassroots recyclers
3: Diagnosis	Situation diagnosed through field visits
4: Baseline	Baseline constructed via standardized files containing data about the grassroots recyclers and their economic and social situations
5: Training and regularization of the grassroots recyclers' labor situation	This step comprises three parts: (a) Four training modules, now national law (b) Support in regularizing grassroots recycler organizations (c) Healthcare in alliance with the National Ministry of Health

Table 6.11 Ciudad Saludable's social and environmental impact

Beneficiaries	As of 2010
Poor recyclers	501
Population reached via awareness programs	4.2 million

Reflection on Designing a Replication Strategy

The Five Rs proposed by Dees et al. [11] can provide a useful framework to systematically analyze Ciudad Saludable's replication strategy. Instructors can use this framework to guide the discussion, posing questions regarding both scaling options along the Five "Rs" (Table 6.12). A white board with two columns (one for each scaling option) and five rows (one for each "R") can help capture the participants' comments. Once the Five "Rs" have been documented, the discussion can turn toward a debate regarding which option Albina should choose. Students should be able to support their decision based on the analysis performed. The discussion can lead to the following observations:

- In terms of Readiness, Receptivity, and Return: Option 1 (the nonprofit model) is more favorable. For both options "Risk" is relatively low.
- In terms of Resources, EUInvestment is unable to invest in a nonprofit. Thus, Option 2 (the hybrid model) is the only option. Despite this issue, PWI is not yet ready to generate enough income. Thus, this option represents a high financial risk for the investor.

Table 6.12 Options for replication

Five Rs [11]	Option 1: scaling by replicating the nonprofit	Option 2: scaling by replicating the hybridized group
Readiness *Has the innovation proved to be successful and not merely dependent on a particular person or a circumstance? Are the key drivers of the innovation's success well understood?*	[• Answer: YES] By 2008, Ciudad Saludable had standardized most of its processes. For example, when companies or municipalities contacted Ciudad Saludable for help tackling their communities' social and environmental issues, the organization implemented the following process: (a) Gather information from local authorities, grassroots leaders, local businesses and poor recyclers, and conduct a detailed analysis of the situation (b) Analyze each recycler and his or her economic and social situation to estimate the impact that Ciudad Saludable could have through its training and support services (c) Create a tailored proposal for the company or municipality, placing grassroot recyclers at the center of the strategy (d) Provide support to the recyclers for 2-4 years (depending on the scope of the project), as a follow-up to the proposal's implementation	[• Answer: NO—the consulting did not yet generate the expected financial returns] Ciudad Saludable covered its costs through income generated from traditional paying customers such as public institutions or private businesses, as well as via grants from public entities and international organizations. To achieve the objective of financial sustainability, Albina had founded Peru Waste Innovation (PWI) in 2008. PWI was a for-profit consulting firm that provided services regarding integrated solid waste management to ensure a widespread replication of the Ciudad Saludable model
Receptivity *Is the new target population interested?*	[• Answer: YES] For this an analysis of the new contexts in which to replicate the model is needed	[• Answer: YES] For this an analysis of the new contexts in which to replicate the model is needed

(continued)

Table 6.12 (continued)

Five Rs [11]	Option 1: scaling by replicating the nonprofit	Option 2: scaling by replicating the hybrid-ized group
Resources *Do the necessary resources as financial, know-how, and human capital exist to implement the project?*	[• Answer: NO] The main resource Albina needs are investors willing to pay for the replication of her business model. When identifying potential investors, she searched for those that were relevant and active in the region, and might be willing to invest in Ciudad Saludable. Albina thought that equity was the best way to leverage value that impact investors saw in the organization in terms of knowledge and social capital. However, EUVestment does not invest in nonprofits	[• Answer: YES] EUVestment was greatly interested in Ciudad Saludable's impact. However, they had an internal policy that prevented them from investing in nonprofit organizations. The founding of PWI increased the possibility to deploy investment
Risk *What happens if it fails? Will there be losses in credibility or reputation?*	[• Answer: RELATIVELY LOW] Ciudad Saludable is an impact success story. Failure would not damage this reputation, as Albina would be able to show her positive intentions to scale	
Returns *Will it be possible to serve more people well? Will this be financially sustainable?*	[• Answer—Impact: YES] Ciudad Saludable has showed great efficiency and success in generating impact. From 2002 to 2010, this was mainly achieved via Ciudad Saludable, which formalized a total of 501 recyclers and educated 4.2 million people in solid waste management through educational and communication campaigns. Another significant achievement was the 2009 approval of Law No. 29419, the first in the world to nationally regulate recycler activities [• Answer—Financial sustainability: NO] As Ciudad Saludable is a nonprofit, it faces problems accessing resources from impact investors such as EUVestment	[• Answer—Impact: YES] Although the hybrid model has not yet been validated, the possibility of fueling Ciudad Saludable's impact through a for-profit branch is in line with its scaling goals [• Answer—Financial sustainability: POSSIBLY] The hybrid model of grouping Ciudad Saludable and PWI as two branches of a single entity could create the necessary financial sustainability and the possibility to replicate this model in different contexts

Discussion Questions

To prepare the case or to structure discussions in class the following four questions can be helpful.

1. *Would you as an impact investor want to invest in Ciudad Saludable in general?* This open-ended question invites participants to reflect on their expectations regarding return. It is likely that those with high expectations for financial return would propose that EUVestment not invest in Albina's initiative.

2. *How would you describe Ciudad Saludable's market approach to scaling?* This question aims to structure the resource analysis into a conceptualization of the hybridized for-profit/nonprofit model. This analysis helps participants understand the hybrid nature of many social enterprises and provides a baseline for reflecting on Albina's two options.

3. *Which of the Five Rs did you identify for both options?* This question guides participants to systematically analyze the case according to the replication strategy presented above.

4. *What are the main cornerstones of Ciudad Saludable's operations and revenue processes if it is to replicate its business model globally?* This question guides participant's attention to Phase II of the market approach to scaling impact: "Operations and revenue processes," and highlights the advantages and disadvantages of a hybrid business model.

Notes

i. See The World Bank's Global Consumption Database http://datatopics. worldbank.org/consumption/.
ii. World Health Organization (WHO) http://www.who.int/pbd/deafness/ news/Millionslivewithhearingloss.pdf.
iii. World Health Organization (WHO) website http://www.who.int/pbd/deaf-ness/news/Millionslivewithhearingloss.pdf.
iv. uSound website http://www.usound.co/.
v. Plan Belgrano website https://www.argentina.gob.ar/planbelgrano.
vi. "Sayajsunjo" means "perseverant women" in the Quechua language.
vii. National Institute of Statistics and Censuses (INDEC) of Argentina.
viii. Ministry of Economy and Public Finances, and Secretariat of Political Economy, 2010. *"Plan de Competitividad Conglomerado Camélidos de la Provincia de Jujuy."* Argentina.

ix. FIDA, 1991. "*Informe de la misión de preidentificación. Programa regional camélidos.*"

x. Fundación Avina (Avina Foundation) is a Latin American philanthropic foundation working towards sustainable development in Latin America by encouraging alliances between social and business leaders.

xi. An Argentine energy company specializing in the industry of exploration, exploitation, distillation, distribution, and production of electricity, gas, oil and hydrocarbon by-products, and the sale of fuels, lubricants, fertilizers, plastics, and other products.

xii. This part is based on the case written on Ciudad Saludable by Carlos Martínez and Felipe Pérez during 2013. The data was mainly changed to fit 2002 and 2010.

xiii. World Bank Group (2016). GDP growth in Peru (annual %). Available at: http://data.worldbank.org/indicator/ (accessed: 24 February 2017).

xiv. World Bank Group (2016) Poverty headcount ratio at $1.90 a day (2011 PPP) (% of population). Available at: http://data.worldbank.org/indicator/ (accessed: 24 February 2017).

xv. In Peru, a province is an administrative subdivision of a department. Each province is civilly governed by a Provincial Municipality, which is headed by a mayor.

xvi. This part is based on the case written on Ciudad Saludable by Carlos Martínez and Felipe Pérez in 2013.

xvii. This part is based on the case written on Ciudad Saludable by Carlos Martínez and Felipe Pérez.

References

1. Casado, F., & Hart, S. L. (Eds.). (2015). *Base of the pyramid 3.0: Sustainable development through innovation and entrepreneurship.* Aizlewood's Mill: Greenleaf.

2. London, T., Anupindi, R., & Sheth, S. (2010). Creating mutual value: Lessons learned from ventures serving base of the pyramid producers. *Journal of Business Research, 6,* 582–594.

3. London, T., Esper, H., Grogan-Kaylor, A., & Kistruck, G. M. (2014). Connecting poverty to purchase in informal markets. *Strategic Entrepreneurship Journal, 8*(1), 37–55.

4. De Soto, H. (2000). *The mystery of capital: Why capitalism triumphs in the west and fails everywhere else* (p. 2000). New York: Basic Books.

5. London, T., & Hart, S. L. (2004). Reinventing strategies for emerging markets: Beyond the transnational model. *Journal of International Business Studies, 35*(5), 350–370.

6. Baker, T., & Nelson, R. E. (2005). Creating something from nothing: Resource construction through entrepreneurial bricolage. *Administrative Science Quarterly, 50,* 329–365.

7. Penrose, E. G. (1959). *The theory of the growth of the firm.* New York: Wiley.

8. London, T., & Jäger, U. (2019). Co-creating with the base of the pyramid. *Stanford Social Innovation Review* (online first). https://ssir.org/articles/entry/cocreating_with_the_base_of_the_pyramid.

9. Kania, J., & Kramer, M. (2011). Collective impact. *Stanford Social Innovation Review,* 63.

10. Lamas, H. (2007). *Desarrollo del encadenamiento productivo de la llama en la provincia de Jujuy.* Economic Commission for Latin America and the Caribbean (ECLAC). Argentina.

11. Dees, G., Anderson, B. B., & Wei-skillern, J. (2004). Scaling social impact: Strategies for spreading social innovation. *Standord Social Innovation Review, 1*(4), 24–32.

12. Castellani, F., Parent, G., & Zentero, J. (2014). *The Latin American middle class fragile after all?* Available at: https://publications.iadb.org/bitstream/handle/11319/6733/The-Latin-American-Middle-Class-Fragile-After-All.pdf?sequence=2. Accessed 24 February 2017.

13. Lopez-Calva, L. F., & Ortiz-Juarez, E. (2011). *A vulnerability approach to the definition of the middle class.* Available at: https://core.ac.uk/download/pdf/6258575.pdf. Accessed 24 February 2017.

14. Dulanto Tello, A. (2013, April). *Asignación de competencias en materia de residuos sólidos de ámbito municipal y sus impactos en el ambiente.* Pontificia Universidad Católica del Perú.

7

Guidelines for Teaching the Market Approach to Scaling Impact

In the previous chapters, we've provided several materials that can be used to design a class or a workshop on scaling a social enterprise. This includes: a detailed description of the market approach to scaling; its theoretical grounding; three phases that comprise a practical guide to creating a market-based scaling strategy; concrete illustrations of each of these phases that can be used as teaching cases; and discussions regarding possible resulting strategies, namely co-creation, collective impact, and replicating business models.

With the proper tools and the guidance of motivated instructors, social entrepreneurs can effectively learn how to tackle new challenges, such as scaling their enterprise's impact. With respect to the pedagogical content introduced below, we define "learning" as the recognition of previously unknown factors that are relevant to scaling impact, or the modification of an existing knowledge base in order to create an effective scaling strategy [1]. We will discuss some of the challenges that instructors may face when working with the materials provided in Chapters 1–6, and introduce the didactical concept of experiential learning as a promising entry point through which to help social entrepreneurs learn new ways to scale the impact of their enterprises through a market approach [2]. While this final chapter focuses on pedagogical tools for teaching the market approach to scaling, its content can be useful to both entrepreneurs and instructors. As it favors an experiential learning approach it highlights the importance of "learning by doing" which is the way most of us learn, what includes entrepreneurs in particular.

The chapter is organized as follows: First, we explore potential settings in which to teach the market approach to scaling social enterprises. Second, we

© The Author(s) 2020
U. Jäger et al., *Scaling Strategies for Social Entrepreneurs*,
https://doi.org/10.1007/978-3-030-31160-5_7

propose experiential learning as the pedagogical framework through which to teach the content presented in this book. Third, we argue that learning the market approach to scaling via an experiential approach prepares entrepreneurs to devise innovative solutions for their most pressing challenges. We conclude by defining the various roles that an instructor adopts when teaching the market approach to scaling impact.

Courses and Workshops on Scaling the Impact of Social Enterprises

To explore potential settings in which to use the material introduced in this book, we will center our discussion on the Latin American region, as this is where the cases introduced in this book are located. This is not to disregard the many other parts of the world in which social entrepreneurs are equally important actors working to scale solutions that address urgent problems akin to those faced by Latin America, such as inequality. Despite the rising need for social entrepreneurs to scale their impact in Latin America, the region is lacking educational programs and trainings that stimulate a culture of social entrepreneurship. In Guatemala, for instance, the relatively low education level among young people is a main constraint to entrepreneurship in general [3]. Likewise, many other Latin American countries lack sufficient incubators and business school trainings. More importantly, there are not enough publicly available training tools that current and future social entrepreneurs can adapt to their contexts to help tackle the ample challenges they face. In short, the region lacks support for a social entrepreneurial culture, platforms through which to present successfully scaled social enterprises as role models, and a systematic provision of opportunities for high-potential social entrepreneurs to scale their business models.

Nevertheless, various emerging actors throughout the region are starting to tackle these problems—including instructors, trainers, consultants, and the entrepreneurs themselves. For these actors, the contents of this book can be used in educational settings, or put directly toward the work being carried out by a given social enterprise. Spaces such as incubators, accelerators, technological parks, and innovation labs are ideal settings in which to offer courses or workshops on a market approach to scaling.

- Incubators: Latin American incubators have evolved from simply offering complementary services to startups to differentiating these services in either technological or economic terms. Subsequently, these models have expanded to include innovation-related topics in various sectors, among them social enterprises. Of the top services offered by Latin American incubators, 25% offer tutoring services, 28% offer mentorships, 7% offer customer relations, 11% offer incubation spaces, and 11% offer financing [4].

- Accelerators: In Latin American countries, accelerators are generally international institutions. Examples include ENDEAVOR, Techba, and New Ventures. These are mainly linked to private investment funds, though a few are linked to universities. The acceleration model requires the presence of leading innovation centers, a critical mass of innovative companies, and the development of an entrepreneurial ecosystem that demands these types of services [4]. Accelerator investment in Latin American startups varies from one country to another. Chile leads, hosting 48% of all accelerators in Latin America; Brazil follows at 17%, Uruguay at 14%, and Mexico at 9%. Prior to 2009, the Latin American acceleration industry was relatively stagnant. From 2009 to 2015, however, the number of accelerators in Latin America increased considerably. According to Gust's report on accelerators in the region, 73% of Latin American accelerators are for-profit organizations—one of the highest percentages in the world. The remaining 27% are public non-profit organizations (Startup Chile, Softlanding UY, or Emprende Fch), or programs launched by universities (UDD Ventures, AUGE in Costa Rica, Chrysalis in Chile, and Macondo Labs in Colombia) [5]. Of all accelerators in the region, 52% are financed exclusively with private capital, and 42% are financed with a mix of public and private funds.
- Technology Parks: The implementation of technology parks in Latin America is relatively recent. There are approximately 150 such parks throughout the region, most of which opened after the year 2000. Many of the most recent are state or municipal initiatives; however, technology parks are more commonly funded by central governments, international organizations, or universities. The majority of technology parks in Latin America are focused on software development, telecommunications, electronic manufacturing, and technical engineering services. Brazil and Mexico are the leading countries in the region, with 22 and 21 parks in operation, respectively.
- Innovation Labs: Successful innovation ecosystems are the result of the synergies created when universities, research and development centers, talented human capital, investors (primarily venture capitalists and angel investors), professional associations, the private sector, and the government work together to achieve sustainable competition between startups. In Latin America, many of these spaces are corporate innovation labs

created by one company or groups of companies in the same industry. These spaces are focused on specific innovations, and follow a traditional private business structure where start-ups focus on economic growth only. A relatively small number of Latin American universities—fewer than 25—have their own innovation labs. The top innovation spaces in Latin America are positioned in specific innovation areas or strategic themes. Table 7.1 presents these spaces and their respective focus areas.

As shown in Table 7.1, only two innovation labs in Latin America are focused on social impact, which is also true for the other spaces introduced above such as incubators, accelerators, and technology parks. Although these spaces are on the rise, they often lack specific services for social enterprises. In this book, we aim to support actors that develop (or want to develop) specific services for social entrepreneurs, particularly those that want to focus on scaling strategies. The book's contents can be adapted to various practical and educational settings. To do so, however, we strongly advocate a pedagogical approach that is centered on experiential learning.

Experiential Learning as a Pedagogical Guideline

Much like business management education in general, social entrepreneurship education has historically been defined as an application-oriented discipline. Thus, the inclusion of practical experience in courses on social enterprises intending to scale seems obvious. However, since the 1960s pressured to position business management as a scientific discipline akin to sociology or economics and, since the 1990s, in view of their desire to appear in academic journals, an increasing number of business management teachers lost their practical orientation. Another shift occurred after the global economic crisis of 2008, when business schools were considered part of the problem rather than the solution, inspiring many management scholars to recover the practical roots of their discipline. Mintzberg's position, which calls for a business management training that systematically helps students both collect and reflect management experience, has become particularly prominent [6]. Others advocate the need to develop a practical approach that combines theory and experience, using critical theories to challenge management assumptions, and experience to apply the real-life problems that students encounter in their day-to-day entrepreneurial settings [7].

Table 7.1 Areas of value creation of established innovation labs in Latin America

Positioning	Specific innovations	Test products	Citizen involvement	Technology	Scaling	Women	Social impact
Lab de Innovación Social Uruguay			×				×
OpenLabs-Tec de Monterrey[a]	×	×					×
Linnear Lab	×			×			
iLab América Latina				×			
LINQ	×	×	×	×			
LabProdam	×			×			
Lab de Gobierno Chile	×	×	×				
Laboratorio de Xalapa							
Lab Río	×						
Open Lab U. de Chile[a]		×	×				
Laboratorio Hacker	×	×	×	×			
iGovSP		×					
ViveLab Bogotá		×	×	×			
Mobilab	×		×				
3IE[a]			×				
Chrysalis[a]	×		×	×			
Incuba UC[a]	×				×		
Startup Farm		×		×			
Startup Mexico	×		×		×		
Wayra				×			
Startup Chile		×			×	×	

[a]Pertains to a Latin American university

Professionalization in business management, specifically in the contexts of social enterprises, is the goal, characterized by the practice of reflecting on what the social entrepreneur does (effectiveness) and how he or she does it (efficiency) [8]. In recent years, many participants in our own courses and workshops have expressed that they understand what they do on a day-to-day basis in their social enterprise when discussing their experiences with instructors and, more importantly, with other social entrepreneurs. Many participants say that it is the first time they've truly felt understood in a business management setting. These sentiments express the importance of fostering settings in which social entrepreneurs can reflect on and share their experiences as they plan for the future.

Experiential learning methods are based on the notion that "change is learning, and learning is change"—or, more generally speaking, "life is learning, and learning is life" [9]. From this perspective, every idea and every day-to-day task is a learning opportunity. The focus isn't *when* someone learns; rather, that life isn't something to be "learned" at all [9]. In this framework, learning isn't a skill that can be taught, but one that every person is born with. This reflects an open-minded curiosity about life, reflected in each and every experience we have along the way. Humans can, therefore, lose their ability to learn, which—unfortunately and paradoxically—often occurs in the education process. The incorporation of specific standards and routines lead us to see different phenomena as unquestionable, fixed in theory. With respect to the material presented in this book, we offer an alternative to this perspective. Learning is ultimately a question of how instructors and social entrepreneurs process the experiences they encounter in their day-to-day lives.

In a business school environment, which typically celebrates lecture-based learning and educational settings in which instructors serve as experts, it is difficult to incorporate experiential learning methods, which some might misinterpret as "childlike." Thus, most instructors who teach social entrepreneurship (or other business management subjects) tend to adopt a positivist worldview. In this worldview, the instructor holds all the strings, so to speak. They objectively identify the "best" scaling practice, and present it to participants as objectively accessible knowledge, using lectures and presentations to define what they consider to be the "best" solution for specific problems. By assuming they possess the correct solution, these instructors often fail to acknowledge that the social entrepreneurs' own experiences in the contexts they are embedded are also valid in terms of generating new knowledge and alternative solutions.

In this book, we argue that effective instructors of topics related to social entrepreneurship must, rather, adopt a phenomenological worldview. Unlike the positivist approach described above, instructors operating on a phenomenological worldview do not assume the existence of objectively accessible knowledge such as principles of scaling. If an enterprise should scale or not depends on the multiple relations the social entrepreneur acts in and the potential to scale that emerge from those [10]. This approach views learning as the collectively processed knowledge that arises before, during and after the learning process. The students themselves are, thus, protagonists of this process—not simply objects that absorb the instructor's knowledge. The students' presuppositions and the cultural context in which their social enterprise operates are placed at the center of the learning, and the object is the social entrepreneurs' self in relation to others and the topic (for example, scaling impact), which is discussed with the instructors, other social entrepreneurs, and anyone interested in the issue.

Experiential learning implies a "non-rational" attitude, in which experience presupposes understanding in the act of learning [11]. According to this framework, social entrepreneurship is more a trade than a profession that cannot be learned in a university, unlike other topics, such as engineering [7]. Effective entrepreneurship is context- and practice-driven. Consequently, from this perspective, social entrepreneurship is a combination of art, craft, and science. Its practitioners need to be able to act effectively from experience in an often chaotic and complex context [12]. Having this skill can be equated to having the right mental software to navigate the context within which a given situation takes place [13].

Obviously, implementing an experiential approach to learning can be demanding. Many instructors struggle to incorporate the complex experiences of social entrepreneurs into their teaching plan. These experiences come with multiple topics, emotions, believes, theories, prejudices, etc. It can be challenging to reduce this variety of information to an essential point. This is why instructors often move away from focusing on the entrepreneurs' experiences and instead teach solutions that are based on theoretical materials on scaling the impact of social enterprises, such as those we've introduced in this book. But teaching the contents of this book does not imply teaching an "objective truth." The theoretical grounding for the market approach to scaling impact and the related three phases simply provide a framework through which to reflect upon and systematically support social entrepreneurs' learning process with respect to how to scale their impact.

Experiential Learning to Tackle Major Challenges

Many experts question whether social entrepreneurs can truly prepare to scale their social enterprise in a way that helps solve major challenges such as climate change and inequality using traditional learning methods, such as reading journal articles and studying theoretical concepts in the classroom. We argue that, through experiential methods, instructors can, in fact, help social entrepreneurs devise innovative and effective responses to these challenges.

Tackling the world's most pressing challenges implies knowledge of many different realities, among them low-income contexts in emerging and developing countries. Therefore, examining social entrepreneurship from the perspective of low-income contexts in Latin America, as we've done in this book, enriches an inclusive, global perspective of major challenges and potential solutions. Furthermore, despite their high rates of poverty and informality, countries with large portions of low-income populations are increasingly being recognized as settings full of economic opportunity. For instance, Raveendran found that, in 2006, India's informal market size in relation to the GDP of its formal markets was roughly 92% [14]. In 2011, ILO estimated that the non-agricultural workforce in informal markets alone—including informally employed people such as domestic servants, had risen to 70%; in Mexico it was 55%, in Costa Rica it was 48%, and in Brazil it was 42% [15]. Many emerging and developing countries are challenged by a structural gap between the formal and the informal markets [16], and more and more countries, such as India, are investing in infrastructure to reduce this gap [17].

For instructors, the challenge begins when they are expected to explain the phenomena that occurs in low-income contexts using management or economic perspectives that were built under first-world paradigms and, thus, are detached from the reality of low-income contexts. Low-income contexts follow standards that are still poorly understood by traditional business theories. Traditional knowledge regarding entrepreneurship can often fall short when it comes to explaining or understanding social entrepreneurship in low-income markets. Typically, many entrepreneurial concepts and instruments assume a formal market with liable contracts, rule of law, property rights, functional market institutions, competition, and market value. The informal markets and impoverished settings of emerging and developing countries, however, do not always follow these assumptions. The profound differences in the values and structures of formal and informal markets make courses and workshops on scaling social impact highly complex, leaving many instructors feeling overburdened.

We might compare the current discussion on the challenges of adapting business management education to encompass the reality of social entrepreneurship in low-income contexts with a situation faced by North American industrialist Henry Ford. Initially, Ford produced his cars in black only—assuming all customers wanted black cars. Today, however, the auto industry thrives on highly individualized marketing techniques. Business researchers and instructors often handle low-income contexts much like Henry Ford treated his early customers. They view low-income regions as if they comprise a homogenous field—all wanting black cars—though it represents different people from different cultures all over the world, each in need of an individualized approach.

An alternative to teaching generalizing concepts is for teachers and their students to become immersed in low-income settings, in order to gain real-world, situational experience. In this sense, the classroom setting is obviously not enough when it comes to teaching about scaling social enterprises. An example of this type of experiential learning is Harvard Business School, which sends its students to advise companies in emerging and developing countries on how to successfully do business in low-income markets. In a similar vein, in Switzerland's University of St. Gallen's highly-ranked Master of Strategy and International Management Program, students must execute a social impact project in an emerging or developing country to gain experience in these extreme contexts. Sometimes, these experiences even turn into concrete and sustainable social initiatives, such as with "Liter of Light," a Colombian initiative supported by St. Gallen students that became a thriving international nonprofit. These examples show a tendency in business schools to include experience with businesses that are tackling major challenges such as those faced by informal markets and poverty in their curriculum. For instructors intending to prepare social entrepreneurs to scale the impact of their enterprises, teaching with respect to these contexts can prove particularly challenging.

The Four Roles Instructors Play When Using Experimental Learning Techniques

Particularly in courses with social entrepreneurs that intend to work on their own business models to scale impact, instructors must be able to incorporate the student's real-life settings and the provided teaching cases, while also drawing from concepts and theories that support reflection on these real-life settings. Each of these tasks require instructors to play a different role. In lectures, they play the role of a rather traditional teacher. With the teaching cases, they play the role of a moderator. In real-life settings, they play the role of a mentor, helping students to reflect on their experiences. Thus, in an experiential model, instructors might play one or different roles, depending on the situation.

To help instructors become aware of their different roles, we will systematize these below, based on two dimensions. First, in some parts of the course, instructors need to impart their own knowledge of social entrepreneurship, social enterprises, and scaling, as introduced in this book. We call this expert-based learning, in which the instructor acts as either a lecturer or an analyst. Second, in other parts of the course, instructors need to focus on experiential learning, as described above, playing the role of a mentor or moderator. The following matrix structures these different learning paradigms and topics, and defines the various roles played by instructors in each of the four fields (Table 7.2). Those roles are a typology, as in practice instructors often play two, three, or four roles simultaneously. This typology helps instructors reflect on their different roles and, therefore, improve their teaching efficiency.

Instructors as Lecturers

Even within an experiential approach to learning, instructors can play the traditional role of lecturers, as students expect them to at least possess a minimal amount of knowledge if they are to help the students solve their scaling challenges—particularly if they are paying for the course or workshop. However, current research on social entrepreneurship shows the limits of lecturing. From a practitioner perspective, instructors have a knowledge

Table 7.2 Topics related to scaling a social enterprise

| | Learning paradigms | |
	Expert-based learning	Experiential learning
Real-life settings	Analyst (e.g., teaching case studies on enterprises operating in low-income contexts)	Mentor (e.g., facilitating field visits to low-income contexts)
Theories/concepts	Lecturer (e.g., giving a presentation on informal market theories)	Moderator (e.g., leading student discussions on experiences in low-income contexts)

gap in terms of providing examples of their own everyday scaling challenges, while students have a knowledge gap in terms of explaining these scaling challenges (of which they have many examples) in theoretical and conceptual terms. Thus, by introducing the theories and concepts, instructors give students the language needed to make sense of the everyday complexity. However, management concepts are often not enough, so it makes sense to include other theories. Instructors might, for example, include anthropological concepts, the same way that a firm might hire an anthropologist to help its strategists determine how to open markets in low-income regions [18]. Another reason to extend the theoretical lens is the relatively rare availability of empirical insight on scaling social impact. In view of the high complexity, diversity, and size of many scaling strategies, it's obvious that practitioners need more research-based insight. However, this will take time to emerge, and instructors must find ways to include scaling issues in their courses now, despite the current scarcity of established concepts and theories.

Instructors as Analysts

Most instructors choose to work with teaching cases, such as those provided in this book. These cases help them introduce social entrepreneurial students to real-life situations in order to provoke a richer discussion on the complexity of their day-to-day work. Instructors facilitate student discussions and help them analyze the essential issues of each case. When the students analyze the cases, with the instructor supporting them in this analytical practice, the instructor is playing the role of an analyst. Although he or she is acting as a quasi-moderator of the student discussions, the main goal is to facilitate an analysis of the case study at hand.

Many business schools have their own databases of teaching cases, and international databases such as the European Case Clearing House also have a variety of similar products. However, much like journal articles, these have a very low citation rate, and many of the teaching cases are rarely used in class. Instructors might have a few favorites that they use repeatedly throughout the years, but this is only a handful of cases. Nevertheless, as with the rarity of defined scaling concepts and theories in this segment of business education, few scholars write cases on social enterprises intending to scale. With this book, we intend to help fill this gap. Nevertheless, instructors will inevitably have to rely on cases that don't precisely fit to their teaching goal. To resolve situations like this, the first author of this book conducted the following experiment: during a class at the University of St.

Gallen in Switzerland, the instructor used social enterprise teaching cases to illustrate a traditional strategy concept, then facilitated a Skype interview between the St. Gallen students and a representative of the social enterprise described in the case. The social enterprise representative, who resided in a low-income region of an emerging country, was able to explain the challenges of this low-income context directly to the students, and responded to their various questions. This interaction deeply changed the discussion. Prior to the interview, the students had been rather critical toward the idea of finding economic opportunities in low-income contexts; after the interview, however, their perspective changed drastically. They began to argue that, while people in low-income contexts may indeed be market actors with fewer opportunities, they are common market actors, nevertheless. Based on this new assumption, the students were then able to develop creative solutions for the problems presented in the case. This led to a better understanding of the results of the course when the interview was not part of the class.

Instructors as Moderators

Including experiential learning in courses on scaling social or environmental impact requires instructors who are willing to focus more on listening to students' experiences and reflections than on transmitting their own knowledge. Expert-based learning is based on research disciplines such as controlling, marketing, etc., whereas experiential learning is context- and situation-oriented [7].

In recent years, we have observed that more and more business schools in the United States offer field visits to emerging and developing Latin American countries. These trips are often costly, and can last from a few days to several weeks. Instructors accompany the students on the trip, during which they visit with social entrepreneurs and other experts within the emerging or developing country. Many of these instructors are themselves experts in social entrepreneurship, but most have no cultural experience with the host country, nor knowledge of its social enterprise markets or low-income contexts. The instructors are, therefore, in the same situation as their students—they are undergoing a first-time experience of social entrepreneurship within the host context and, like the students, are processing new information. Thus, in these situations, effective instructors approach the new context as their students' peer and, rather, act as a moderator to help the students make sense of these experiences on the spot. Generally, the instructor has no more knowledge of the context than their students do, but they do have learning tools and methodologies they can transmit to their students along the way.

What instructors *can* do when taking the moderator role is to teach students about qualitative methodologies for gathering information, such as interview techniques or methodologies of observations. These techniques help students observe phenomena as closely as possible and reduce prejudices. In addition, they can draw from existing theories and concepts to help students make sense of the host country context. They might even incorporate a professor from the cultural context of the host country to co-teach a segment of the course.

Instructors as Mentors

As touched on above, not only do instructors lack sufficient management theories and concepts related to social enterprises intending to scale in low-income contexts, but they also lack enough teaching cases to support the students' related analytical processes. Conducting costly field visits to social enterprises, while helpful, without adequate knowledge can also prove inefficient as the instructors do not fully leverage the learning potential these visits can offer.

Another option is to design courses in which the instructors include experiential learning in combination with real-life examples. The downside of these examples is the huge complexity that instructors must navigate. For example, when visiting social enterprises in low-income contexts— an extreme version of a real-life example—students will likely undergo extremely foreign experiences that can shake the foundations of their own worldviews and lead to deeply personal responses such as fear, uncertainty, or hope. Learning is, therefore, primarily oriented toward self-reflection and hands-on experiences. In this way, the students are encouraged to develop innovative ideas that transcend the boundaries of concepts and theories [19]. Instructors can never fully prepare for these highly complex, real-life situations. They must act didactically and effectively in the specific situation at hand, and cannot merely focus on their areas of expertise. In this way, instructors are confronted with the entrepreneurial practice in its full expression: unexpected, complex, dynamic, multidimensional, culturally diverse, and not always subject to theoretical boundaries or instructor expertise.

What instructors *can* prepare for, is to play a mentorship role in the midst of unexpected confrontations with real-life situations in a teaching setting. Like business leaders, they must be capable of responding to the situation at hand and helping students make sense of it in relation to their learning experience. Their role is, thus, that of a mentor who focuses on the students' own personal development within the experience at hand. In this context of helping students process unexpected situations, preparing a lecture is hardly helpful. The students cannot yet analyze the situation, as they are living it—they have no time to gather all the information; real-life situations are ever changing. Nor can instructors help moderate the students' learning experience, as they do not have the time to formulate the appropriate concepts and theories through which to structure the learning process.

Instructors who decide to embrace the complexity of the four teaching roles described above must invest significant time in personal and pedagogical preparations, and must have the courage to transcend the boundaries of their own expertise. It may be because most instructors of social entrepreneurship courses and workshops are former consultants or other practitioners who are accustomed to simultaneously playing the role of lecturer, analyst, mentor, and moderator. Most of these instructors do not have typical curriculum vitae for a business school teacher, as the "typical" business school teacher is unprepared to take on all these roles at once.

Teaching social entrepreneurs how to scale their enterprise is clearly a highly complex endeavor with significant demands on instructors, regardless of whether they play the role of lecturer, analyst, moderator, or mentor. Most instructors who rely entirely on their own knowledge as experts, for example, would likely have a hard time acting as mentors in the field. To lead these sessions, instructors must be intellectually and logistically flexible enough to provide on-the-spot responses to highly complex, real-life entrepreneurial phenomena. In any case, field visits to social enterprises in emerging or developed countries must be carefully prepared—both prior to the course and as the trip itself unfolds.

Taking an experiential approach to teaching social entrepreneurs how to scale their enterprise is, thus, a challenging path. But it is also a vital one. In this book, we hope to have provided instructors with useful theoretical tools, process guides, and teaching cases that can help orient this process with respect to a market approach to scaling impact. Every context—from the developing world to highly developed countries—needs more spaces that support the social entrepreneurs in their countries in their efforts to scale their impact. This can be one way to respond to the global social and environmental challenges of our times. Nevertheless, as we mentioned in our preface, there is no such thing as a universal principle to scaling impact—neither for entrepreneurs nor for instructors.

The decision of whether to scale or not to scale depends on the multiple relations around which a given social enterprise works, and out of which potentials to scale can emerge. But if we understand that our social enterprise, bank, venture capitalist, university, company, nonprofit, international nongovernmental organization, or whatever organization we work with has the potential to scale impact, then we need to favor the creation of scaling plans. We all need to foster our capacity to realize our full potential as entrepreneurs, investors, instructors and individuals; to contribute more to solving the social and environmental challenges of our times.

References

1. Euler, D., & Hahn, A. (2004). *Business didactics* [Wirtschaftsdidaktik]. Bern, Stuttgart, and Wien: Haupt.
2. Kolb, D. (1984). *Experiential learning: Experience as the source of learning and development.* Englewood Cliffs, NJ: Prentice Hall.
3. Rodríguez, L. (2010). *Políticas públicas para promover el empleo juvenil y el emprendedurismo de los jóvenes en México.* Available at: http://prejal.oit.org.pe/prejal/docs/emp_juvenil_y_emprendedurismo_mexico.pdf.
4. Lagunes, L., Solano, F. Herrera, M., & San Martín, J. (2014). *González L. Innovación y Emprendimiento a la Luz del Contexto Latinoamericano.*
5. Gust.com. *Global Accelerator Report 2015.* Available at: http://gust.com/latam-accelerator-report-2015/.
6. Mintzberg, H. (2005). *Managers not MBAs: A hard look at the soft practice of managing and management development.* San Francisco, CA: Berrett-Koehler Publisher.
7. Raelin, J. A. (2007). Toward an epistemology of practice. *Academy of Management Learning & Education, 6*(4), 495–519.
8. Drucker, P. F. (2007/1955). *The practice of management.* Oxford: Butterworth-Heinemann.
9. Chia, R. (2003). From knowledge-creation to the perfection of action: Tao, Basho and pure experience as the ultimate ground of knowing. *Human Relations, 56*(8), 953–981.
10. Whitehead, A. N. (1997/1925). *Science and the modern world.* New York: Free Press.
11. Whitehead, A. N. (2008/1929). *Process and reality* [Prozess und Realität]. Frankfurt am Main: Suhrkamp.
12. Chia, R. (2005). The aim of management education: Reflextions on Mintzberg's managers not MBAs. *Organization Studies, 26*(7), 1089–1109.

13. Hofstede, G., & Hofstede, G. J. (2005). *Cultures and organizations: Software of the mind.* New York, Chicago, San Francisco, Lisbon, London, Madrid, Mexico City, Milan, New Delhi, San Juan, Seoul, Singapore, Sydney, Toronto: McGraw-Hill.
14. Raveendran, G. (2006, May). *Estimation of contribution of informal sector to GDP.* New Delhi, India: National Commission of Enterprises in the Unorganized/Informal Sector.
15. ILO Department of Statistics. 2011. *Statistical update on employment in the informal economy.* Geneva: ILO Department of Statistics.
16. London, T., Anupindi, R., & Sheth, S. (2010). Creating mutual value: Lessons learned from ventures serving base of the pyramid producers. *Journal of Business Research, 63,* 582–594.
17. Sathe, V. (2011). The world's most ambitious ID project: India's project Aadhaar. *Innovations, 6*(2), 39–66.
18. Hart, S. L. (2010). *Capitalism at the crossroads: Next generation business strategies for a post-crisis world.* Upper Saddle River, NJ: Prentice Hall Pearson.
19. Chia, R. (1996). The teaching paradigm is shifting in management education: University business schools and the entrepreneurial imagination. *Journal of Management Studies, 33*(4), 409–428.

Index